Poverty in the Early Church and Today

Poverty in the Early Church and Today

A Conversation

Edited by
Steve Walton and
Hannah Swithinbank

t&tclark

LONDON • NEW YORK • OXFORD • NEW DELHI • SYDNEY

T&T CLARK
Bloomsbury Publishing Plc
50 Bedford Square, London, WC1B 3DP, UK
1385 Broadway, New York, NY 10018, USA

BLOOMSBURY, T&T CLARK and the T&T Clark logo are trademarks of
Bloomsbury Publishing Plc

First published in Great Britain 2019

Cover image © Dhandevi Seaming (32) reading bible at her home, ShivNagar
community, Tikapur, Western Nepal. TF Partner: Sagoal. Photo by Ralph Hodgson

A catalogue record for this book is available from the British Library.

A catalog record for this book is available from the Library of Congress.

ISBN: HB: 978-0-5676-7776-1
ePDF: 978-0-5676-7775-4
ePUB: 978-0-5676-7773-0

Typeset by Newgen KnowledgeWorks Pvt. Ltd., Chennai, India
Printed and bound in Great Britain

To find out more about our authors and books visit www.bloomsbury.com
and sign up for our newsletters.

Contents

How This Book Works

The Editors

Poverty is one of the most significant challenges our world today faces, and it is a particular challenge for Christians, who follow the Jesus who urges giving to the poor and who includes people in poverty among his highest concerns. The essays in this book offer a fresh angle on debates about poverty by bringing together people who have expertise and experience in alleviating poverty today with people who have expertise in the ancient worlds of the Bible. We bring them together in order to have a conversation about how Christians today might think about and act on poverty issues, informed by the way our ancestors-in-faith responded to poverty in their places and times.

We are not simply interested in holding up modern practices to a supposed early Christian example. Rather, we are interested in the complex ways in which the early Christian ideas and practices relate to modern ideas and practices and vice versa. In other words, the conversation in this book aims to address both continuities and discontinuities between the ancient world and today. We are most interested in coming to grips with the full complexity of the matter, in order to inform and engage our readers, whom we hope will include church leaders, people working in non-governmental organizations (NGOs) concerned with poverty and thoughtful people, both Christian and not.

We designed the book in order to be most beneficial to individuals and organizations currently involved in addressing poverty in its many forms, as a space for critical thought and discussion. Therefore, we ground our thinking in a rigorous study of poverty and its alleviation in both earliest Christianity and today's world, while presenting the fruit of this study accessibly for those who do not have formal training in these areas. In this light, the heart of the conversation consists of eight sections.

Our book opens with two forewords, which are themselves thoughtful reflections on poverty, by Graham Tomlin, the Anglican Bishop of Kensington (London), and Cardinal Vincent Nichols, the Catholic Archbishop of Westminster. Justin Thacker then reflects on the ways we identify poverty and offers a valuable theological assessment.

The body of the book is a series of sets of four essays, in which we pair an expert in early Christianity in its Jewish and Graeco-Roman settings with an expert in modern strategies for addressing poverty and benefaction. They each address the same topic from their respective areas of expertise in a substantial essay, and then each author responds to their partner much more briefly, identifying points which are mutually informing and stimulating. In this way, we hope we shall both model and encourage profitable conversation between those primarily engaged in today's world and specialists in the biblical world.

Francis Campbell then discusses what it means to be a Catholic university in today's world of poverty, a 'case study' of Christian engagement with poverty. Finally, Craig Blomberg and Francis Davis review and reflect on the whole collection of essays as (respectively) a New Testament scholar and a Christian social thinker.

This book grew out of a conference 'Engaging with Poverty in the Early Church and Today' held at St Mary's University, Twickenham (London) in December 2015, and we are very grateful for the hospitality of the university. The project was the brainchild of Professor Chris Keith, Director of the St Mary's University Centre for the Social-Scientific Study of the Bible, and Mr David Parish, chair of the Hampton Fuel Allotment Charity, and became a partnership in money and kind between the university, Tearfund, Caritas (Diocese of Westminster) and the Bible Society, and we gratefully acknowledge the contributions of each of the partners. We are also thankful to Professor Francis Campbell, Vice Chancellor of St Mary's University, Twickenham, for his support and encouragement, including his own essay in this volume. Scott Robertson kindly provided the index for the volume.

During the conference, we contributed a portion of the registration fees to Riverside, a local Christian charity which works with single parents in poverty. Ellie Hughes, who writes in this book, was then the Director of Riverside's ministry. In similar vein, royalties from this book will be split between Tearfund and Caritas (Diocese of Westminster) to support their Christian engagement with people in poverty today.

Lent, 2018

Reflecting on Poverty

Bishop Graham Tomlin

A little while ago, I spent a day at homeless drop-in centre in one of the parishes I have responsibility for here in London. When we hear the word 'homeless', we probably imagine ragged, unkempt people with plastic bags, straggly beards and dirty clothes, people with little employment capacity, living in poverty and who have spent a good deal of their lives unemployed. In any gathering of people in the average homeless centre, there may be a fair number who fall under that description, but during that day, I found my preconceptions of homelessness, poverty and the reasons for it beginning to erode quite quickly. I am ashamed to say I tweeted early that day that I was going to spend the day with 'a bunch of homeless people' to which one person replied that they were very uncomfortable with that description – and they were exactly right.

Talking to several people over the day, I began to realize that 'homeless' is a fairly blunt category. This homeless drop-in centre had around sixty or so regulars but they were all there for different reasons. One elderly woman was not homeless – in fact, she had a very nice flat – but was desperately lonely since her husband died, and came along to find some people to talk to. Another had walked out of an old people's home because he had kept getting drunk and had fallen out with those in charge. Others were sleeping on friends' floors, some had recently arrived from other countries, a few were asylum seekers, unable to work while their cases were being heard and just wanted somewhere to stay dry and some company on another aimless and frustrating day.

I met an architect with an encyclopaedic knowledge of the dates of London City churches, a teacher of English as a Second Language and a retired research chemist. All the world was there. The one thing in common was some back story, something that had gone wrong in their lives. I heard one story of a man who had come to the centre who had been CEO of a large international airline. His child had died in an accident, the stress led to the break-up of his marriage, he then started drinking, which led to him losing his job, and soon he had lost family, home, income, job – in fact, everything – and he was now on the streets. Whether it was a bereavement, unemployment, a marriage breakdown, mental health issues, a physical accident or a chronically bad temper, something had led them to this point. Usually alcohol or drugs were involved in some way, a short-term comfort, but ultimately making the problem worse. What strikes you is how easily it could happen to anyone – even to you or me. In a sense, there are no such thing as homeless people, just people with different problems, who find it difficult to handle life when it gets really hard.

The day impressed upon me how complex poverty is and how many types there are. Alongside economic poverty there is also the poverty of loneliness, purposelessness, or mental and psychological poverty. It also showed me that while Christians (and others) speak of 'the poor', that, too, is a blunt category. There might be a great deal of discussion around how to deal with poverty and how to help 'the poor'; but in the end, the poor are *people*, each with their own story, their own reasons for being economically disadvantaged, some of which are told in this volume, all having to deal with the debilitating and demoralizing effects of poverty in their own way.

A friend who works in disadvantaged areas of the United Kingdom once said to me that the problem is not so much that the rich do not help the poor, as they do not know the poor. A book on attitudes to poverty in the ancient and modern worlds is an excellent contribution to the complex set of issues surrounding poverty; yet my hope is that this book will not just provide intellectual stimulation but will also lead to a desire in those who read it not just to understand poverty but also to experience it, even if vicariously.

On my day at the homeless centre, the other people present were the volunteers, people who give time and energy to serve their guests, wash their feet, give legal or housing advice, cook breakfast, listen to their stories. Each one of us had our own problems and issues as well. None of us are self-sufficient and were never meant to be. We are all, whatever our economic circumstances, in need of a Saviour, someone who understands our story with its highlights and failures, who, 'though he was rich, yet for your sakes he became poor, so that by his poverty you might become rich' (2 Cor. 8.9). That Saviour ministers to us through each other, through the words of life, encouragement and gospel we offer one another and through the gestures of love – a meal given, a new set of clothes given, a hand shaken – all bringing the possibility of change.

This transformation comes not just through remote donations, standing orders or cheques signed, however valuable they may be, but also through human contact, face to face, in which the incarnate Christ makes himself present in that interaction, both for the giver and the receiver, both as recipients of grace. Each word or act of love offered in the name of Christ becomes a word or act done to Christ and for Christ, as we work out our salvation with fear and trembling.

At the end of the day, people experiencing poverty of whatever kind need dignity, not dependence. They need to be treated as precious human beings, created and loved by God as they are, and dignity comes through human contact, not just through handouts. Only then will they find the dignity that enables them to take the hand that helps them out of poverty into self-respect and the ability to make their own contribution to the society in which they live.

If this book helps its readers not just to understand poverty but also to get to know one or two people for whom poverty is their daily experience, then it will have done its job well.

Graham Tomlin, Bishop of Kensington

Foreword

Cardinal Vincent Nichols

The Church has, from its beginning, been committed, in the name of Christ, to care for those in poverty. This book contributes to that commitment by bringing together present-day thinkers and activists with scholars of Scripture to reflect on this important theme. I welcome this book.

Catholics believe that faith must be put into action. The shape of this faith-in-action has been developed and brought together as Catholic Social Teaching, which identifies and expounds key themes, concerns and practices arising from our faith.[1]

The dignity of human beings made in God's image and remade in the image of Christ by the Holy Spirit is a core principle in such thinking and action. Further, human existence is not meant to be individualistic, but personal, corporate and communal. Reflection in this book clarifies the working out of this principle and the way commitment to human dignity, and community, can transform people caught in poverty by empowering them to respond to its challenges.

Pope St John Paul II writes of Jesus:

> ... who, while *being God*, became like us in all things, devoted most of the years of his life on earth to *manual work* at the carpenter's bench. This circumstance constitutes in itself the most eloquent 'Gospel of work', showing that the basis for determining the value of human work is not primarily the kind of work being done but the fact that the one who is doing it is a person.[2]

Catholics and other Christians, thus, have the highest possible motivation to enable people in poverty to move out of dependence into interdependence and community, for in this they follow in the path of our Lord and Saviour Jesus Christ. As Pope Francis has written,

> Our faith in Christ, who became poor, and was always close to the poor and the outcast, is the basis of our concern for the integral development of society's most neglected members.[3]

---

[1] See, e.g., the Catholic Social Teaching website (http://www.catholicsocialteaching.org.uk, accessed March 2018).

[2] *Laborem Exercens* (On Human Work) §6 (italics original) (http://w2.vatican.va/content/john-paul-ii/en/encyclicals/documents/hf_jp-ii_enc_14091981_laborem-exercens.html, accessed March 2018).

[3] *Evangelii Gaudium* (The Joy of the Gospel) §186 (http://w2.vatican.va/content/francesco/en/apost_exhortations/documents/papa-francesco esortazione-ap_20131124_evangelii-gaudium.html#II.%E2%80%82The_inclusion_of_the_poor_in_society, accessed March 2018).

This is a key factor, as a number of the essays in this book realize, in opening pathways to work as an expression of human personhood, made in God's image and known by God.

I have the honour to be Chancellor of St Mary's University, Twickenham, which both hosted and co-sponsored the conference which produced the essays in this book. As a Catholic university, we are deeply committed to open education and learning to students from backgrounds of significant poverty, as our Vice Chancellor, Francis Campbell, makes clear in his essay in this book. I am delighted to commend this book. I wish it well in influencing and transforming attitudes and action by Christians of every tradition in the service of Christ among people in poverty.

✠ *Cardinal Vincent Nichols, Archbishop of Westminster*

Abbreviations

1 Apol.	Justin Martyr, *First Apology*
2 Tars.	Dio Chrysostom, *Second Tarsic Discourse*
AB	Anchor Bible
ABCD	Asset-based community development
Acts Phil.	*Acts of Phileas*
ANF	*Ante-Nicene Fathers*
Ann.	Tacitus, *Annals*
Ant.	Josephus, *Antiquities of the Jews*
Apos. Trad.	*Apostolic Tradition*
Aug.	Suetonius, *Divus Augustus*
BAFCS	The Book of Acts in its First Century Setting
BBR	*Bulletin of Biblical Research*
BDAG	Bauer, Walter, Frederick W. Danker, W. F. Arndt and F. W. Gingrich, eds, *A Greek-English Lexicon of the New Testament and Other Early Christian Literature*, 3rd edn (Chicago: University of Chicago Press, 2000)
BNTC	Black's New Testament Commentary
BR	*Biblical Research*
BTB	*Biblical Theology Bulletin*
ch./chs	chapter/chapters
Cher.	Philo, *On the Cherubim*
CIJ	*Corpus Inscriptioum Judaicarum*
CIL	*Corpus Inscriptionum Latinarum*
Decalogue	Philo, *On the Decalogue*
DRC	Democratic Republic of Congo
EC	*Early Christianity*
ed.	editor/edited by
Ep.	Pliny the Younger, *Epistles*
Epig.	Martial, *Epigrams*
ERT	*Evangelical Review of Theology*
EvQ	*Evangelical Quarterly*
GDP	Gross Domestic Product
GNS	Good News Studies
HALOT	Koehler, Ludwig, Walter Baumgartner and Johann J. Stamm, eds, *The Hebrew and Aramaic Lexicon of the Old Testament*, 4 vols., trans. Mervyn E. J. Richardson (Leiden: Brill, 1994–1999)
HBT	*Horizons in Biblical Theology*
Herm. *Simil.*	Hermas, *Similitudes*

Hist	*Historia*
Hist.	Sozomen, *Ecclesiastical History*
Hist. eccl.	Eusebius, *Ecclesiastical History*
HTR	*Harvard Theological Review*
ICC	International Critical Commentary
IGRP	*Inscriptiones Graecae ad res Romanas Pertinentes*
Int	Interpretation (commentary series)
Int	*Interpretation* (journal)
J.W.	Josephus, *Jewish War*
JBL	*Journal of Biblical Literature*
JBQ	*Jewish Bible Quarterly*
JCP	Jewish and Christian Perspectives
JJS	*Journal of Jewish Studies*
JRS	*Journal of Roman Studies*
JSJSup	Supplements to the Journal for the Study of Judaism
JSNT	*Journal for the Study of the New Testament*
JSNTSup	Journal for the Study of the New Testament Supplement Series
JSOTSup	Journal for the Study of the Old Testament Supplement Series
JTS	*Journal of Theological Studies*
L&N	Louw, Johannes P., and Eugene A. Nida, eds, *Greek-English Lexicon of the New Testament Based on Semantic Domains*. 2 vols., 2nd edn (New York: United Bible Societies, 1988)
LCL	Loeb Classical Library
LHBOTS	Library of Hebrew Bible/Old Testament Studies
LNTS	Library of New Testament Studies
LXX	Septuagint (Greek Old Testament)
MT	Masoretic Text (of the Hebrew Bible/Old Testament)
NCB	New Century Bible
NCBC	New Cambridge Bible Commentary
NGO	Non-governmental organization
NIBC	New International Biblical Commentary
NICNT	New International Commentary on the New Testament
NICOT	New International Commentary on the Old Testament
NIGTC	New International Greek Testament Commentary
NIV	New International Version (editions of 1984 and 2011)
NovT	*Novum Testamentum*
NRSV	New Revised Standard Version
n.s.	new series
NTM	New Testament Monographs
NTS	*New Testament Studies*
Off.	Cicero, *De officiis*
P. Mert.	Bell, H. Idris, and Colin H. Roberts, *A Descriptive Catalogue of the Greek Papyri in the Collection of Wilfred Merton* (London: Emery Walker, 1948)
Perist.	Prudentius, *Liber Peristphanon* (=*Crowns of Martyrdom*)

Resp.	Plato, *Republic*
RSV	Revised Standard Version
RTR	*Reformed Theological Review*
s.v.	under the word (Latin *sub verbo*)
SNTSMS	Society for New Testament Studies Monograph Series
SNTW	Studies in the New Testament and its World
SP	Sacra Pagina
TDNT	Kittel, Gerhard, and Gerhard Friedrich, eds, *Theological Dictionary of the New Testament*, 10 vols., trans. Geoffrey W. Bromiley (Grand Rapids: Eerdmans, 1964–1976)
THNTC	Two Horizons New Testament Commentary
TNIV	Today's New International Version
trans.	translator/translated by
TynBul	*Tyndale Bulletin*
UN	United Nations
WBC	Word Biblical Commentary
WUNT	Wissenschaftliche Untersuchungen zum Neuen Testament
ZNW	*Zeitschrift für die neutestamentliche Wissenschaft und die Kunde der älteren Kirche*

Contributors

John M. G. Barclay, Lightfoot Professor of Divinity, University of Durham, UK.

Craig L. Blomberg, Distinguished Professor of New Testament, Denver Seminary, CO, USA.

Francis Campbell, Vice Chancellor, St Mary's University, Twickenham (London), UK.

Lynn H. Cohick, Provost/Dean and Professor of New Testament, Denver Seminary, CO, USA.

John Coleby, Director, Caritas (Diocese of Westminster), UK.

Francis Davis, Professor of Religion and Public Policy, University of Birmingham, UK; and Fellow, Helen Suzman Foundation, South Africa.

Fiona J. R. Gregson, St John's, Harborne, Diocese of Birmingham, UK.

Katie Harrison, Director, ComRes Faith Research Centre; formerly Corporate Communications Director, Tearfund, UK.

Christopher M. Hays, Professor of New Testament, Fundación Universitaria Seminario Bíblico de Colombia.

Helen Hekel, Digital Project Manager, Communications for Development Team, Tearfund, UK; formerly Programme Coordinator, Sexual and Gender-based Violence Team, Tearfund, UK.

Ellie Hughes, Founder, Riverbank Trust, Richmond upon Thames, UK.

Bruce W. Longenecker, Professor of Religion and W. W. Melton Chair, Baylor University, TX, USA.

Virginia Luckett, Director, UK Churches' Team, Tearfund, UK.

Vincent Nichols, Cardinal Archbishop of Westminster, UK.

Hannah Swithinbank, Leader, Theological and Network Engagement Team, Tearfund, UK.

Justin Thacker, Lecturer in Practical and Public Theology, Cliff College, Calver, Derbyshire, UK.

Myrto Theocharous, Professor of Hebrew and Old Testament, Greek Bible College, Athens, Greece.

Stephen Timms, MP, House of Commons, Westminster, UK.

Graham Tomlin, Bishop of Kensington and President of St Mellitus College (London), UK.

Steve Walton, Associate Research Fellow, Trinity College, Bristol, UK; formerly Professor in New Testament, St Mary's University, Twickenham (London), UK.

Part One

Poverty Then and Now

Two Concepts of Poverty: A Theological Analysis

Justin Thacker

Individual versus relational concepts of poverty

Some years ago, I knew a widow in Uganda called Charity.[1] Charity lived in a ramshackle dwelling with a dirt floor, no electricity and a shared, outside long drop toilet. One of her children had died of malaria and out of her three remaining children, Charity could only afford to pay the school fees for one of them. One of her children had recently been taken to hospital, showing evidence of early malnutrition. Charity primarily cooked with wood and charcoal, and she did not own a TV, telephone, bike, motorbike, refrigerator or car. According to one well-established definition, Charity's household was suffering from multidimensional poverty.[2] This index seeks to define poverty in a more meaningful manner than mere economic measures. It consists of ten indices in three domains covering health, education and living standards. It has been widely praised as moving definitions of poverty beyond an obsession with gross domestic product (GDP) per capita. One possible response, then, to Charity is to observe the multiple deprivations in which she finds herself and seek to remedy them.

Charity could be provided with an improved dwelling, perhaps a stone- or brick-built house. It could be connected to the recently developed electricity grid and might have a stone floor and an inside, flushing toilet. A direct cash transfer might help her with the school fees or better nutrition for her children, and perhaps a micro-loan would enable her and her family to build up a small enterprise and in time find the funds to purchase one of the 'luxury' goods mentioned in the multidimensional definition of poverty.

The reason I tell this story, however, is that this is only one way to interpret the poverty that Charity experienced. For as I got to know Charity, one of the things that

---

In addition to the discussion here, see more fully Justin Thacker, *Global Poverty: A Theological Guide* (London: SCM, 2017).

[1] In order to protect anonymity, some of the details of this case have been changed. The overall thrust of the example, though, is of a real person whom I knew well.

[2] S. Alkire et al., 'Global Multidimensional Poverty Index 2015', *Oxford Poverty and Human Development Initiative* (June 2015) (http://www.ophi.org.uk/wp-content/uploads/Global-MPI-8-pager_10_15.pdf, accessed May 2016). See also http://www.ophi.org.uk/multidimensional-poverty-index/mpi-2015/ (accessed February 2017).

became clear was that she was very intelligent and hardworking. Initially, this puzzled me, for I could not understand how Charity could be so bright and yet only find employment in a very low-status, poorly paid position. On one occasion, I commented on her clear intelligence and her relative lack of status within her work, and she told me her story. The senior manager at her workplace had demanded that Charity sleep with him. She refused, and as a result, she was told she would stay in that low position despite her clearly having the ability to take on a more demanding role.

I tell this story because it illustrates two different ways in which we can conceive of poverty. On one level, Charity undoubtedly did suffer from a series of individual material deprivations. This 'poverty as individual lack' framework represents the dominant paradigm for understanding poverty in much of the literature. At the same time, one can also interpret her poverty in terms of disempowerment and a failure of relationships. Transparently, her relationship with that senior manager was deeply flawed, but, in addition, the whole relational dynamic of the workplace was also flawed. How was it possible for one individual to wield such power? Where were the necessary checks and balances? The relational dysfunction did not just end at the institution's gates though. Charity did not have access to due process of law, which speaks of a wider relational breakdown within the whole of her community affecting in particular widowed women, and of a gender discrimination that continues to plague much of our world. Indeed, one could extend this argument even further to argue that Charity's material deprivation is actually the result of a dysfunctional relational dynamic not just at a local or even national level but also includes the whole globe across both space and time. It has been argued by some that one of the reasons why 'big man leadership' exists in a range of African communities is because during the colonial era, it was the West that fomented the development of internal elites and a strategy of internal corruption.[3] In short, it was because of the way in which our Western forebears acted some 200 years ago, combined with the relative absence of good global governance today, that Charity exists in a state of multidimensional poverty. On this understanding, then, the nature of her poverty is fundamentally (dis)relational.

We have then two distinct ways in which to conceive of poverty. Following Amartya Sen, Alkire and others have helpfully moved us beyond an understanding of poverty as just economic deprivation towards a broader conception that encompasses the multiple indices that she and others have developed. However, even with a multidimensional understanding of poverty, there remain these two different conceptual frameworks that impact any discussion of poverty. The first of these is what is best characterized as an individualistic concept of poverty. Within this understanding, the object of concern is the individual or perhaps the family unit, and poverty is described in terms of the multiple deprivations that such an individual (or family) might experience: lack of adequate nutrition, lack of access to healthcare, lack of clean water, poor sanitation and so on. This is the primary form of poverty analysis in the biblical, theological and social scientific literature.

---

[3]   James M. Cypher and James L. Dietz, *The Process of Economic Development*, 4th edn (London: Routledge, 2014), 87.

There is, though, another way to conceptualize poverty, and that is to think of it in relational terms. Conceptually, this means not just noting that this person lacks access to clean water but also exploring why, in relational terms, this is the case. Is it due to gender disempowerment, tribal allegiances, local favouritism, national – or even international – policies? All of these could represent the ultimate reason why an individual (or family) lacks access to clean water. Under a relational framework of thought, one does not just seek to meet the particular material deprivation that is being experienced, but rather one seeks to bring about a state in which right (or at least healthier) relationships exist between the relevant parties. Returning for a moment to Charity, one could, in principle, directly address all of her multiple deprivations. In the short and possible medium term, this would be beneficial. Or, one could ensure that her relationship with that senior manager was healthy – which of course might and probably would mean his dismissal from a position of power – thereby enabling her to use her God-given potential to flourish. In the rest of this chapter, I will be exploring how in recent biblical scholarship these two concepts of poverty have been in play, and I also discuss the theological significance of this. In the process, I argue that as biblical theologians, we should more clearly be seeking to frame our concepts of poverty in relational terms, not least because such a relational understanding implicates us in the West in the ongoing maintenance of poverty to a far greater extent than we may realize.

Oakes's deprivation concept of poverty

In 2004, Peter Oakes published a paper in which he argued for a more 'sociological' and 'multidimensional' definition of poverty than was currently doing the rounds in New Testament scholarship.[4] In particular, he had in mind a paper by Friesen which had sought to develop an economic poverty scale for Graeco-Roman society.[5] In response, Oakes drew on work by Peter Townsend to argue for a broader conception of poverty that identifies a wide range of deprivations. He quotes with approval Townsend's definition of poverty as 'the lack of the resources necessary to permit participation in the activities, customs and diets commonly approved by society'.[6] In the course of developing this argument, Oakes lists examples of such deprivations:

- adequate diet for survival
- adequate diet for good health
- diet suitable to status
- adequate living space
- living space suitable to status
- support for immediate family

---

[4] Peter Oakes, 'Constructing Poverty Scales for Graeco-Roman Society: A Response to Steven Friesen's "Poverty in Pauline Studies"', *JSNT* 26.3 (2004): 367–71, here 371.
[5] Steven Friesen, 'Poverty in Pauline Studies', *JSNT* 26.3 (2004): 323–61.
[6] Peter Townsend, *Poverty in the United Kingdom* (Harmondsworth: Penguin, 1979), 88.

- support for extended family
- provision of dowry
- purchase of medical help
- freedom to control use of time
- liberation from slavery
- liberation from abusive relationship
- freedom from likelihood of periodic want
- retention of inherited land
- carrying out of religious obligations.[7]

While it is undoubtedly clear that many of these deprivations have a social dimension – liberation from an abusive relationship being the obvious example – it is also clear that the focus of attention is the individual experiencing these deprivations. It is person Y who has an inadequate diet or poor living space or is prevented from carrying out their religious obligations. This individualistic approach to poverty analysis is also one that characterizes the work of Amartya Sen, on whom Oakes also draws. Oakes nominates the deprivations listed above as 'inabilities' and so writes regarding his ordered poverty scale that it 'can be characterized by combinations of inabilities'.[8] It is unclear whether this was intentional or not, but such language echoes that of Sen and his capabilities approach to poverty. In a seminal work on international poverty, Sen – a Nobel Prize-winning economist – describes poverty as 'deprivation of basic capabilities'.[9] Perhaps an even clearer parallel between the two authors can be observed when we compare their respective definitions of poverty:

(Sen) For example, in the capability view, the poverty line may be deemed to represent the level at which a person can not only meet nutritional requirements, etc., but also achieve adequate participation in communal activities.[10]

(Oakes) I took current sociological work on poverty in places such as Britain and India[11] and argued that it is best defined in terms of deprivation, that is, the economically enforced inability to participate in the normal activities of society.[12]

This approach to poverty in New Testament scholarship has been the dominant paradigm and is often simply assumed.[13] There is of course much to commend it,

[7] Oakes, 'Constructing', 371.
[8] Ibid.
[9] Amartya Sen, *Development as Freedom* (Oxford: Oxford University Press, 1999), 20.
[10] Amartya Sen, 'Poor, Relatively Speaking', *Oxford Economic Papers* 35 (1983): 153–69, here 167.
[11] Sen's primary studies on poverty were undertaken in India, and, therefore, it is quite likely that this is a reference to Sen's work.
[12] Peter Oakes, 'Methodological Issues in Using Economic Evidence in Interpretation of Early Christian Texts' in *Engaging Economics: New Testament Scenarios and Early Christian Reception*, ed. Bruce Longenecker and Kelly Liebengood (Grand Rapids, MI: Eerdmans, 2009), 9–34, here 30.
[13] See, e.g., Bruce Longenecker, *Remember the Poor: Paul, Poverty and the Graeco-Roman World* (Grand Rapids, MI: Eerdmans, 2010), especially ch. 3, '"The Least of These": Scaling Poverty in the Graeco-Roman World'.

not least, as Longenecker points out, its heuristic value in helping us analyse Graeco-Roman society.[14]

Individual versus relational poverty in international development

However, there remains a problem with this approach, which is best illustrated by analysing in more depth the individualism that characterizes it. In respect of international development, which Sen defines as the 'process of expanding the real freedoms that people enjoy',[15] which he goes on to explain are 'the capabilities – to choose a life one has reason to value',[16] he writes, 'The analysis of development presented in this book treats the freedom of individuals as the basic building blocks.'[17] Sen's concern is to protect the individual freedoms of individual people to choose a life that they have reason to value. This is what he means by capabilities. Poverty, then, represents the inability to exercise such freedoms. The obvious critique of this approach is that it would appear to tend towards an individualism in which what matters is what *I* choose to value, not what is of value to my whole community, let alone my group, my nation or the world. Sen's purpose in this is to avoid a utilitarianism in which the individual becomes merely the tool of the state for some greater good. Alkire and Deneulin defend Sen by arguing that he is merely offering us a form of ethical individualism – what ultimately matters ethically is the individual – rather than some form of methodological or ontological individualism.[18] Nevertheless, the possibility of critiquing Sen's framework as too individualistic remains, for in respect of any freedom I wish to exercise, one cannot avoid the relational aspects of that capability. I may choose to value education and so choose to pay for my child to attend school, but in so doing I am also contributing to the salaries of teachers, the learning experience of other children and the potential loss of business to other traders who now do not receive my money as it is being spent on education. My point, therefore, is not so much that we should reject an individualistic analysis of poverty as such. It is more that such an ethical individualism does not sufficiently comport with reality.

Klaasen draws attention to this point when he juxtaposes the Alkire/Sen definition of development, concerning which he writes, 'There is not a strong sense of mutually enriching interaction', with one developed in South Africa: 'a process of planned social change designed to promote the wellbeing of the population as a whole'.[19] He writes,

---

[14] Longenecker, *Remember*, 53.
[15] Sen, *Development*, 3.
[16] Ibid., 74.
[17] Ibid., 18.
[18] Séverine Deneulin and Sabina Alkire, 'The Human Development and Capability Approach', in *An Introduction to the Human Development and Capability Approach: Freedom and Agency*, ed. Séverine Deneulin and Lila Shahani (London: Earthscan, 2009), 22–48, here 35.
[19] John Klaasen, 'The Interplay between Theology and Development: How Theology Can Be Related to Development in Post-Modern Society', *Missionalia* 41.2 (2013): 182–94, here 185.

'Sen's definition of development restricts development to the increase of the choices of the individual . . . Unlike the capability approach that compartmentalizes the person, development of the person happens in relationships with other persons and the rest of creation, including structures, societal units or material resources.'[20]

Klaasen writes from an African perspective, and although he bases his argument on Trinitarian theology and definitions of personhood derived from the Cappadocian Fathers, it is perhaps not surprising that he writes such theology in that particular social context, for, of course, a relational ontology is precisely what is found in the African concept of *Ubuntu*, 'I am because we are.' Ilo explains it thus:

> Ubuntu is today one of the most current categories from African communitarian ethics in reconciling communities, in building interdependent relationship, and encouraging the service of charity in truth. It is being embraced in international development discourse as a way of showing the mutuality of human living on earth, and the bond that could be established across racial, economic, political, and religious lines based on love and friendship. It is also another way of expressing the triple bottom line of people, prosperity, and planet (God + 3BL) as irreducibly inter-twined in any authentic and sustainable development praxis.[21]

Newbigin draws clearly the contrast between this conception and the Western individualistic model:

> For African society, the human person is seen as a partner in a whole network of relationships binding him or her horizontally across a widely extended family and vertically to the ancestors who have died and to children yet to be born. To be human is to be part of this closely woven fabric of relationships. By contrast, the Western post-Enlightenment understanding of the human person centers on the autonomy of the individual who is free to make or to break relationships at will.[22]

The key phrase here is 'irreducibly intertwined'. Sen appears to advocate an approach in which the individual *qua* individual evaluates the freedoms that they desire and is enabled to pursue those freedoms. For him, that is *development*. But, as Ilo indicates, such freedoms are 'irreducibly intertwined' with the freedom of others. The coffee I choose has an impact on the wage earned by a day labourer in Kenya, and therefore whether his or her child can pay for the medicines they require. Given this state of affairs, *development* has occurred not when all individuals have maximal capabilities – for such a situation is theoretically, let alone practically, impossible. Rather, *development* has occurred when in our relating to one another we do so with justice and righteousness.

---

[20] Klaasen, 'Interplay', 192.
[21] Stan Chu Ilo, *The Church and Development in Africa*, 2nd edn (Eugene, OR: Pickwick, 2014), 265.
[22] Lesslie Newbigin, *The Gospel in a Pluralist Society* (London: SPCK, 1994), 187–8.

Green's relational definition of the poor in Luke

In contrast to the somewhat individualistic concept of poverty expressed by Sen, and to some extent followed by Oakes and Longenecker, Joel Green, in his analysis of the poor in Luke, strikes a somewhat different note. In 1994/1995, Green published two chapters in two different books (with some overlapping material) that addressed the question of the 'poor' in Luke-Acts.[23] He draws attention to the way in which most New Testament scholarship interpreted Luke's use of the 'poor' in largely, or even exclusively, economic terms. 'Our tendency today is to define "the poor" economically, on a scale of annual household income or with reference to an established, national or international poverty line.'[24] However, Green argues that this is to interpret Luke through our own cultural lenses and that in reality, Luke's concept of 'the poor' was far more multidimensional than that (though that is not the terminology he uses). The real issue for Luke was not so much economic prosperity but 'status honor', one's standing and acceptance within the community, and so he writes,

> Status honor is a measure of social standing that embraces wealth, but also other factors, including access to education, family heritage, ethnicity, vocation, religious purity, and gender. In the Graeco-Roman world, then, poverty is too narrowly defined when understood solely in economic terms.[25]

In support of this argument, he points, in particular, to the pericope of the poor widow (Lk. 21.1-4) and highlights the contrast between this 'poor' widow and the 'rich' teachers of the law oppressing her. While the latter are characterized by honour, power and standing, she is characterized by dishonour, shame and exploitation. In other words, while she certainly did suffer from economic poverty, that was not the whole of the picture that Luke presents to us, and not wholly what he means when he describes her as 'poor'.[26] In addition, he notes how Luke repeatedly juxtaposes the word 'poor' with a range of words that flesh out its meaning. These include: captive, blind, oppressed, hungry, mournful, persecuted, lame, deaf and leper.[27] He concludes by saying, 'The impression with which one is left is that Luke is concerned above with a class of people defined by their dishonourable status, their positions outside circles of power and prestige, their being excluded.'[28] He notes how Zacchaeus, though materially wealthy, could be included within the Lukan 'poor' because he enjoyed the status of social outcast.[29]

---

[23] Joel B. Green, 'Good News to Whom?', in *Jesus of Nazareth Lord and Christ*, ed. Joel B. Green and Max Turner (Grand Rapids, MI: Eerdmans, 1994), 59–74; Joel B. Green, 'To Proclaim Good News to the Poor: Mission and Salvation' in his *The Theology of the Gospel of Luke* (Cambridge: Cambridge University Press, 1995), 76–101.

[24] Green, 'To Proclaim', 79–80.

[25] Green, 'Good News', 65.

[26] Ibid., 67.

[27] Ibid., 68.

[28] Ibid.

[29] Ibid., 72.

What is certainly clear in the Lukan narratives is that even when the focus of Luke's attention is someone who is economically poor, Luke frequently draws attention to the relational dynamics of their poverty. So as already indicated, the woman with two small coins is presented as someone whose house has been devoured by the powerful. Similarly, the leper in Lk. 5.12-14 is healed, but also touched and thereby restored to the socio-religious community. For Luke, then, economic poverty is never the only thing which matters. He does not, for instance, portray Jesus as merely healing the leper or merely observing the poor widow's plight. Rather, he always draws attention to the relational aspects of their material poverty.

Green's versus Oakes's definitions of poverty

What is interesting about Green's analysis vis-à-vis Oakes is that while both emphasize the multidimensional aspects of poverty that go significantly beyond mere economic measures, the emphasis in Green seems to lie in the relational dynamics of such poverty rather than in the individual deprivations that may be experienced. So while Oakes talks in terms of an inability to participate in society due to a 'lack of resources', Green writes,

> 'Poor' has become a cipher for those of low status, for those excluded according to normal canons of status honour in the Mediterranean world. Although 'poor' is hardly devoid of economic significance, for Luke this wider meaning of diminished status honour is paramount . . . 'Poor' is not to be narrowly understood along economic lines, but also as a measure of belonging, a matter of group definition. In the Third Gospel, 'good news to the poor' is pre-eminently a gracious word of inclusion to the dispossessed, the excluded.[30]

My point in all this is not to criticize Oakes and commend Green as if they are sitting on two different sides of some putative debate in which I am in favour of Green. Rather, I suspect somewhat unconsciously that two distinct conceptions of poverty are in circulation. As such, it is not that Oakes has intentionally *decided* for the individualistic conception and Green has *decided* for the relational (though, of course, I may be wrong about that and there is far more intentionality than I perceive). Rather, their different emphases (and it is only a difference of emphasis) lies in the respective origins of their work on this issue. Oakes, it would appear, draws heavily on Townsend and Sen – both of whom have drunk deeply at the Enlightenment well of knowledge, and so both reflect the Western individualism that characterizes most enlightenment thinking since Descartes. In contrast, Green is, I would suggest, performing a perhaps less-conditioned exegesis of the relevant texts. I am not suggesting that Green can bracket out his Western, and doubtless individualistic, education, but his goal is more clearly to simply elucidate what the texts say. And in this regard, his conclusions reflect the Graeco-Hebraic background to the Lukan narrative – a background that is not

---

[30] Ibid., 69.

tainted by Enlightenment individualism but reflects, in particular, the more relational ontology that characterized Jewish thinking of the first century. It is for this reason I suggest that Green's description of poverty is more relational.

Of course, another way to characterize this difference in emphasis would be suggesting that Oakes's framework is more informed by a Pauline analysis, while Green's analysis is based on Lukan texts. Perhaps it could be argued that Luke's Galilean emphasis reflects a rural concept of poverty while Paul's more urban context reflects poverty as experienced there. The argument would be that status honour and, therefore, relationships, are more significant factors in rural than urban contexts. The problem with this argument is that intuitively one would expect the precise opposite: that the rural environment would have relatively less social stratification than urban environments, and, as such, status honour would comparatively be less of a factor in the rural (Lukan) context than the urban (Pauline) one. Hence, it is hard to argue that Paul was individualistic in a way that Luke was not. While we know far more of the personal history of Paul than we do of Luke, it is not at all clear that they occupied different cultures. Indeed, it is almost certain that they both lived and breathed Hellenized Judaism. To that extent, the difference between Oakes and Green cannot be ascribed to their respective fields of study: Pauline and Lukan texts.

The corporate image of God

Theologically, this difference in emphasis finds a ready parallel in differing interpretations of the *imago Dei* ('image of God'). For most of Christian history, the disputes regarding the *imago Dei* terminology have focused on the precise locale of God's image. Westermann provides a careful history of this debate and notes the way in which the *imago Dei* has been variously located in particular spiritual capacities (e.g. the soul or mind), corporeal capacities (e.g. ability to stand upright or communicate), functional capacities (e.g. as representatives of God on Earth) and relational capacities (e.g. as counterparts to God) of humans.[31] The third of these has the greatest support in terms of other Ancient Near Eastern texts.[32] However, it is in regard to the last that I would like to develop some thoughts here. Westermann comments, 'The uniqueness of human beings consists in their being God's counterparts. The relationship to God is not something which is added to human existence; humans are created in such a way that their very existence is intended to be their relationship to God.'[33] Westermann does not mention him, but such language echoes of course the work of John Zizioulas. In discussing the ontological nature of Trinitarian theology, Zizioulas writes, 'The person is no longer an adjunct to a being, a category we *add* to a concrete entity once we have first verified its ontological hypostasis. *It is itself the hypostasis of the being*.'[34]

---

[31] Claus Westermann, *Genesis 1–11* (London: SPCK, 1984), 147–58.
[32] This concept has particularly been developed in J. Richard Middleton, *The Liberating Image: The Imago Dei in Genesis 1* (Grand Rapids, MI: Brazos, 2005).
[33] Westermann, *Genesis 1–11*, 158.
[34] John Zizioulas, *Being as Communion* (Crestwood: St Vladimir's Seminary, 1985), 39 (emphasis original).

For Zizioulas, this mean that our fundamental identity is as persons-in-relation. We do not, first of all, exist and then discover our relationships to God or others, but our identity as extant persons is bound up with our relationship to God.

All of this is standard fare in much contemporary theological anthropology, at least that influenced by the twentieth-century Trinitarian revival.[35] However, it is possible to take Westermann's description of the *imago Dei* even further by adding one more idea: 'The uniqueness of human beings consists in their being God's counterparts. The relationship to God is not something which is added to human existence; humans are created in such a way that their very existence is intended to be their relationship to God [and other human beings]'.[36] If we add this description – and, at least according to Westermann, there are form critical reasons for doing so[37] – then we have transitioned into a direction for *imago*-speak that has been most fully expounded by Jürgen Moltmann and, in particular, his concept of a corporate *imago Dei*. For most of Christian history, it has undoubtedly been the case that even though we have debated the precise capacity that corresponds to the image of God, there has been a consensus that the relevant capacity is one that exists in the individual human being. A particular man or woman has a soul, intellect, ability to communicate, ability to represent God on Earth, ability to relate to God – and in that capacity lies their image of God. In contrast, Moltmann makes the case for a corporate sense of *imago Dei*. In other words, it is not the individual human that images God in some way, but that we image God collectively as humans in relation to one another. He describes the earlier forms of *imago* thinking as showing 'a tendency towards monotheism in the concept of God, and a trend towards individualism in anthropology'.[38] Moltmann sums up this way of thinking thus:

> The individual human in his spiritual subjectivity corresponds to the absolute subject, God. So it is to the spiritual subjectivity alone that the dignity of the likeness to God is ascribed. Human relationships, mediated through body and soul, are secondary to this. Every individual soul must be esteemed as an *imago*.[39]

In contrast to this, his argument for a corporate sense of the *imago* proceeds along these lines. The Jewish Scriptures had no concept of a separated body and soul. As such, the *imago Dei* must rest in the whole of our humanity – both body and soul, or, more precisely, a whole human being. Yet, humans are created as both male and female, and this characteristic seems to be a particular focus of the *imago* narrative – 'in the image of God he created them; male and female he created them' (Gen. 1.27). For Moltmann, this means that the image of God does not reside in the 'sexless soul', nor does it reside in the individual man *qua* man, for men alone do not represent the image of God on Earth. Rather, the image must reside in humans *as* men and women. And if the image only exists in both men and women, then that means the image necessarily

[35] For an alternative perspective see Stephen Holmes, *The Holy Trinity* (Milton Keynes: Paternoster, 2012).
[36] Westermann, *Genesis 1–11*, 158.
[37] Ibid., 156–7.
[38] Jürgen Moltmann, *God in Creation* (London: SCM, 1985), 234.
[39] Moltmann, *God in Creation*, 239.

requires humans *as* community. In this way, the *imago Dei* is not an individualistic concept, some attribute of a single human. Rather, the *imago Dei* refers to the whole human community as it exists in relation both to God and to one another. Indeed, we could add – and to the rest of non-human creation – but that is a topic for another day.

Contrasting this corporate view with the individualistic anthropology that pervades much theological discussion, Moltmann writes, 'But if we instead interpret the whole human being as *imago*, we then have to understand the fundamental human community as *imago* as well.'[40] And so he writes,

> This community already corresponds to God, because in this community God finds his own correspondence. It represents God on earth, and God 'appears' on earth in his male-female image. Likeness to God cannot be lived in isolation. It can be lived only in human community. This means that from the very outset human beings are social beings . . . Consequently, they can only relate to themselves if, and to the extent in which, other people relate to them. The isolated individual and the solitary subject are deficient modes of being human, because they fall short of the likeness to God.[41]

As we have seen then, in parallel to the individualistic and relational concept of poverty already noted, there exists an individualistic and relational/corporate concept of the 'image of God' (*imago Dei*).

This point is well illustrated by Kang's work regarding HIV stigma. He draws attention to the fact that increasingly the social scientific literature is no longer conceiving of HIV-AIDS as a purely medical, individualistic problem: a disease to be cured. Rather, HIV-AIDS is considered primarily as a social phenomenon.[42] Kang then links this to Moltmann's Trinitarian concept of the *imago Dei* and, in the process, argues that our efforts to address the social dimensions of HIV-AIDS are of a piece with our efforts to image the corporate *imago Dei*.

> HIV-stigma cannot be singularly framed as an intrinsic spoiled identity based on illness. . . . As such, efforts to reduce or mitigate the destructive vestiges of stigma that linger must address social relationships that are embedded in socio-economic and political structures that insidiously exclude and devalue these groups. Moltmann's doctrine of the social *imago Dei* provides an important framework to challenge and guide how Christians begin addressing this complex web of factors.[43]

Kang's example serves to demonstrate the practical import of this reframing of the concept of poverty. It reminds us that poverty is not merely a problem affecting *them*,

---

[40] Moltmann, *God in Creation*, 241.
[41] Ibid., 223.
[42] Ezer Kang, 'Human Immunodeficiency Virus (HIV) Stigma: Spoiled Social Identity and Jürgen Moltmann's Trinitarian Model of the *Imago Dei*', *International Journal of Public Theology* 9 (2015): 289–312, here 289.
[43] Kang, 'Human', 311–12.

for which we have the solution. Rather, poverty is a problem affecting all of us – albeit in different ways.

Swart, a South African theologian, has written of this in terms of a 'double movement' in our poverty alleviation efforts. The first is a movement towards the poor, providing relief and assistance; the second is a movement towards the wealthy and a call for repentance and change in our complicity in sustaining economies of deprivation. In this context, he writes,

> Within the aforementioned framework, the most important innovation has certainly been the shift away from the conventional perspective that development should be viewed as the exclusive 'problem of poor people' and 'poor communities'. Instead, the point has been emphasized that development should be considered as much if not more so a 'problem of the rich' and 'rich communities' and their preservation of the current capitalist system. In turn, this shift in emphasis has led to the rather radical social theological insight of the necessity of a new 'double movement' in development in which the imperative of renewal, conversion, and change should as much be directed to the life-worlds of the economically rich and privileged.[44]

This point has also been made by Rowan Williams, the former Archbishop of Canterbury. He is not especially well known for his writing on poverty and international development, but in an important excursus on this topic, he makes the rather telling point that when we work with someone in a situation of poverty seeking to free them from the ravages of nature, the one being liberated is not whom we might think:

> We are not trying to solve someone else's problem but to liberate *ourselves* from a toxic and unjust situation in which we, the prosperous, are less than human. The way forward is not simply the shedding of surplus wealth on to grateful recipients but an understanding that we are trying to take forward the process by which the other becomes as fully a 'giver' as I seek to be, so that the transaction by which I seek to bring about change in the direction of justice for another is one in which I come to be as much in the other's debt as they are in mine.[45]

This is a profound point, and one that far too often seems to escape the international development community. In 2016, the *Guardian* newspaper published a pseudonymous blog in which the author bemoans critiques of the aid industry and wrote this, 'You can parse it many ways, but in simple English the purpose of the aid system is to facilitate the continued flow of resources between donors and beneficiaries . . . The purpose of

---

[44] Ignatius Swart, 'Meeting the Challenge of Poverty and Exclusion: The Emerging Field of Development Research in South African Practical Theology', *International Journal of Practical Theology* 12.1 (2008): 104–49, here 134. See also Bretherton, who argues that a faithful response to poverty is not so much altruism as 'repentance': Luke Bretherton, 'Poverty, Politics and Faithful Witness in the Age of Humanitarianism', *Int* 69.4 (2015): 447–59, here 453.
[45] Rowan Williams, 'A Theology of Development', 5 (emphasis original) (http://clients.squareeye.net/uploads/anglican/documents/theologyofdevelopment.pdf, accessed July 2015).

the aid system is to move resources – money, stuff, knowledge or expertise – from the hands of donors to the hands of beneficiaries. It is that basic.'[46]

In contrast, for Williams, in a situation of poverty there exists a double (at least) condition of slavery in which humans are not fully imaging God as intended. In the first place, the one subject to creation – the one experiencing any of the multiple indices of deprivation mentioned earlier – is not fully imaging God, because to fully bear the likeness of the Creator is to exist in a state whereby creation is stewarded by us, rather than we being subjects of creation. But *at the same time*, those of us in the rich West are also not fully bearing the likeness of the Creator. We are, in Williams's words, being 'less than human', because we too are embroiled in a situation in which the corporate flourishing of humanity is not taking place and we are participants in that corporate failure. Paul reminds us that when one part suffers, all parts suffer with it (1 Cor. 12.26). Thus, what is being proposed here is that the image of God is only fully displayed when *every* human is in a state of creaturely flourishing, characterized by good relations with one other and the planet.

The fundamental problem, then, with the paradigm presented by the *Guardian* blog is that the authors assumes that we – those of us in the rich West – have arrived, and that the job of the aid community is to help others climb up the same ladder that we ourselves have climbed.[47] The value of Swart's and Williams's point is that it forces those of us who live in the West to recognize not just that we are part of the problem, but that we are in need of salvation too. When one is working with an individualistic concept of poverty, then the solution to poverty rapidly becomes providing individuals with more things – especially things that the West has come to value. In the process, the individual becomes an object of charity, an aid recipient, someone to whom we extend our largesse. In contrast, a relational concept of poverty reminds us that corporately we are failing to display the *imago Dei*, that the problem is not *them*, but *us*, or, more precisely, *all of us*, and that the solution to poverty is not about trying to make them like us but consists in bringing about right relationships across the whole of our globe. In short, the transformation that is required is a transformation of all.

---

[46] J, 'Is Humanitarian Aid Really Broken? Or Should We All Just Calm Down?', *The Guardian*, 6 Jan 2016 (http://www.theguardian.com/global-development-professionals-network/2016/jan/06/is-humanitarian-aid-really-broken-or-should-we-all-just-calm-down?CMP=share_btn_tw, accessed May 2016).

[47] In terms of development theory, this approach is called modernization theory, and while it is rejected by many scholars, it is alive and well in much practitioner thinking. Such an approach has been criticised by Melba Maggay, a Filipino theologian; cf. Melba Maggay, 'The Influence of Religion and Culture in Development in the Phillipines', in *Carnival Kingdom: Biblical Justice for Global Communities*, ed. Marijke Hoek, Jonathan Ingleby, Carol Kingston-Smith and Andy Kingston-Smith (Gloucester: Wide Margin, 2013), 177–205.

2

Poverty and Its Causes in the Early Church

Lynn H. Cohick

Introduction

The title of this essay, 'Poverty and Its Causes in the Early Church', is wonderfully provocative, for it demands not only a definition of poverty but also an explanation for why such a situation exists. Then, as now, 'poverty' is a relative term, and defining it entails a reflection on the economic, moral, social, gender and political aspects of the poor person. The ancient Roman world rarely reflected on the causes of poverty. Instead, the elite focused on such topics as the moral questions surrounding wealth, the civic responsibilities of the wealthy and the moral failings of those who laboured for a living. The New Testament (NT), likewise, does not weigh in on this specific debate about the causes of poverty per se.[1] Instead, it focuses on the needs of the poor person, including physical care and justice, and the requirements of those with means to provide aid. This book is dedicated to exploring these needs and requirements, and I am especially eager to hear the work of those who engage in poverty issues today. This essay will hopefully provide a historical backdrop for these discussions and highlight the primary evidence used by theorists in determining the economic profile of the earliest Christians.

When I began this exploration into the questions surrounding ancient poverty and wealth, I created a list of possible causes of poverty present in the age of the early church. I reckoned my three years living in rural Kenya had alerted me to systemic issues of poverty, to which I could add my knowledge of the Hellenistic and early Roman Imperial periods. My research affirmed that, in some cases, my list was accurate. For example, natural disasters such as drought or flooding can wreak havoc on food supplies.[2] Poor sanitary conditions and lack of medical knowledge, coupled

---

[1] Steven J. Friesen, 'Injustice or God's Will? Early Christian Explanations of Poverty', in *Wealth and Poverty in Early Church and Society*, ed. Susan R. Holman (Grand Rapids, MI: Baker Academic, 2008), 17–36, here 18, observes that he could not find 'a single study on early Christian analyses of the causes of poverty'.

[2] Peter Garnsey, *Cities, Peasants and Food in Classical Antiquity: Essays in Social and Economic History*, ed. with addenda by Walter Scheiden (Cambridge: Cambridge University Press, 1998), 275, who concludes that 'famines, thus defined, are, and always have been, rare: they are genuine catastrophes'. Garnsey concludes that famine is linked to the 'collapse of the social, political and moral order'

with rather routine epidemics, took many able-bodied labourers from the work force and brought families to ruin.[3] These factors fall under the categories of human ignorance and 'acts of God', and generally are not the focus of research on the ancient economy or concepts of wealth and poverty. Instead, government policies, taxes and laws, the Roman military and cultural values informing 'the good life' all play roles in creating wealth and causing poverty in the period of the early church.

Scholars analyse poverty in this period using at least three different approaches: social scientific models, economic analysis and archaeological research. The results can be roughly divided into two rather distinct pictures. On the one hand, classicists using theories from economics conclude that between roughly 200 BCE and 200 CE, the Roman economy flourished at levels not again reached until the early Industrial Era. Archaeological evidence, at the very least, does not contradict this conclusion and often seems to strengthen it. On the other hand, those drawing on social science models emphasize conflict between elite and peasant, with its attending injustice and displacement of the landless subsistence farmer. This approach rightly warns readers today to avoid imposing their own economic biases and assumptions onto the ancient world; however, in some cases, the social scientific models' expectations of class conflict and oppression may posit such activity in the absence of any solid evidence.

This paper argues that the late Republic and early Roman Imperial period (first century BCE to second century CE) was a time of economic upturn that included widespread trade and developing ceramic and textile industries offering employment and livelihood to many. I am persuaded that the majority of households were not at the brink of starvation and ruin by debt, although populations suffered widespread hunger at times due to epidemics or war. For example, Josephus tells us that Queen Helena from Adiabene, a recent convert to Judaism, helped those in Jerusalem during a crisis. Josephus states that 'many people died for want to money to procure food. Queen Helena sent some of her servants to Alexandria with money to buy a great quantity of grain, and others of them to Cyprus to bring back a cargo of dried figs . . . which she immediately distributed to those that need' (*Ant.* 20.2.5).[4] Individuals faced poverty for several reasons, including from (1) forces that weakened the body, such as disease and malnutrition, and (2) lack of opportunity to find work or benefit from one's labour, often related to both (3) government policy or injustice that benefited only those in power and (4) the clash of ideologies as Rome imposed its cultural, social and political will on subject ethnicities who held opposing fundamental views. I will focus primarily on the latter two causes. The essays from Fiona Gregson and Christopher Hays will go much more into depth in this area.

---

(280). See also Peter Garnsey, *Famine and Food Supply in the Graeco-Roman World: Responses to Risk and Crisis* (Cambridge: Cambridge University Press, 1988).

[3] Galen, *De Rebus Boni Malique Suci* 1.1–3, notes that the countryside could face a food shortage even as the city had stored food to sustain them. Eating unwholesome foods, such as roots, twigs and grasses, led to skin diseases, tumors, fevers, dysentery and abscesses. Garnsey notes that the 'effect of famine is largely indirect' and that 'infection [is] the real killer' (*Cities*, 283–84).

[4] This famine was probably 46–48 CE, although it may have started in Fadus's time, 44 CE. Claudius ruled 41–54 CE.

Additionally, the institution of slavery played a key role in the Roman economy, and its economic impact is so vast that it properly requires a separate treatment.[5] The slave is quite often the face of the poor; however, most studies reserve the categories of poverty and 'the poor' to free men and women, and to freedmen and freedwomen (i.e. those who had been freed from slavery). This is due perhaps in part to the connection we make today between poverty/wealth and labour choices and conditions. Thus, while we cannot treat its impact in this short essay, we must keep in mind slavery's pervasive impact on wages and labourers' opportunity to work their land and freedom to innovate.

Definitions of poverty

Our study focuses on the causes of poverty, a topic embedded within a larger conversation. To look at poverty, one must determine what counts as wealth; both are relative terms that reflect opposite poles of a given group of people. Poverty often implies deprivation, as Peter Oakes recognizes when he defines poverty as 'the economically enforced inability to participate in the normal activities of society.'[6] Oakes concludes that researching economy involves 'the study of the allocation of scarce resources.'[7] He rightly notes that social position does not easily map onto the economic situation of the individual; for example, in rather rare cases, one finds a wealthy slave. He warns, 'Any attempt to isolate economics from other social factors such as politics would be doomed.'[8] Mik Larsen follows Oakes, citing Adam Smith's characterization that the poor lack the ability 'to participate fully in society.'[9] Larsen discusses the complexity of defining poverty from the literature of the day. Some ancient authors argued that poverty in the abstract could be a virtuous and noble state, but actual poverty in the present could be a threat to social order and stability. Additionally, one reads much about 'wellborn poverty', which befalls the upper classes, and 'voluntary poverty' chosen by the wealthy whose morality is thereby exemplified by their frugality.[10] Urban poor lacked land and, thus, were derided as failing to be self-sufficient.[11] As Harris laments, 'While it is possible to write the *cultural* history of

[5] Moses I. Finley, *The Ancient Economy*, updated edn (Los Angeles: University of California Press, 1999), 95–122, includes a lengthy chapter devoted to the complexity of the ancient system of slavery and its impact on Roman economy. See also Daron Acemoğlu and James A. Robinson, *Why Nations Fail: The Origins of Power, Prosperity, and Poverty* (New York: Simon & Schuster, 2012), who note that Rome's reliance on slave labour contributed to the 'extractive' nature of its economy and thus its downfall.
[6] Peter Oakes, 'Methodological Issues in Using Economic Evidence in Interpretation of Early Christian Texts', in *Engaging Economics: New Testament Scenarios and Early Christian Reception*, ed. Bruce W. Longenecker and Kelly D. Liebengood (Grand Rapids, MI: Eerdmans, 2009), 9–34, here 30.
[7] Oakes, 'Methodological Issues', 12.
[8] Ibid., 11.
[9] Mik Larsen, 'The Representation of Poverty in the Roman Empire' (PhD diss., University of California Los Angeles, 2015), 5.
[10] Larsen, 'Representation', 8, 154.
[11] Ibid., 21.

poverty – to put it telegraphically, what people thought about poverty and the poor – its *economic* history is too slippery to grasp.'[12] Nevertheless, I shall try to apprehend it by looking at an ancient Roman's life.

Economic models and theories of the ancient Roman economy

Eumachia's business and trade

In first-century CE Pompeii, the guild of fullers celebrated the generous gifts of their patron, the wealthy Eumachia, by erecting a statue dedicated to her. Eumachia did not come from a senatorial or equestrian family. Elizabeth Will notes, 'The family estate included a pottery factory large enough to produce bricks, shipping jars and dishes for international export.'[13] Eumachia appears to be the only heir of her father's wealth and business, and she used it in part to build a finely crafted edifice, whose Corinthian column capitals have been judged 'as the purest and most elegant found in Pompeii'.[14] Eumachia represents the category of women Suetonius speaks of in his *Life of Claudius*. Suetonius notes that to keep Rome fed, Claudius promised profit to merchants who shipped grain to the city by assuming the risk should the boat be lost in a storm. Moreover, he promised ship builders key legal exemptions: 'to a citizen exemption from the *lex Papia Poppaea*; to a Latin the rights of Roman citizenship; to women the privileges allowed the mothers of four children. And all these provisions are in force today' (*Claud.* 18–19). Eumachia's inscriptions, building projects and family businesses invite further exploration.[15] We turn now to examine this period from the economist's categories of production, distribution and consumption.[16]

Production, distribution and consumption

Production in the ancient world looked quite different (not surprisingly) than what the term conjures up today.[17] In general, businesses were not looking to cut labour costs by investing in technology, as several stories reveal. In one case, Emperor Tiberius is shown a sample of flexible or unbreakable glass. The maker assumes he will get a

---

[12] W. V. Harris, *Rome's Imperial Economy* (Oxford: Oxford University Press, 2011), 30.
[13] Elizabeth Lyding Will, 'Women in Pompeii', *Archaeology* 32 (1979): 34–43, here 38.
[14] Will, 'Women', 38.
[15] For helpful reviews of the major scholars and theories, see Helen Rhee, *Loving the Poor, Saving the Rich: Wealth, Poverty, and Early Christian Formation* (Grand Rapids, MI: Baker Academic, 2012); and Michael J. Sandford, *Poverty, Wealth, and Empire: Jesus and Postcolonial Criticism*, NTM 35 (Sheffield: Sheffield Phoenix, 2014).
[16] Keith Hopkins, 'Taxes and Trade in the Roman Empire (200 B.C.–A.D. 400)', *JRS* 70 (1980): 101–25, here 102, argues for a more mutually beneficial relationship between city and surrounding countryside. 'This simple model implies a whole series of small-scale changes in production, distribution and consumption, whose cumulative impact over time was important.'
[17] Dennis P. Kehoe, 'The Early Roman Empire: Production', in *The Cambridge Economic History of the Graeco-Roman World*, ed. Walter Scheidel, Ian Morris and Richard Saller (Cambridge: Cambridge University Press, 2007), 543–69, esp. 543–47, offers a useful summary.

reward, but Tiberius hands him his head, literally, for Tiberius worries that with this innovation, gold will be reduced to the value of mud (Petronius, *Satyricon* 51). In another case, Suetonius notes that Vespasian declined to reward a mechanical engineer who devised a way to transport heavy columns at little expense, saying, 'You must let me feed my poor commons' (*Vesp.* 18). Thus, technological advances that boosted production tended to be modest and rare. Moreover, as Eumachia's building project indicates, surplus was often spent on conspicuous consumption or lavish public edifices.

Cities grew as the economy expanded, for the population overall grew about 33 per cent in the period from Augustus to the Antonines.[18] Economic growth involved both population increase and per capita increase, which was quite rare until the Industrial Revolution. Instead, what we usually see is Malthus's theory played out, which postulates that as a population grows, standards of living and food supplies dwindle. This leads to a decrease in population, which drives up standard of living – to start the cycle all over again.[19] Morley, Jongman, Alcock and others, however, suggest that for this brief period in history, Malthus's theory does not hold. Instead, the economy grew and many benefited.[20] This growth, generating the need for building supplies and food, water and clothing, occurred as the Roman government mined great quantities of silver, especially in Spain. These amounts would not be matched until the beginning of the Industrial Revolution. Moreover, Romans quarried more marble during this period than any other culture has done.[21]

Merchants and builders oversaw the constructing of the numerous public building in city centres or aqueducts or infrastructure projects. These people might have been freedmen or women working on behalf of their former owner, or enterprising individuals. For example, Eumachia's family likely owned the land from which they dug the clay to make bricks or jars. It is possible that they handed over the manufacturing of the bricks to another. Slaves might have worked Eumachia's vineyards, as was common in Italian estates along the coast at this time. However, by the second century, competition from vineyards in other parts of the empire caused the large estates in Italy to diversify into livestock and cereal production, which required less slave labour.[22]

---

[18] The plague that swept through the empire during Marcus Aurelius's rule (161–180 CE) is often named as the reason for the decrease in production and the overall malaise of the economy.

[19] Robert Thomas Malthus (1766–1834), wrote in 1798 'An Essay on the Principle of Population as It Affects the Future Improvement of Society, with Remarks on the Speculations of Mr. Godwin, M. Condorcet, and Other Writers' (http://www.esp.org/books/malthus/population/malthus.pdf, accessed March 2017). He argued that human population growth would always exceed humans' ability to grow enough food, hence famine would be a permanent experience for some or many. His ideas continue to be debated, as seen in David Rieff, *The Reproach of Hunger: Food, Justice, and Money in the Twenty-First Century* (New York: Simon & Schuster, 2015).

[20] Susan Alcock, 'The Eastern Mediterranean', in *The Cambridge Economic History of the Graeco-Roman World*, ed. Walter Scheidel, Ian Morris and Richard Saller (Cambridge: Cambridge University Press, 2007), 671–98, here 686, notes that the evidence points 'for an overall increase in productive activity in the early imperial east, as well as continuing the reassessment and deconstruction of the "consumer city" model for classical antiquity'.

[21] Willem M. Jongman, 'The Early Roman Empire: Consumption', in *The Cambridge Economic History of the Graeco-Roman World*, ed. Walter Scheidel, Ian Morris and Richard Saller (Cambridge: Cambridge University Press, 2007), 592–618, here 592.

[22] Kehoe, 'Early Roman Empire: Production', 555.

The fullers who honoured Eumachia were part of the clothing production process. It could be that Eumachia owned sheep, but if so, she likely did not oversee the production of wool and cloth. Indeed, she may have leased the land to a herdsman or a merchant who took all the risks of caring for sheep and producing the cloth. Looms were inexpensive and could be set up in homes, where the initial spinning of wool was done. Those involved in the process of taking the sheared wool and working it into cloth, including weavers and artisans, organized into guilds (*collegia* or *synodoi*).[23] Alcock notes that in the Eastern Empire, over one hundred occupations are listed on tombstones, leading her to conclude the existence of *collegia* as a 'dense network of manufacturing activities at work'.[24] These artisans would not have enjoyed a high wage or high status, but they would also not have lived at or below subsistence levels.

In the late Republic and early Imperial periods, wine was shipped extensively across the Mediterranean. Eumachia's business participated in this expansion, for after producing wine and amphoras in which to store it, her business shipped the wine across the Empire. Shipwrecks recently excavated in the south coast of France and Spain reveal extensive economic activity between 200 BCE and 200 CE, at a level not reached again until the sixteenth century. Hopkins notes, 'There was more sea-borne trade in the Mediterranean than ever before, and more than there was for the next thousand years'.[25] Broadly speaking, archaeology indicates the distribution of foodstuffs and pottery on a large scale to the general population within and between regions of the Roman Empire. Previously these materials had been produced and consumed locally, or had not been consumed by the majority of people.

The wine, food and pottery often followed the distribution paths of the Roman military, which might be thought of as a centre of demand that required more goods than could be supplied locally. Morley estimates that the military used about one half of the total imperial budget in the mid-first century CE, with many of the troops stationed at the empire's frontiers.[26] Additionally, one could think of Rome as a centre of demand, and even more, Morley suggests that cities in the provinces sought to imitate Rome and, thus, created broad distribution patterns.[27] About 10–12 per cent of the population lived in cities, but it was in the cities that the elite competed with each other to emulate Rome.

When the product arrived at the market, who was able to purchase it? Jongman argues that the empire at this time experienced a per capita income level that was 'remarkably high for a pre-industrial economy' and that this income level was enjoyed by 'relatively large segments of the population'.[28] Jongman presents an interesting

---

[23] Kehoe, 'Early Roman Empire: Production', 566.

[24] Alcock, 'Eastern Mediterranean', 685.

[25] Hopkins, 'Taxes and Trade', 106, referring to the study by A. J. Parker, *Ancient Schipwrecks of the Mediterranean and the Roman Provinces*, British Archaeological Reports International series 580 (Oxford: Hadrian, 1992).

[26] Neville Morley, 'The Early Roman Empire: Distribution', in *The Cambridge Economic History of the Graeco-Roman World*, ed. Walter Scheidel, Ian Morris and Richard Saller (Cambridge: Cambridge University Press, 2007), 570–91, here 575.

[27] Morley, 'The Early Roman Empire: Distribution', 574.

[28] Jongman, 'Early Roman Empire: Consumption', 596–7.

case for his theory of broad and modest to moderate prosperity by looking at meat consumption, which 'rose dramatically during the late Republic, to reach a peak in the early empire'.[29] Jongman argues that the elite cannot be responsible for the large increase in meat consumption because they could not possibly consume that much – and the very poor would not have the surplus money to purchase meat. Jongman concludes that it is those numerous ordinary people who had enough surplus income to purchase meat in significant quantities.

Using a different approach than Jongman, Scheidel and Friesen attempt to quantify the Roman GDP and connect that with income level groups, from elite to impoverished. They note that 'the Roman economic performance approached the ceiling of what was feasible for ancient and medieval economies and their more recent counterparts in the Third World but failed to anticipate even the early stages of the path toward modern economic development'.[30] Scheidel and Friesen postulate a vibrant middling group of about 10 per cent of the population. This group, as well as the elite 3 per cent of the population, controlled about 50 per cent of the income, with the remaining roughly 85–90 per cent of the population at various levels of subsistence.

Yet, as Bruce Longenecker rightly notes, a weakness in this theory is the decision to treat the urban and rural 'middling' group as a single unit. Longenecker suggests, 'It seems unrealistic to imagine complete parity between urban and rural population percentages.'[31] Additionally, Longenecker reminds us that at least some individuals who might qualify as very poor are nevertheless part of households 'and consequently were not exposed to the harsh realities of poverty to the same extent as those . . . who lived beyond household structures'.[32]

Social scientific models' critique of an economic model

Peter Oakes, moreover, rightly points out that a focus on resources might fail to account for much of the data we have in the sources, including the NT. Instead, we need to use the messier but more representative category of behaviour. As an example, Oakes states that we might know that a person has no cloak, that is, he or she lacks a resource, and thus, we might label this person at subsistence level. However, that person might have sold the cloak to fulfil religious vows deemed more important than owning a cloak. Thus, behaviour and resource must be considered together to ascertain an adequate picture of the relative economic level of the person.[33] John Barclay also urges consideration of the social configuration of society and, thus, Paul's churches, because 'wealth is only *one* factor in determining who "counted for

[29] Jongman, 'Early Roman Empire: Consumption', 614.
[30] Walter Scheidel and Steven J. Friesen, 'The Size of the Economy and the Distribution of Income in the Roman Empire', *JRS* 99 (2009): 61–91, here 74.
[31] Bruce W. Longenecker, *Remember the Poor: Paul, Poverty, and the Graeco-Roman World* (Grand Rapids, MI: Eerdmans, 2010), 51.
[32] Longenecker, *Remember*, 54. See also his detailed critique of Freisen's 2004 Poverty Scale (317–32).
[33] Peter Oakes, 'Constructing Poverty Scales for Graeco-Roman Society: A Response to Steven Friesen's "Poverty in Pauline Studies"', *JSNT* 26 (2004): 367–71, 368.

something" in the churches'.[34] Barclay is concerned not only with wealth or lack of it, but also with power within the churches, a social capital issue, if you will.

Barclay laments briefly the lack of comparative data from contemporary 'third-world' urban churches in these studies.[35] I will use his comment as an invitation to recount a conversation with my Kenyan friend Jane that haunts my study of poverty in the early church. My friend is married but separated, with four children, and holds a good job as a dental technician in a local clinic. We knew each other for three years, and in those last two the skies withheld most of their rain. The dust was an inch or two thick and the family gardens or *shambas* had nothing but withered vegetables. I asked her how people were doing in the village. She answered with no trace of irony, 'God is so good; no one has starved to death.' I had no response; nothing seemed suitable. But given the perimeters of this essay, I realize that I am a long way from being able to discern subsistence level. By my view, Jane was really poor; she lived in a mud and stick hut with tin roof, no electricity, no running water, no tarmac roads. Yet I think in her environment, she would neither be considered dirt poor, nor below subsistence level, nor even at subsistence level. She might be considered slightly above subsistence because she had work and owned some things, and could send her kids to school. Jane puts a face on the complexity of determining levels of poverty in the early church. Jane lived in a rural village, not in urban Nairobi. Her village life provides a transition for us to look at first-century Galilee.

Economy in Judaea and Galilee in the first century CE

The issues faced by the explorer of the first-century CE Galilean and Judaean economy are closely aligned with the questions and perspectives noted above to analyse the Roman economy.[36] Yet we also encounter two new concerns. First, specific changes in pottery remains suggest a demographic shift from the Hasmonean period to the Herodian period (mid-second century BCE to mid-first century CE), and these changes can be usefully mapped onto the increasing concern for purity codes discussed in the Jewish literature of this period (including the NT). Second, we find a keen interest in peasant economies. Douglas Oakman, a strong proponent of the peasant economy view, stresses the precarious subsistence existence of most of the (Jewish) residents of Galilee and Judaea. Taking issue with Oakman's views are a number of archaeologists and historians who suggest that robust trade characterizes first-century Galilee and Judaea and, even more, that the goods traded were enjoyed by most of the villagers.

The balance of evidence, as I hope to show below, favours the view that first-century Jews in Galilee, until the years immediately prior to the First Revolt (60–66 CE), enjoyed a standard of living above subsistence level, high enough to allow purchases

---

[34] John Barclay, 'Poverty in Pauline Studies: A Response to Steven Friesen', *JSNT* 26 (2004): 363–6, here 366.
[35] Barclay, 'Poverty', 365.
[36] Philip A. Harland, 'The Economy of First-Century Palestine: State of the Scholarly Discussion', in *The Handbook of Early Christianity: Social Science Approaches*, ed. Anthony J. Blasi, Jean Duhaime and Paul-André Turcotte (Walnut Creek, CA: AltaMira Press, 2002), 511–27, here 511.

of imported pottery and wine and oil – and that the interest in purchasing specific products was tightly tied to religious purity concerns. This modestly prosperous environment grows unstable for at least two reasons: Rome's rapacious and unjust governors, and nationalistic ideology that swept across much of the Roman Empire's frontiers. These two conditions eventually lead to much poverty and displacement of Jews with the failure of the First Revolt.

Archaeological evidence from Galilee in the first century CE

Galilee in Jesus's day was populated mainly by Jews but included cities with sizable gentile populations, such as Tiberius and Sepphoris. Looking at the archaeological evidence in specific cities, Sharon Mattila focuses on the small town of great biblical fame, Capernaum.[37] In Jesus's day, perhaps 1,000 lived here along Lake Gennesaret's shores, compared to 7,500 to 8,000 in Sepphoris to the west. She points to the two excavated homes in Capernaum, dating to the third or fourth century CE, and notes that the Triple Courtyard House in Capernaum is about 50 per cent larger than the roughly contemporaneous Patrician House from Meiron which is often viewed as the home of a moderately well-to-do family.[38] Rhodian jar fragments from the second century BCE and free-blown glassware from the late first century CE in domestic spaces prompt Mattila's contention that 'at least some of the villagers in Jesus's Capernaum probably lived at a level significantly above subsistence.'[39] Additionally, she notes the high number of stone jars (approximately 150) found in this small town. A few of these jars were quite large and, thus, quite expensive.

Moreover, the evidence points to a local economy shaped by religious convictions. Capernaum bought wine and oil based on purity concerns that mandated Jewish kosher laws superintended the harvest, production and distribution containers of the liquids.[40] Additionally, stone containers were produced in great numbers to hold the ritually pure wine and oil. Mattila concludes that as the concern for purity and halakah rose, the 'introverted trade patterns' grew stronger.[41]

The archaeological evidence supports Josephus's claims about large quantities of olive oil produced in Galilee and exported to Jewish communities in Syrian Antioch. Josephus rails against his political rival, John of Gischala, who has a stranglehold on olive oil production in upper Galilee and charges high prices to Jews in Antioch (*J.W.* 2.21.2). Josephus's rant reveals a perennial problem, namely suppliers taking advantage of a crisis.[42] As I noted above, a drought developed during our three years in Kenya.

---

[37] Sharon Lea Mattila, 'Revisiting Jesus' Capernaum: A Village of Only Subsistence-Level Fishers and Farmers?', in *The Galilean Economy in the Time of Jesus*, ed. David A. Fiensy and Ralph K. Hawkins (Atlanta: Scholars, 2013), 75–138, here 75–78.

[38] Meiron is in the far north of Galilee; see Eric M. Meyers, James F. Strange and Carol L. Meyers, *Excavations at Ancient Meiron, Upper Galilee, Israel, 1971–72, 1974–75, 1977*, Meiron Excavation Project 3 (Cambridge, MA: American Schools of Oriental Research, 1981). Mattila, 'Revisiting', 120.

[39] Mattila, 'Revisiting', 95.

[40] Ibid., 98, notes that because Capernaum was on the shores of 'living water' there was no need to construct *miqwāōt*.

[41] Mattila, 'Revisiting', 105.

[42] Lk. 12.16-21 speaks of a rich man hoarding grain (see Josephus, *Life* 13).

A Kenyan friend spoke of having a large quantity of maize (corn) harvested and stored. As the food shortages grew, he was unwilling to release the maize for sale, waiting for the prices to rise even more. I confess I was stunned. This Christian businessman stated his intentions without any sense of discomfort or confliction.

Analysis of archaeological evidence

Challenging the view presented above, Douglas Oakman and Richard Horsley argue that the archaeological data can reflect villages under the power of the wealthy elite in the cities (Oakman)[43] or the presence of high taxation that burdened the villages (Horsley).[44] In his work, Oakman points to Josephus's report that in 66 CE, insurgents burned the Jerusalem Archives, which included debt records (*J.W.* 2.17.6), and did the same in Sepphoris. These debts grew from 'taxes, tributes, tithes and religious dues, land rents, as well as "borrowed money"'.[45] Oakman suggests that 'ancient peasants preferred barter in kind'.[46] He concludes that Rome's monetary policy reserved silver for paying taxes and debts and left the copper tokens in use for buying and selling. This effectively kept the silver out of the peasants' pockets, following Gresham's Law ('bad money drives out good').[47] Oakman explains that the Gospels speak only indirectly about the damage done by extensive debt, because the Roman occupation would come down hard on dissenters. Jesus used parables, then, to address critical issues indirectly.[48]

I remain unconvinced by Oakman's analysis. A second look at Josephus's information provides an alternative reading. Insurgents burned the debt archives in Jerusalem *after* attacking the palaces of the high priest and Agrippa I and Berenice, indicating the overarching intent of the insurgents – namely the overthrow of the Jewish 'collaborators' and Rome's rule (*J.W.* 2.17.6). A secondary, albeit important goal, was to gain the support of Jerusalem's populace, and removing debt records would help achieve that. However, in Sepphoris, Josephus speaks of the Galilean insurgents burning and looting. He makes no mention of actions against an archive holding debts; instead, he stresses the desire to destroy those who side with the Romans (*Life* 67). Fiensy correctly observes that 'the problem with the application of many of these models for the social-science critics is that the model has become the evidence'.[49]

---

[43] Douglas E. Oakman, *Jesus, Debt, and the Lord's Prayer: First-Century Debt and Jesus' Intentions* (Eugene, OR: Cascade, 2015).

[44] Richard A. Horsley, 'Jesus and Galilee: The Contingencies of a Renewal Movement', in *Galilee through the Centuries: Confluence of Cultures*, ed. Eric M. Meyers (Winona Lake, IN: Eisenbrauns, 1999), 57–74.

[45] Oakman, *Jesus, Debt*, 18.

[46] Douglas E. Oakman, 'Execrating? Or Execrable Peasants!', in *The Galilean Economy in the Time of Jesus*, ed. David A. Fiensy and Ralph K. Hawkins (Atlanta: Scholars, 2013), 139–64, here 156.

[47] Sir Thomas Gresham, in 1558, argued that if coins made of metals of differing values are given the same value as legal tender, the cheaper metal coins will be used for buying and selling, and the coins made of more expensive metal will be stockpiled or sent abroad – effectively removed from circulation (https://www.britannica.com/topic/Greshams-law, accessed March 2017).

[48] Oakman, *Jesus, Debt*, 33, notes that 'public speech in an oppressive and conflicted political situation – like that of Jesus in Roman Palestine – cannot address any serious problem in material, social, or power relations without a certain indirection or obfuscation'.

[49] Fiensy, *Christian Origins*, 84.

Religious nationalism foments revolt against Rome

James Bloom suggests the rampant Jewish nationalism fomenting unrest played a larger role than taxes or debt in bringing on the First Revolt.[50] He pays close attention to the apocalyptic fervour, which went hand in glove with the antagonism against pagan shrines and temples located in Galilee and especially Judaea. To push this a bit further, I suggest that the uprising in Galilee and Judaea in the late 60s CE was of a piece with similar revolts on the frontiers of the empire, such as that in Britain led by Boudicca, queen of the Iceni in the early 60s. These uprisings took the Romans by surprise, perhaps in part because they occurred after the initial conquest had been made. Further, the rebels' native religion seems to have played a key part in the events; at the very least, Rome saw the cult sites as the epicentre of the revolt or a main reason for the insurrection.

Why did Rome allow certain cults and destroy others? Martin Goodman notices that the native people in authority were not always the wealthiest in that society. Goodman argues, 'In essence, when faced by societies in Judaea, Gaul and Britain where high status was accorded to many who were not rich, the Romans could explain such societies to themselves only by assuming that their "unnatural" attitudes were the result of religious fanaticism.'[51] Goodman's perceptive analysis recognizes the tight connection between economic wealth and high social status expected by elite Romans. The Romans explained the strong nationalistic fervour in both Britain and Judaea, which resisted Romanization of their culture, as the result of the 'stubborn and vicious religious instincts of the inhabitants'.[52]

Moreover, it appears that the insurgents viewed Roman culture and political manoeuvring with increasing distaste. Stephen Dyson notes that Boudicca's forces devastated three cities and destroyed the imperial cult temple in Camulodunum (Tacitus, *Ann.* 14.31.6–7).[53] This occurred after her husband's death and the refusal by Rome to honour his will. The king left half his estate to his two daughters and the other half to the Emperor. Rome rejected the terms of the will and the possibility of female rule, and made clear their position by publicly raping the daughters in front of their mother. Additionally, a financial panic of some sort ran through the land, and loans were called. Seneca was involved, although it is unclear whether the loans were personal or imperial (Dio Cassius, *Roman History*, 62.2.1).[54] Religious tensions, nationalistic fervour, Romanization and financial mismanagement of personal or imperial loans boiled over in revolt.

---

[50] James L. Bloom, *The Jewish Revolts against Rome, A.D. 66–135: A Military Analysis* (Jefferson, NC: McFarland, 2010), 17.

[51] Martin Goodman, *The Ruling Class of Judaea: The Origins of the Jewish Revolt against Rome A.D. 66–70* (Cambridge: Cambridge University Press, 1987), 240.

[52] Goodman, *Ruling Class*, 244.

[53] Stephen L. Dyson, 'Native Revolts in the Roman Empire', *Historia* 20 (1971): 239–74, here 260, does not believe that the destruction of the sanctuary was key in fomenting revolt.

[54] Dyson, 'Native Revolts', 259.

Conclusion

The human-made causes of poverty in the early church reveal themselves to be problems endemic to human culture, namely, misguided governmental policies, human greed and corruption and human ideological commitments that breed conflict and war.[55] The early Pauline churches were urban communities that participated in the relative prosperity of the early Roman Empire. Jesus's Galilee boasted villages and small cities of about 1,000–8,000 inhabitants that enjoyed lively exchange of goods, often made by and for Jews who valued purity customs. Here, one finds families with modest incomes and enough surplus money to buy luxury tableware or stone jars and very few living at the edge of subsistence.

How does this information help us understand the early Christian communities? At minimum, it affirms that within the early Christian communities, one would expect to find a range of modest income levels that were above subsistence level. And this analysis opens the door more widely to appreciate the possible differences between churches in their specific cities. For example, Paul expresses no compunction in asking the Corinthians to share with those believers who are facing hardship in Judaea. He makes it clear that his churches have 'plenty' at the moment and, thus, should respond with generosity to those overcome in Judaea (2 Cor. 8.13-15).[56] John Barclay's essay in this book focuses on Paul and the gift.

Paul connects his mainly gentile churches to the Jewish believers in Judaea with his call for almsgiving. Other essays explore this, as Bruce Longenecker speaks to benefaction and Steve Walton looks at patronage. On the whole, the Jews in Judaea and Galilee from Herod the Great's time (king of Judaea 37–4 BCE) until the First Revolt (66–70 CE) seemed to live above subsistence level, enough to maintain purity habits that required specific production and distribution networks. Jesus's Galilee was not overrun with destitute peasants; instead, many of Jesus's fellow Jews had modest means and even a bit of surplus. The debate between Jesus and other religious leaders revolved around how to spend this money. For Jesus knew, 'where your treasure is, there your heart will be also' (Mt. 6.21).

---

[55] Willem M. Jongman, "'Gibbon Was Right": The Decline and Fall of the Roman Economy', in *Crises and the Roman Empire*, ed. Olivier Hekster, Gerda de Kleijn and Daniëlle Slootjes (Leiden: Brill, 2007), 183–200, here 198, suggests that in the late second century, the decrease of population (perhaps because of the plague in the 160s) did not lead to more peasants having their own land but 'the emergence of a new social, political and legal regime, where oppression replaces the entitlements of citizenship'.

[56] Paul speaks of the Macedonians' 'extreme poverty' (2 Cor. 8.2). For an excellent discussion of the social and economic situation in Philippi, see Peter Oakes, *Philippians: From People to Letter*, SNTSMS 110 (Cambridge: Cambridge University Press, 2001).

3

Causes of Poverty Today

Katie Harrison[1]

Introduction

Definitions of poverty are hotly debated and widely documented. Having worked with some of the world's poorest people for almost fifty years, we at Tearfund are clear that poverty is both absolute (not having enough to live well) and relative (having less than those around you). Among the millions of people served by non-governmental organizations (NGOs) like ours are many very different experiences of poverty. Their circumstances and locations vary. Some will leave poverty behind; many will not. But what they all have in common is a sense of lack. People cannot have or do things necessary for their survival, like eating. Or they cannot exercise any kind of power – through purchasing, voting or influencing – because they just do not have any.

> Poverty is hunger. Poverty is lack of shelter. Poverty is being sick and not being able to see a doctor. Poverty is not having access to school and not knowing how to read. Poverty is not having a job, is fear for the future, living one day at a time. Poverty is losing a child to illness brought about by unclean water. Poverty is powerlessness, lack of representation and freedom.[2]

We have learnt a lot from the people we serve, and we have developed an understanding of human flourishing based on the scriptural concepts of being made in the image of God (Gen. 1.26-27) and living a full life (Jn 10.10). Put simply, a full life is one where people are able to exercise creativity and productivity, and to live in community with those around them.[3] This, we believe, is the opposite of poverty, for when people leave poverty behind, their journey is not only towards something material; it is towards a life which is also richer socially, intellectually and spiritually. Once we have enough

---

[1] At the time of writing this essay, Katie Harrison was on the staff of Tearfund.
[2] D. Narayan et al., 'Voices of the Poor: Can Anyone Hear Us?' (Washington, DC: World Bank, 2000). For more information, see http://go.worldbank.org/H1N8746X10 (accessed December 2017).
[3] Cafod, Tearfund and Theos, 'Wholly Living: A New Perspective on International Development' (London: Theos, 2010), http://whollyliving.tearfund.org (accessed December 2017).

money that our financial situation ceases to cause us to panic, our fulfilment comes from other things. Money is not the answer to all our human problems, but a complete lack of it is devastating.

Without an environment which encourages people to flourish in this way, it is easy for people to give up. Many of my colleagues would say that the biggest barrier to development is fatalism. If people believe not only that poverty is not only how life will always be and that they cannot change it (apathy) but also that it is somehow their preordained destiny (fatalism), they can become trapped in passivity and lose their belief in their own agency.

The answer, in our opinion, lies in restoring healthy relationships at every level. People are held back from fulfilling their own potential and from participating fully in society when relationships break down – both at a personal and a structural level. When people do not have a healthy understanding of their own identity and capacity, they are unable to explore and fulfil their potential. When families break down, children are vulnerable to trafficking and exploitative labour, and will often miss out on school. And when citizens and governments, or employees and businesses, do not trust each other, corruption and exploitation can flourish. Thus, individuals, families and communities become resigned to living with lack and, for generations, people miss out.

Often as a result of low expectations or of facing extremely challenging circumstances, people who are poor can become caught up in harmful habits which exacerbate their problems and further separate them from the people around them, holding them back from fulfilling their own potential. This cycle is as evident in poor communities in developed countries as it is in the world's poorest countries, as the UK's Centre for Social Justice found:

> It became apparent that many of these acute social problems – worklessness, family breakdown, educational failure, addiction, serious personal debt – were very closely connected. Wherever we found one problem, we tended to find another. Where we found two we tended to find three, and so on. They were interconnected: we know that a child who experiences family breakdown is less likely to thrive at school. A school leaver who has struggled is more likely to be unemployed often or for long periods, and more likely to get into debt thanks to low or unstable income. Where unemployment and debt took root we saw how people are more susceptible to drifting into drug and alcohol abuse. This was a tragic pattern we encountered continually in people's lives and the charities helping them. Furthermore, the pathways to poverty facilitate an intergenerational transmission of disadvantage. Too often deprivation is destiny for those born into the poorest parts of the UK.[4]

So this vicious circle continues: relationships break down, people become poor, frustrations mount, people sometimes engage in harmful habits and alienate those

---

[4]   C. Guy and A. Burghart, *Breakthrough Britain 2015: An Overview* (London: Centre for Social Justice, 2015), 2; available at https://www.centreforsocialjustice.org.uk/core/wp-content/uploads/2016/08/CSJJ2470_BB_2015_WEB.pdf (accessed December 2017).

around them, relationships suffer even more, people become isolated or habits become entrenched and passed on to their children. And so whole communities remain poor for generations.

What makes people poor?

Here are three of the hundreds of people whom I have met while working for Tearfund: the grandfather in Uganda who lives hundreds of miles from the city's markets where he could get a good price for the produce from his smallholding; the young mother in a makeshift camp in Lebanon who gave birth on the traumatic journey from Syria while fleeing bombs and shellings; and the parent whose house, business and young son were washed away by flooding in Malawi.

All three, and millions more like them, are poor. They have no access to basic services. Two of them have no electricity in their home, all struggle to get clean water. A functioning latrine – even a long drop – is a luxury. The two who live in Africa have never known any kind of prosperity. In fact, the Ugandan grandfather is now the richest he has ever been, despite living in a basic home in the middle of nowhere. The Syrian woman used to live in a comfortable home, which she and her husband built, decorated and furnished together. Now she is in a muddy tent in the Bekaa Valley, where it sometimes snows so heavily in winter that the snowdrifts cover her inadequate home. All three are living in poverty because of structural causes. The economic, governance and environmental systems in which they live have failed, and they are poor as a result.

Conflict, climate change and poor governance are among the causes of poverty for these three people. The horrors of life in Syria, where we hear that women are being raped in the streets and children suffer extreme psychological trauma from having witnessed barbaric cruelty, forced our friend and her family to flee to neighbouring Lebanon, leaving behind the comforts of their middle-class life.

Rapidly changing unpredictable weather conditions, with no early warning systems or flood defences, wiped out all that the Malawi family held dear, including their only son. Further, a lack of infrastructure – long and badly maintained roads with very little public transport, barriers to markets, absence of affordable patient capital, anti-competitive practices, no electricity – means that the Uganda grandfather's business relies on travelling traders to act as middlemen to take his goods to market instead of his being able to build up the business and move up the value chain.

These are known as *structural causes* because they are based on a failure of human structures to protect people's safety and enable them to prosper. The systems of government and private sector business have failed to deliver protection and basic services, or to provide the infrastructure within which people can thrive.

The roles of government and business are crucial. Tearfund's *Restorative Economy* report celebrates the successes of the markets in creating more opportunities for people to leave poverty in the last generation than at any other time in human history, while at the same time calling for greater resource efficiency in order to generate sustainable development for generations to come:

Markets have been crucial in enabling people to lift themselves out of poverty. In developing countries, 90 per cent of jobs are created by the private sector. And the countries that have done best over the past two decades are ones that established the right enabling environment to foster private sector growth: contracts that are enforced, customs systems that work, educated workforces and dependable infrastructure, from roads to broadband.[5]

So, a capitalist framework which relies on self-determination for the capable and safety nets for those in need must at the same time recognize that there will always be functions for which government is responsible. Whether they choose to provide services directly or through public-private partnerships, there are some responsibilities which a government must hold. In *Philanthrocapitalism*, Matthew Bishop and Michael Green argue that a scene in US political drama *The West Wing* misunderstands this:

> In the penultimate episode of *The West Wing*, a favourite TV show of policy wonks, a multibillionaire Gates-like character tried to head-hunt White House chief of staff C. J. Cregg to run his foundation. She initially declines, but urges him to build roads in Africa. There is plenty of evidence that roads and railways are good for an economy and good for poor people, but C. J.'s advice was wrong. Infrastructure is hugely expensive to build and costs a lot to maintain, as the English philanthropists in the Renaissance found out. All the philanthropic capital in the world could not build enough roads to make a real difference in Africa – and within five years they would be falling apart with no one to maintain them. Public and for-profit private capital should build roads.[6]

A heartbreaking paradox of poverty is the natural resource trap, as posited by Paul Collier.[7] He argues that some countries which are the most rich in natural resources remain worse off than those with less because their bounty attracts conflict for those resources, exacerbated by lack of transparency by officials who are happy to receive secret payments or use surpluses of natural resources for their own benefit. Equally, some governments in countries with high levels of natural resources don't believe they need to operate a tax system, and so their citizens are less likely to hold them to account. And other industries become less competitive because of over-reliance on the natural resource.

Despite their abundance of natural resources – in 2010, exports of oil and minerals from Africa were estimated at $333 billion, nearly seven times the value of international aid ($48 billion) to the continent[8] – some countries remain poor because

[5] A. Evans and R. Gower, *The Restorative Economy: Completing our Unfinished Millennium Jubilee* (Teddington: Tearfund, 2015); available at www.tearfund.org/economy (accessed December 2017).
[6] Matthew Bishop and Michael Green, *Philanthrocapitalism: How the Rich Can Save the World and Why We Should Let Them* (London: A&C Black, 2008), 281.
[7] Paul Collier, *The Bottom Billion: Why the Poorest Countries Are Failing and What Can Be Done about It* (New York: Oxford University Press, 2007).
[8] Tearfund, Unearth the Truth (2012), https://learn.tearfund.org/~/media/files/tilz/research/ unearth_the_truth_-_november_2012.pdf (accessed January 2018).

human structures – including governments and businesses – fail to work together effectively to make sure that all citizens have access to decision-making and to basic services. Essentially, this is because of broken relationships at institutional levels which, when exacerbated by broken relationships between ethnic and tribal groups as in places like the Democratic Republic of Congo (DRC), mean that natural resources like minerals bring no tangible benefits to millions of people. In a 2015 survey by Transparency international, 22 per cent of Africans reported having paid a bribe in the past year.[9] The DRC is an example which demonstrates this complexity of broken relationships: its conquest and pillaging by European colonists and its painful struggles for independence from colonialism and subsequent divisions between communities within the borders set for it by its former colonists providing the background from which many of today's problems have emerged – problems exacerbated by ongoing external engagement that often takes advantage of internal tension and strife.[10]

In addition, the balance of protecting citizens and workers from harm while at the same time giving enough freedom for people to innovate and thrive is a responsibility held by both governments and businesses. For example, the commonly held consensus that the way out of poverty is through work holds true only when workers are paid fairly and are not exploited. Try telling a labourer in a sweatshop or rice field in Asia that if they work harder they will leave poverty behind. It is simply not true. Often, people are poor because systems failed. Governments or businesses let them down.

What keeps people poor?

Once in poverty, people remain there for various reasons.

Inequality

People who are poor are almost always excluded from opportunities and have limited access to essential services, from pre-birth onwards. Consistently, people without means receive lower standards of healthcare and education. Where people live without essential infrastructure and basic services, their children are more likely to die.

---

[9] Transparency International, 'People and Corruption: Africa Survey 2015', https://www.transparency.org/whatwedo/publication/people_and_corruption_africa_survey_2015 (accessed January 2018). Reported in *The Economist*, 3 December 2015 (https://www.economist.com/news/middle-east-and-africa/21679473-gloomy-news-transparency-international-scale-corruption-africa, accessed January 2018).

[10] See, e.g., Thomas Pakenham, *The Scramble for Africa* (London: Weidenfeld & Nicolson, 1991); A. Hochschild, *Leopold's Ghost: A Story of Greed, Terror and Heroism in Colonial Africa* (Boston and New York: Houghton Mifflin Harcourt, 1999); and Martin Meredith, *The State of Africa: A History of the Continent since Independence* (London: Simon & Schuster, 2013), which describe the colonial and postcolonial history of the DRC. For a more contemporary analysis of the DRC, including the ongoing conflicts' roots in the nation's history see, e.g., Jason Stearns, *Dancing in the Glory of Monsters* (Philadelphia: Public Affairs, 2012); Lise A. Namikas, *Battleground Africa: Cold War in the Congo, 1960–1965* (Stanford, CA: Stanford University Press, 2013); Emizet Francois Kisangani, *Civil Wars in the Democratic Republic of Congo 1960–2010* (Boulder, CO: Lynne Rienner, 2012), Thomas Turner, *Congo* (Cambridge and Malden: Polity, 2013).

WaterAid report that, globally, 'diarrhoea caused by dirty water and poor toilets kills a child under five every two minutes' – that is over 700 children per day.[11]

Diarrhoea is, of course, both preventable and treatable and is not a cause of death in countries where there is adequate and easily available healthcare. For this reason, it is a good example of the unnecessary injustice and the debilitating nature of poverty. For millions of people in many countries, if you are born poor, you stay poor – if you survive into adulthood at all, that is.

For children who make it to the age of five, the global lottery of access to education looms. To be fair, and Hans Rosling is particularly strident in rebuking NGOs for failing to celebrate sufficiently the world's progress in this area, primary school education is now far more widely accessible than ever before. Nine out of ten primary school age girls are enrolled in primary school.[12]

That is a huge achievement, and it is significant that the statistic applies to girls. Gender has always been, and continues to be, a barrier to economic progress in many countries, which is why there has been such an emphasis recently on offering women routes to market. For example, once a girl has completed primary school education, in many countries she will then drop out of the education system. She may be expected to work in the home or the family business. She may be married off in the hope of a better life for her or for financial gain for her parents. In some communities, she will be invited to go with a friendly uncle to the city for work; effectively, she is trafficked to labour in a factory or a brothel.

Even in a family which values education, a girl may find that once she reaches puberty she misses a week each month of her schooling, because schools in many rural areas of poor countries have no lavatories and she cannot bear the thought of people seeing her trying to replace her sanitary towel behind a tree. As she starts to fall behind with her schoolwork due to frequent absences, she becomes less motivated and gives up altogether. Because there is not a toilet. Because she is a girl. Thus, half of the community (the women) remain uneducated, their earning power is limited and everyone misses out. All because of a lack of basic sanitation.

The odds are stacked against people in extreme poverty because of broken relationships. A lack of understanding between men and women means that the school buildings have not been designed to work for everyone: there are no latrines. Broken relationships between civic authorities and citizens mean that there is inadequate infrastructure and children die because of lack of clean water supply.

In many countries where Tearfund works, children who grow up in unstable families, or where their needs for education and care are not met, are more likely to be trafficked, married against their will at an early age, or forced to work. These children miss out on their education and are vulnerable to physical and sexual abuse, because of broken relationships within their own families.

Sadly, this principle remains broadly true everywhere in the world. Many poor people do not live in poor countries; in fact, some countries are extremely mixed and

[11] See https://www.wateraid.org/uk/facts-and-statistics (accessed December 2017).
[12] Speech by Hans Rosling to Overseas Development Institute (ODI), London, 23 October 2015; available at http://www.odi.org/events/4281-data-lecture-hans-rosling (accessed December 2017).

so the poverty of their poorest communities is masked by their overall prosperity. For example, in 2010, one-third of the world's 1.2 billion extremely poor people lived in India alone.[13] Broken relationships between those with power and those living in poverty mean that, while globally the middle class is growing at an unprecedented rate,[14] not everyone benefits and there remains an unacceptable level of poverty even in countries where some people prosper.

Even in the world's most advanced democracies, poor children face more barriers than those from richer families and are less likely to achieve academically or economically. In the UK, the Sutton Trust found that disadvantaged young people are less likely to continue with post-16 academic study than those from more advantaged families.[15] They also report that three-quarters of the UK's highest-ranking judges were educated at private schools rather than the state sector.[16]

Thomas Piketty, Joseph Stiglitz and others all document the effects of extreme economic disparity, and particularly the impact on economic, academic and professional progress of social capital.[17] Children born into privilege have an advantage over those who are not because of their parents' connections or because they have better access to sports and hobbies and are therefore more likely to gain enviable university places or job opportunities. People in the 'sharp elbowed' middle classes are more likely to have access to education and health services. They know how to negotiate for specialist services when they need to and how to protest against services being withdrawn.[18] A powerful middle class which knows how to use the system generates further disparity with those who do not.

Boris Johnson, a Conservative MP and former Mayor of London, and an unlikely bedfellow of Piketty and Stiglitz, complained in 2015 of a lack of social mobility in the UK:

> Professional middle class jobs [are] dominated by families who have professional middle class jobs. Big top universities dominated by families who've been at top universities. You see it I'm afraid in the law, in journalism, in Parliament, in just about every profession. You see it in acting, for heaven's sake . . . you see it in

[13]   T. Too-Kong, *The Millennium Development Goals Report* (New York: United Nations, 2014); available at   http://www.un.org/millenniumgoals/2014%20MDG%20report/MDG%202014%20English%20 web.pdf (accessed December 2017).

[14]   Globally, the size of the middle class could increase from 1.8 billion people to 3.2 billion by 2020 and to 4.9 billion by 2030. Homi Kharas, *The Emerging Middle Class in Developing Countries*, OECD Development Centre Working Paper 285 (Paris: OECD, 2010), 27; available at http://www.oecd.org/ dev/44457738.pdf (accessed December 2017).

[15]   Katalin Toth, Kathy Silva and Pam Sammons, *Background to Success* (London: Sutton Trust, 2015); available at http://www.suttontrust.com/researcharchive/background-to-success/ (accessed December 2017).

[16]   Sutton Trust, Press Release, Nov 2015; available at http://www.suttontrust.com/newsarchive/ the-sutton-trust-and-prime-call-for-better-engagement-in-social-mobility-initiatives/   (accessed December 2017).

[17]   Thomas Piketty, *Capital in the Twenty-First Century* (Cambridge, MA: Harvard University Press, 2014); Joseph E. Stiglitz, *The Price of Inequality* (New York: Norton, 2013).

[18]   A. Hastings and P. Matthews, '"Sharp Elbows": Do the Middle-Classes have Advantages in Public Service Provision and if so How?' (Glasgow: University of Glasgow, 2011); available at http://eprints. gla.ac.uk/57021/ (accessed December 2017).

sport, it's decades since we had in this country a culture of bright kids from poor background in huge numbers bursting down the doors, exuberantly bursting down the doors of the establishment.[19]

This widespread understanding across political ideologies of the dangers of inequality is important. In a world where political and economic systems have historically – intentionally or otherwise – conspired to keep poor people poor, perhaps an answer lies in generating some unlikely alliances between thought leaders and policymakers across political and cultural spectrums.

In the same speech about inequality in London, and confirming our point about the vicious circle of poverty, disadvantage and risk, Johnson said,

> It is a fact that when bad things happen, they are more likely to happen to you if you are poor. You're more likely to be burgled if you are poor. You're more likely to be murdered if you are poor. Your kids are more likely to be killed in a road traffic accident if you are poor. Your kids' school is more likely to be in an area with heavily polluted air if you are poor. And you are more likely to die in a domestic fire if you are poor.

Unequal power structures, where the needs of poor people are ignored and little or no safety net provided in order for them to gain a level footing and participate in society, keep people poor.

Fatalism

In Tearfund's long experience of working as a distinctively Christian NGO and of working through local churches, we have found that there is more to tackling poverty than economic activity. The plains of Africa, Latin America and Asia are littered with the remains of good intentions. Wells installed and no longer used, schools constructed then abandoned, clinics built but now unstaffed and empty.

There are lots of reasons why many development interventions do not work. Fundamentally, we have found that the best way out of poverty, in a community where it has become a way of life for generations, is for the people in that community to lead themselves and each other on a journey towards prosperity.

When outsiders come in and do things to or for people, there may be some short-term gain, but often the benefit is short-lived. But when people work together in a community to save money and create a micro-economy, or to lobby local authorities and raise funds for healthcare or education, then their progress is far more likely to be tangible and sustainable. It seems obvious: when people do something for themselves, especially when there has been an element of sacrifice and hard work, they are more likely to commit to its success and to use the service well.

---

[19] Speech by Boris Johnson, 'Inequality in London' at the Centre for Social Justice, 2015; video available at https://www.youtube.com/watch?v=CDe-9GSCPYY (accessed December 2017).

But it is not that simple. In many places, the first barrier to overcome is people's beliefs about their own agency. Time after time, we find that people have become accustomed to poverty and cannot imagine achieving anything else. It is a long and sometimes painful journey, even when sensitively facilitated by local workers, to bring a community towards a recognition that the power to change their standard of living could lie in their own hands.

Habits are ingrained, beliefs are long-held and traditions held dear. Our methods start first with the local church using biblical and theological reference points to help churchgoers understand the potential of their existing resources, before broadening the conversation using secular language to include people not in the church. It can take people a while to grasp that they have some decision-making power and to find the ability to dream, hope and do.

That is partly because of the daily drudge of poverty. People might work hard, doing thankless repetitive, physically arduous tasks in the home and garden, walking miles to fetch water, tending often unproductive smallholdings. It is tiring. And the consequences of poverty which we have already examined work against them – lack of healthcare, limited diet, low levels of education.

However, there is an increasingly wide recognition across the sector that some of the most crucial keys to unlocking people's potential are in the mind. The World Bank's Development Report for 2015 is entitled *Mind, Society, and Behavior*[20] and examines a wide range of development interventions where 'nudge' techniques to prompt people to do or not so something have been used.[21] These incentivization or social marketing programmes have often succeeded in encouraging people to change behaviour patterns: to save money, take medications regularly, send their children to school. Persuasion techniques of many different kinds have often succeeded in changing some habits. In the UK, the government's Behavioural Insights Team developed a text message system for Job Centres to use to encourage unemployed people to attend recruitment interviews. Personalizing the messages and wishing the jobseeker good luck nearly trebled attendance rates.[22] Attempting to change behaviours by persuasion can bring about some change. Personalizing and wishing the beneficiary well shows the value of relationship and adds additional value.

That said, apart from some research into the effects on academic attainment of the caste system in India, we at Tearfund would argue that the World Bank report does not go far enough to identify the root causes of attitudes which hold people back. There are reasons why some people have not developed productive habits, and tinkering with the effects is helpful but not as effective as addressing the causes. As we have seen,

---

[20] World Bank, *World Development Report 2015: Mind, Society, and Behavior* (Washington, DC: World Bank, 2015); available at http://www.worldbank.org/content/dam/Worldbank/Publications/WDR/WDR%202015/WDR-2015-Full-Report.pdf (accessed December 2017).

[21] Richard H. Thaler and Cass R. Sunstein, *Nudge: Improving Decisions about Health, Wealth, and Happiness* (New Haven: Yale University Press, 2008), which argues that human decision-making is not wholly logical and rational but swayed by assumptions, ideas, fallacies and social influence and interaction. 'Nudge techniques' seek to nudge people, gently and almost unconsciously, to make 'better' decisions.

[22] The Behavioural Insights Team, *Update Report 2013–2015*, http://www.behaviouralinsights.co.uk/wp-content/uploads/2015/07/BIT_Update-Report-Final-2013-2015.pdf (accessed January 2018).

partly people have not had the opportunity, education or access to helpful services which would help them to navigate the systems already available, however informal. This in itself contributes to a downwards spiral of lack of self-belief or of expectation that life could be different and requires of the rest of us a greater level of compassion – to respond to the challenge of poverty with humanity, as Matthew Taylor argues.[23] Alternatively, they have lived with repeated cycles of poverty, conflict and exploitation in their families, communities or countries which have meant that, historically, every time someone has tried to achieve something, they've been thwarted.

Most common, in our experience, is a combination of both of these which culminate, along with cultural or religious beliefs, in a perception of oneself and one's place in the world which is essentially passive: this is how things are, nothing has worked before, I do not have anything with which to try to change my future, and in fact I am not supposed to. This is my lot. My destiny is settled, and this is where I belong. These fundamental beliefs about personal identity and capacity are not easily changed. But unless people are able to rethink their assessment of themselves, their capacity to change and their ability to hope and bring about new things, they will remain trapped in poverty.

Is there a way out?

It is because of the need for such fundamental change that our distinctive approach at Tearfund brings in the actor we have not yet examined but which this book explores more fully: the local church. The church can be a version of civil society with a role to unite and mobilize people around a common cause, reaching towards a way of life that is better than we have known before and with a determined belief that the future can be better than the past, although it must be said that the church has often failed. In many places, the church has been part of the problem. Implicitly or sometimes explicitly, churches have condoned wife beating, child abuse and marital rape.[24] Churches have preached harmful approaches to money, either through poverty gospel – Jesus had no place to lay his head, so you are more holy if you have nothing – or a prosperity gospel through which only a few people benefit, and inequality becomes as marked in the church as it is in wider society.

However, the church's message is one of redemption, of restoring that which was dirty and shameful to a noble, honourable and beautiful state. Indeed, the church can and, in our experience, often does become what it was always meant to be: a group of people united in their desire to thrive and to bring others to find fulfilment in the

---

[23] Matthew Taylor, 'Blog: The Poor – Always with Us?' (RSA, 22 July 2015); available at https://www.thersa.org/discover/publications-and-articles/matthew-taylor-blog/2015/07/the-poor---always-with-us/ (accessed December 2017).

[24] This is clear from a number of Tearfund's reports into sexual and gender-based violence, including 'Breaking the Silence' (2013) (https://learn.tearfund.org/~/media/files/tilz/hiv/breaking_the_silenceweb_final.pdf?la=en, accessed January 2018); 'Silent No More' (2011) (https://learn.tearfund.org/~/media/files/tilz/hiv/silent_no_more_english.pdf?la=en, accessed January 2018); and 'Our Daughter's Voices' (2016) (https://learn.tearfund.org/~/media/files/tilz/sgbv/our_daughters_voices_e_web.pdf?la=en, accessed January 2018).

creativity, productivity and community which together make up a full life. Thus, even though those interviewed about their experiences as survivors of sexual and gender-based violence acknowledge that the church has failed them, they are also often able to see the potential of the church to be welcoming, redemptive and transformational. For example, in Goma in the DRC, Tearfund's partner HEAL Africa has been working for a number of years alongside local churches to provide emotional, medical and practical assistance to survivors who describe the church as 'supportive and compassionate' and as 'contributing to our internal healing'.[25] When the church operates at this level, we see people's attitudes change and their levels of personal initiative and collective momentum increase.

This transformation does not necessarily mean changing one's religion, although sometimes that happens as people embrace their own decision-making capacity and choose a path they want to follow. It does, however, mean addressing some difficult questions about personal and family history, and finding the ability to dream some dreams and then put them into practice. Those are not easy for any of us, and for people who have always known the back-breaking daily grind of relentless poverty, they are particularly difficult.

Happily, we often see these social and emotional benefits in people outside the church as well as those who subscribe to Christian beliefs. A thriving local church can bring transformation to those in the wider community as well as to those within its doors – and it all comes back to relationships. This is clearly seen where churches and communities are trained to advocate for themselves at the local and national levels. Tearfund's 2016 report, *Bridging the Gap*, found that advocacy training within a church and a community mobilization approach gives individuals and communities confidence, leads people to seek out the information they need in order to advocate and promotes unity and change within the community (including those often excluded elsewhere) and improved relationships with decision makers.[26]

For example, in Recife, Brazil, there is an informal settlement near a river. This community has no sanitation system or formalized waste collection, so human and solid waste is disposed of in the river. The river often floods after heavy rain, which is made worse by the waste it contains. The flood waters enter and destroy local homes and carry disease. The local church has mobilized the community to clean up the river and prepare for potential floods. They have also set up a scheme supporting women to turn discarded plastic bottles into a range of crafts and household items, from handbags to Christmas decorations. Finally, the church brought together fifteen local churches to develop the 'Clean River, Healthy City' campaign. They worked with students from the city's main university in Recife, created publicity materials for local schools and churches about the environment and the problems of waste and brought together the city council, public authorities, schools, churches and local associations for a public hearing on river conditions in June 2016. Their most recent achievement was to secure a public hearing with State Legislative Assembly of Pernambuco (the state in which

---

[25] Tearfund, 'Silent No More', 9.
[26] Tearfund, 'Bridging the Gap', 4 (https://learn.tearfund.org/~/media/files/tilz/topics/advocacy/2016-tearfund-bridging-the-gap-en.pdf, accessed January 2018).

Recife is located) in April 2017 for the community to call for a clean-up of the river.[27] This has been possible because the local church has spent a number of years building relationships and earning the trust of the local communities.

Within a community of trust, where people are able to discuss amicably and take decisions together, the relationships at family and community level act as levers of power and enable people to represent themselves confidently to local and national authorities to access the services they need.[28] Often, they will meet the authorities halfway, such as building a clinic on the basis that the government will staff and equip it. Collective organization to develop plans and raise the quality of life together helps create a shared vision and move a community on from a sad history to a hopeful future.

Restored relationships create the environment necessary for people to flourish. A person's transformed relationship with their own self and a clear understanding of their worth and potential as an individual is both the cause and the effect of a hopeful and truly prosperous life. In tackling the causes of poverty, we must focus on the ways in which we want people to flourish: to have not just material prosperity but also dignity, agency and the opportunity to use their resources and talents. We must also look at our own contributions to systems that contribute to global poverty, for example, the ways we make lifestyle choices that create waste or demand cheap products, or the ways our Western governments assume that their citizens' comforts are more important than the well-being of those in poorer countries. The essays that follow in this collection look at some of the ideas and practices that can help us to pursue this goal.

---

[27] Tearfund, 'Why Advocate on Waste and a Circular Economy?' (2017), 8 (https://learn.tearfund. org/~/media/files/tilz/circular_economy/2017-tearfund-why-advocate-on-waste-and-a-circular-economy-en.pdf?la=en, accessed January 2018).
[28] Tearfund, 'Bridging the Gap', 17–20.

4

Response to Lynn H. Cohick

Katie Harrison

One of the things that struck me most about Lynn Cohick's paper was that although, as she identifies, the ancient and modern worlds have different ways of conceiving of poverty and demanding justice, the *causes* of poverty are largely the same. As Lynn listed the reasons why individuals in the ancient world faced poverty – ill health, lack of opportunities to work, poor governance and corruption and ethnic tensions and conflicts – I recognized each of them from the world I encounter in my work every day. However, I wonder if seeing these causes regularly in the contemporary world really makes clear the importance of the opportunity to choose as a richness? Lynn writes about the way that in the story of the widow's mite, the widow was still able to give, but actually, I think, some people today do not have that choice.

I also found it interesting though that we both put more emphasis on structural issues in discussing the causes of poverty and in people's opportunities to become free from poverty. Nevertheless, we both agreed that matters of the mind and heart are key for overcoming poverty, and this is personal as well as structural: perhaps this is an indicator of how tricky it can be to talk about agency and responsibility without getting drawn into what you might call a 'blame game'.

I am glad that Lynn, in her response, picks up on the phrase, 'Dream better dreams': I think that is an important part of people overcoming the fatalism we have talked about. Dreams engage the heart and the mind. They can provide an inspiration and an impetus for change. Lynn's response described some of the dreams of Christians in the ancient world. These are also some of the dreams of Christians today: it is one of the reasons why we believe that the church is such a powerful actor in overcoming poverty. Further, I would add, I think it is an important idea and activity for those of us who do not lack material things. What dreams could or should we dream that would move us to live in ways that help others to overcome poverty?

5

Dream Better Dreams: Response to Katie Harrison

Lynn H. Cohick

'Dream some dreams and put them into practice.' Thus Katie Harrison sums up her well-argued position on the way out of poverty in the modern world. She rightly perceives that poverty is both absolute (no food or water) and relative, a matter of lacking what others have. With this encompassing description of poverty, she addresses the social and emotional barriers to eliminating poverty, alongside highlighting the structural impediments that keep individuals and communities in destitution. Harrison points to the failures of government and private sector business as contributing to community impoverishment. Lack of infrastructure, such as decent roads and reliable electricity and sanitation, weakens families' earning potential. Lack of healthcare and education limit potential. Businesses that deny workers fair pay trap their employees in poverty. War and natural disasters such as floods and fires cause great destruction and refugees plunge into poverty.

Fixing these structural problems, however, is only half the battle, according to Harrison. A key strategic piece in the war against poverty is addressing the fatalism that permeates the poor communities. This lack of hope results in passivity. A good anti-poverty programme, therefore, must also address the social needs of people in poverty. Harrison suggests building relationships and encouraging creativity as ways to boost productivity as both the individual and community work their way out of poverty. She advocates for more decision-making opportunities for poor people. Harrison's multipronged approach addresses the numerous contributing causes of poverty, including individual, familial, communal, corporate and governmental causes.

When it comes to studying the causes of poverty in the ancient world, what counts as poverty is not always comparable with our modern context. For example, the social component of poverty is difficult to study, as we lack access to the voice of the poor themselves. Additionally, discriminators between rich and poor are different, as both suffered from poor healthcare and lack of clean water and sanitation. Money could not buy health, although it could support pilgrimages to healing shrines. Wealth did not prevent infant mortality, as it can today, because the accepted practices for childbirth and childcare were faulty, even dangerous, to the mother and child. Nor was education necessarily the way out of poverty as it is so often today. Land ownership counted for much, as did an able body that could do manual labour.

There are also differences in cultural values that suggest that poverty might be differently described. The ancient world did not value innovation, or individualism (and the creativity associated with it) as we do today. For example, Harrison rightly notes the importance today of poor people's voice in decision-making. The ancient world would not have articulated the situation this way. Rather, people in poverty asked for justice, for courts to uphold contracts and property rights. Further, they might riot against a corrupt king. Nevertheless, the idea that the individual had a vote in matters of government is a modern one rooted in democracy. Again, Harrison decries modern sex trafficking. In the ancient world, such practices were institutionalized in the slave industry; many men and women slaves were prostitutes. In my paper, I do not address the institution of slavery and its impact on the Roman economy, as the topic is too vast. Yet, Harrison's keen observation on the impact of modern sex trafficking provides the opportunity to expose the ancient world's reliance on slave labour within its overall economy.

Christians in the ancient world dreamed new dreams, of life eternal in peace with Christ in the new heavens and new earth. They dreamed of unity as citizens of heaven. This meant that their small communities strove to reduce social hierarchy within their group and re-evaluate who received honour and why. The new community neither valued the biological family as highly as did the Romans nor put the state above all. Instead, the church valued 'family' with its new, fictive kinship relationships and cherished the kingdom of God as its proper allegiance.

6

'Do Good to All' (Gal. 6.10): Assets, Capital and Benefaction in Early Christianity

Bruce W. Longenecker

Introduction

Did benefaction arise within early Christianity? If so, what might it have looked like in relation to other forms of financial initiatives within the Graeco-Roman world? In approaching these basic questions, I want to propose that benefaction is evident within early Christianity, although much of it did not look too much like the kinds of benefaction that commanded the most attention in the Graeco-Roman world. This is true in several respects: the form it took, its motivational structures, its resource base and its primary targets. This essay explores these features of benefaction in early Christianity.

Benefaction in the Graeco-Roman world and in early Christianity

Benefaction, like most things, came in a variety of shapes and sizes in the Graeco-Roman world. For this reason, nothing more than a very basic overview can be offered here. But with that said, and generally speaking, the type of benefaction that really mattered in the Graeco-Roman world was civic euergetism – that is, the initiatives that benefitted urban centres, being funded usually by those who controlled enormous resources. These initiatives, involving vast sums of money, could include paying for the erection or renovation of temples, bathing complexes, statues to deities and members of the imperial family; or the underwriting of spectacles, such as gladiatorial competitions and theatrical performances; and so on. Initiatives at this end of the spectrum involved expenditures that (generally speaking) only the wealthiest elite could afford. The price tag was extremely high; those eligible to pay were extremely few.

The health of ancient urban centres was not utterly reliant on elite initiatives. Although the point is debated, a strong case has been made that taxation was generally a reliable income stream for urban development in the Graeco-Roman world.[1] But however we adjudicate that issue, there is no dispute that the civic infrastructure was significantly enhanced by initiatives of civic euergetism undertaken by elite benefactors.

In an ideal world, the system of civic benefaction was to be characterized by economic balance. The elite accessed significant income streams and were expected to combine them into a much larger collection of resources for public use through sizable donations that strengthened the fabric of civic life. The old French adage *noblesse oblige* captures the sentiment of things pretty well – those who have deep pockets are expected to undertake initiatives on behalf of their communities. It is against this very general background, elaborated further below, that we can begin to consider the issue of benefaction in Christianity in the pre-Constantinian period.

We see none of this macro-scale benefaction being carried out by Christians in the earliest centuries of the Common Era. This is not to be heard as a criticism. It is simply a reflection of the fact that not many Christians were among the economically privileged in those centuries (e.g. 1 Cor. 1.26). There is some truth to Paul Veyne's description of things when he writes:

> Paganism was aware of the poor man only in his most commonplace shape, that of the beggar encountered in the street . . . [It] had abandoned without much remorse the starving, the old and the sick . . . All this changed with the coming of Christianity, in which almsgiving resulted from the new ethical religiosity . . . Old people's homes, orphanages, hospitals and so on are institutions that appear only with the Christian epoch.[2]

Institutions of this kind, however, are primarily post-Constantinian phenomena, arising in the aftermath of the Christianizing of the empire in the fourth century and beyond. At that point, the super-elite had motivation to join the Christian church, and their huge slush funds were put to good use (as noted by Veyne in the quotation above).[3] But this was not characteristic of Christianity prior to the Constantinian revolution. In the first three centuries of the Common Era, if our focus is on macro-level beneficence (i.e. things required of politicians, who were predominately drawn from circles of the elite), Christian initiatives will be (almost?) absent from our inventory.

This is not to suggest that generosity was absent from Christian identity during those centuries. In fact, judging from certain strands of evidence, generosity was precisely the character trait that frequently marked out Christian communities. We could trudge our way through various New Testament (NT) passages to illustrate the point. Having done that elsewhere,[4] I will only cite here a brief passage or two from beyond the NT to make the point.

[1] On this, see especially Hertha Schwarz, *Soll oder Haben? Die Finanzwirtschaft kleinasiatischer Städte in der römischen Kaiserzeit am Beispiel von Bithynien, Lykien und Ephesos (29 v. Chr.–284 n. Chr.)* (Bonn: Habelt, 2001).
[2] Paul Veyne, *Bread and Circuses: Historical Sociology and Political Pluralism* (London: Penguin, 1990), 31 and 33. For similar estimates, see Bruce W. Longenecker, *Remember the Poor: Paul, Poverty, and the Graeco-Roman World* (Grand Rapids, MI: Eerdmans, 2010), 63–64.
[3] See, e.g., Peter Brown, *Poverty and Leadership in the Later Roman Empire* (Waltham: Brandeis, 2001).
[4] See Longenecker, *Remember*, 140–56.

At some point between 125 and 140 CE, the philosopher Aristides of Athens had this to say about Christians (*Apology* 15):

> They love one another. They do not neglect widows. Orphans they rescue from those who are cruel to them. Every one of them who has anything gives ungrudgingly to the one who has nothing. If they see a travelling stranger they bring him under their roof. They rejoice over him as a real brother, for they do not call one another brothers after the flesh, but they know they are brothers in the Spirit and in God . . . If one of them sees that one of their poor must leave this world, he provides for his burial as well as he can. And if they hear that one of them is imprisoned or oppressed by their opponents for the sake of their Christ's name, all of them take care of all his needs. If possible they set him free. If anyone among them is poor or comes into want while they themselves have nothing to spare, they fast two or three days for him. In this way they can supply the poor man with the food he needs.

The rhetoric is so effusive that we might imagine Aristides (himself a Christian) to have exaggerated his case about Christian beneficence. But our scepticism must be tempered by other data. For instance, Lucian of Samosata, a critic of Christianity, had this to say about Christians (*Peregrinus* 13):

> The earnestness with which the people of this religion [i.e., Christianity] help one another in their need is incredible. They spare themselves nothing to this end. Apparently their first law-maker [Jesus] has put it into their heads that they all somehow ought to be regarded as brothers and sisters.

Lucian's depiction of Christians differs from Aristides's in its extent (i.e. it is shorter than Aristides) but not in its content. Evidently, Christians were engaging in noticeable (or, as Lucian calls them, 'incredible') beneficence initiatives and, consequently, were known to be doing so.

Three things need to be noted. First, the kinds of beneficence that we see in early Christianity are, generally speaking, of a very low-grade type. In Aristides's examples, for instance, it involves attending to widows, rescuing orphans, resourcing those who have nothing, extending hospitality, paying for burials, caring for the imprisoned and oppressed, and fasting to build up a small pot of assistance money. NT examples could be brought alongside to demonstrate similar low-grade forms of beneficent initiative.[5] In the discourse of the apostle Paul, these small gestures for others, carried out by ordinary people in small, simple and relatively insignificant ways, are discussed in terms like 'remember the poor' (Gal. 2.10), 'bear one another's burdens . . . [and] work for the good of all' (Gal. 6.2, 10), 'pursue the good' for the benefit of others (1 Thess. 5.15), be known for 'your generosity in sharing with . . . all' (2 Cor. 9.13) – or, in later epistles, 'share with the needy' (Eph. 4.28) and 'devote yourself to

---

[5] In this regard, Phoebe, whom Paul identifies as 'a benefactor of many and of myself as well' (Rom. 16.2), would probably have been relatively exceptional among the majority of early Jesus-followers.

good works in order to meet urgent needs' (Tit. 3.14). Notions of benefaction are probably in play to one extent or another in these exhortations. That is significant, since such minute gestures of beneficence almost runs against the grain of the term 'benefaction', at least as it was employed in ordinary parlance within the Graeco-Roman world. If elite benefaction was broadly civic in focus, forms of beneficence among Christian communities in the pre-Constantinian period seem to have targeted a much narrower subset within that civic focus – that is, the destitute. (Benefaction of a more widespread and pronounced kind was generally an unworkable form of benefaction for Christians in the pre-Constantinian world.)[6] What we are seeing in the early Jesus movement and beyond is the reframing of benefaction so that it applies to the smallest gestures of the ordinary, the underprivileged and even the poor. Here, the narratives of the socially insignificant are being placed front and centre.

Second, we can probably draw a straight line from Aristides's characterization of Christians in a pre-Constantinian context to Veyne's characterization of institutions of care 'that appear only with the Christian [post-Constantinian] epoch'. When the super wealthy began to populate a religion whose character had been shaped by three centuries of caring for the poor, the combination of care and super-wealth resulted in the creation of forms of care provision never before evidenced.

Third, even the ordinary was taken notice of, in a fashion comparable to the notice given to the grand forms of benefaction. This is embedded within Lucian's comments (noted above), which suggests that care for the needy was one of the distinctive identity markers of Christian communities in the second century. The same is evident two centuries later. Seeking to extricate Christianity from the post-Constantinian empire, the pagan emperor Julian (332–363 CE; emperor 360–363) nonetheless testified to the respectability of Christian social action. Noting the way in which the poor were 'neglected and overlooked' by pagan sectors of society and the way that Christians (and Jews) 'devoted themselves to benevolence', Julian also took note of the way that 'the impious Galileans [i.e., Christians] support not only their poor, but ours as well', not least since 'everyone can see that our people lack aid from us' (*Ep.* 22.430D).[7] In Julian and Lucian we find two of Christianity's earliest critics testifying that micro-level care for the needy was a distinguishing feature of Christian communities and was being noticed.[8] Crudely speaking, the moral assets of Christian communities were being turned into social capital.[9]

---

[6] See, e.g., Travis B. Williams, *Good Works in 1 Peter: Negotiating Social Conflict and Christian Identity in the Graeco-Roman World*, WUNT 2/337 (Tübingen: Mohr Siebeck, 2014).

[7] See also also the fifth-century Christian historian Sozomen, *Hist.* 5.16.5. See further P. Johnson, *A History of Christianity* (New York: Touchstone, Simon & Schuster, 1976), 75; D. Ayerst and A. S. T. Fischer, *Records of Christianity, Vol. I: The Church in the Roman Empire* (Oxford: Blackwell, 1971), 179–81.

[8] Classical scholars remind us that the elite literature from the early imperial period regularly demonstrate 'a general lack of understanding of the realities of conjunctural [or structural] poverty'.

[9] Perhaps the author of 1 Peter would have been pleased about this. In a context of difficult relationships with non-Christians, that author thought that if Christians were 'eager to do good' (3.13) within their society, that would deflect some potential criticism against them.

Motivating benefaction in the Graeco-Roman world and early Christianity

With the huge expenses of civic euergetism in view, the twenty-first-century observer might be inclined to ask, Why would people have undertaken such hugely expensive initiatives? The answer is simple: because the elite were enmeshed within the unending quest to maintain and increase their social status. The Roman orator and philosopher Cicero (106–43 BCE) attributed the motivation to 'the lure of honour' (*Off.* 1.44). Approximately a century later, Dio Chrysostom (40–115 CE) noted that public benefactors give of their resources 'in the pursuit of crowns and precedence and purple robes' (*2 Tars.* 29). His contemporary Pliny the Younger (61–113 CE) said much the same when he spoke of 'the boast of their good deed' as motivating elite benefaction (*Ep.* 1.8.15). The Jewish philosopher Philo of Alexandria (25 BCE–50 CE or so) depicted the motivational structures that embedded civic benefaction in this way:

> Those who are said to bestow benefits sell rather than give; and those who seem to us to receive them [i.e., those benefits] in truth buy [them]. The givers are seeking commendation or honour as their return and look for their benefits to be repaid, and so under the false name of a gift, they in truth carry out a sale. (*Cher.* 122–23)

The primary currency of the Graeco-Roman world was not money per se, but status. More precious than gold, public honour was the most coveted social commodity, and it drove the system of benefaction throughout the Graeco-Roman world. As Philo observed (as noted above), capturing social capital was integral to the whole process of elite benefaction. The social honour that came with these sizeable initiatives of benefaction was so significant that others further down on the scale of economic security seem often to have sought to imitate the civic euergetism of the grand elite, setting up smaller-scale initiatives of their own in order to reap some of the status benefits that came with those initiatives.[10]

In the ideal scenario, a balanced benefaction fostered healthy relationality between the elite and their civic beneficiaries. The reality, however, was much different much of the time. There were a hundred and one variations on a theme in this regard, but the popular adage that 'power corrupts' captures the sense that accruing social esteem

---

[10] There are a number of instances in which groups undertook initiatives of benefaction by pooling their money. Jews in Smyrna, for instance, were known to have done this in the early second century (*CIJ* 742; see E. Leigh Gibson, 'Jews in the Inscriptions of Smyrna', *JJS* 56 (2005): 66–79; more broadly, Tessa Rajak, 'Jews as Benefactors', in *Studies on the Jewish Diaspora in the Hellenistic and Roman Periods*, ed. Benjamin Isaac and Aharon Oppenheimer (Tel Aviv: Ramot, 1996), 17–38. Gestures of civic benefaction could at times even be initiated by slaves – some of the more fortunate slaves, no doubt, but slaves nonetheless. These benefactions could take the form of collectively donating the base of a statue to a local temple (*CIL* 10.824 and 10.826), enhancing public devotion to the Roman deities (*CIL* 10.888; 10.890; 10.901; 10.902) or serving as caretakers of the neighbourhood deity cult whose shrines stood at the intersections of urban streets to protect the local residents from an influx of evil (*CIL* 4.60; 4.7425; 4.7855). Sometimes the non-elite were able to add fairly insignificant amounts of money to elite initiatives of benefaction, being recognized on inscriptions as a consequence.

often went hand in hand with being complicit, in what we today would think of as abuses of human rights.[11]

This is not the place to overview the voices of protest against this system, voices found on occasion within the literature of the Graeco-Roman world.[12] But we can make a gesture to those voices of protest by calling again on the Jewish philosopher Philo to make the point (*Decalogue* 2.4):

> Cities are full of countless evils, both acts of impiety towards God and wrongdoing between man and man. For everything is debased, the genuine overpowered by the spurious, the true by the false . . . so too in cities there arises that most insidious of foes, pride, admired and worshipped by some who add dignity to vain ideas by means of gold crowns and purple robes and a great establishment of servants and cars, on which these so-called blissful and happy people ride aloft, drawn sometimes by mules and horses, sometimes by men, who bear the heavy burden on their shoulders, yet suffer in soul rather than in body under the weight of extravagant arrogance.

Christians, too, raised their voice against the economic system that prioritized the interests of the elite. Pride of place goes to the fiery Apocalypse of John, or Revelation. Within his symbol-rich narrative, the author of Revelation decries the religious, military and economic structures that combined in an all-encompassing system that he deemed to be engulfing the whole world. This system, which Walter Wink insightfully labels 'the Domination System', is attributed by the author of Revelation to the corrupting power of the Satan within God's world.[13]

The system is one that the kings and merchants of this world engorged themselves on, being filthy rich because of 'the power of [the system's] luxury' (Rev. 18.3).[14] But telling in this regard is the inventory of the resources contributing to the luxuries of the Domination System, an inventory that the author constructs in Rev. 18.12-13. The

---

[11] For examples of the poor being resources for elite advancement, see Longenecker, *Remember*, 19–35. One interesting example is the plundering of possessions. As Peter Garnsey notes, the plundering of possessions was carried out legally through official confiscation, whereby those deemed to stand opposed to the expansion of Roman power had their possessions striped from them and given to those favorably disposed to the Roman project (Peter Garnsey, 'Peasants in Ancient Roman Society', in his *Cities, Peasants and Food in Classical Antiquity* (Cambridge: Cambridge University Press, 1998), 91–106). Examples of this are evident in the material record (e.g. the Villa of the Papyri in Herculaneum; see Andrew Wallace-Hadrill, *Herculaneum: Past and Future* [London: Frances Lincoln/Los Alto, CA: Packard Humanities Institute, 2011], 115) and the literary record, even in the NT itself (see Heb. 10.32-34).

[12] On this, see Bruce W. Longenecker, 'Peace, Security, and Prosperity: Advertisement and Reality in the Early Roman Empire', in *An Introduction to Empire in the New Testament*, ed. Adam Winn (Atlanta: SBL, 2016), 15–46.

[13] Walter Wink, *Engaging the Powers: Discernment and Resistance in a World of Domination* (Minneapolis: Augsburg Fortress, 1992), 87–104.

[14] It is interesting to observe that in Petronius's novel *Satyricon*, one character complains that the civic aediles, 'who play "you scratch my back and I'll scratch yours", are in league with the bakers' (*Satyricon* 44). The point is simply that the bakers are conscripted to support the power aspirations of the elite by regaling the local populace with bribery bread in the name of the elite. Compare the less sinister inscription from Pompeii: 'I beg you to elect Gaius Julius Polybius as aedile; he brings good bread [to the people]' (*CIL* 4.429).

inventory comprises more than two dozen entries. Towards the top are entries that we might well expect to see in the most highly prized position: gold, silver, jewels and pearls. Towards the middle of the inventory reside the entries appropriate to middling-level resources: costly wood, bronze, iron and marble. Almost at the bottom of the inventory appear the much more common resources of the empire: olive oil, flour, wheat, cattle and sheep. But it is the last entry that is most interesting, as well as most difficult to interpret. We do not need to debate whether the Greek phrase (*sōmatōn, kai psychas anthrōpōn*) is best rendered 'slaves – and human lives' (NRSV), or 'slaves, that is human beings', or 'human beings sold as slaves' (NIV 1984 and 2011) or 'slaves and souls of men' (Douay-Rheims). The point is that the author's list of commodities is meant to be shocking to healthy Judaeo-Christian sensitivities. In the Domination System, insecure human lives are not regarded as valued creatures of the sovereign creator. Instead, insecure human lives are captured as hostages within a system of economic exchange that benefits the elite who have managed the system to their own benefit. Human beings are simply cogs in the wheelhouse of elite domination, in which benefaction plays a central role. The author of Revelation admits that the Domination System looks splendid and impressive.[15] But behind it and undergirding it, even invisibly and unperceptively, is the ultimate anti-God power, the power of the Satan (compare the narrative movement from Revelation 12 to Revelation 13–14).

There is tragedy in all of this, from the author's point of view. Economic structures are managed by the elite, for whom the powerless are simply assets in their economic capital. People are being viewed in terms of an inverted scale of worth. But more than tragedy is involved here. Ultimately, there is idolatry – worship directed to something other than its only worthy recipient. The idolatrous tragedy and the tragic idolatry of it all is not simply that human lives are improperly placed on a skewed scale of worth; it is the skewed scale of worth itself is deemed to be a Satanic construct. In a race to capture value, worth, honour and capital, the whole world has come under the beguiling sway of a satanic deceit, thereby becoming complicit in the valuing of human life according to its placement in the system that oversees the commoditization of assets. This, the Johannine author contends, is not how the sovereign deity assesses worth. Social Darwinism, in which the fittest survive by feeding off of the resources of the insecure, is the system of the Satan. For this reason, a heavenly voice urges Christians to remove themselves from the Domination System: 'Come out of her, my people, so that you do not take part in her sins' (Rev. 18.4).

Whereas Revelation is one of the most countercultural voices in the Christian canon, a much different ethos emerges from the Lukan Gospel, with its generally 'positive, robust, world-affirming character' (although its prophetic voice should not be overlooked).[16] But despite their differences in posture, both are in agreement that Christian moral identity is averse to the Domination System. So, with its message of

---

[15] See Rev. 17.6, where *ethaumasa* should probably be translated 'filled with amazement'.

[16] Richard Hays depicts in the following fashion: 'The church is not a defensive community withdrawing from an evil world; instead, it acts boldly on the stage of public affairs, commending the gospel in reasoned terms to all persons of goodwill and expecting an open-minded response', in his *The Moral Vision of the New Testament: A Contemporary Introduction to New Testament Ethics* (San Francisco: HarperOne, 1996), 134.

'good news to the poor' glorious articulated by Jesus (Lk. 4.18), the Lukan Gospel makes this aversion evident in notable fashion, and specifically with regard to benefaction:

> A dispute also arose among them [Jesus's disciples] as to which one of them was to be regarded as the greatest. But he said to them, 'The kings of the Gentiles lord it over them; and those in authority over them are called benefactors. But not so with you; rather the greatest among you must become like the youngest, and the leader [must become] like one who serves.' (Lk. 22.24-26; cf. Mk 10.42-44)

Why does Luke depict Jesus as challenging the benefaction system, as managed by the 'kings of the gentiles' and 'those in authority'? Notice that Jesus does not simply call for a restoration or reformation of the benefaction system. He does not simply exhort benefactors to be good-hearted people. Instead, in a short soundbite, he challenges the very structures supporting the benefaction system of the Graeco-Roman world. His clipped challenge may derive from a recognition of the abusive injustices of that system – a system that fed all-pervasive structures whereby the wealthy extracted resources from the reserves of others in order to enhance their social capital.[17] But Jesus does not simply decry the injustices; instead, he 'goes for the jugular' of the system itself, undermining its notions of worth and value that pervade the structures propping up the kingdoms of this world.

Accordingly, despite their different postures regarding the character of Christian communities in relation to society, the Lukan Gospel and the Johannine Revelation mesh well together in their critique of the Domination System. The prophetic criticism voiced by heavenly deity of Revelation ('Come out of her, my people') reverberates with the voice of Jesus of Nazareth ('not so with you').

Critical exhortations of this kind are not sustained throughout the whole of the early Christian literature. At times, more accommodating models are advocated, seeking a positive interface between the Christian message and the surrounding culture. And some sympathy might be reserved for the early Christians who sought to work within the structures of society rather than to abandon them and set up small enclaves of alternative societies. Just as there are strengths in each modelling of Christian engagement with society, so too there are weaknesses in each. But standing over all models, it seems, is the revaluing of worth that lies at the heart of the Christian 'good news' and the concern that Christian initiatives reflect revaluation, in contrast

---

[17] The author of 1 Timothy explores this theological terrain when speaking of those who strive to be rich as 'trapped by many senseless and harmful desires' (1 Tim. 6.9). Previous to this charge (in 6.5), an economic component is already in play when the author speaks of envy among those 'deprived of the truth who suppose that religion [*eusebeian*] is a way of making profit'. (The word *eusebeia* is used positively in 6.6, connoting 'piety' or 'godliness'. In 6.5, however, a positive characteristic [i.e. 'godliness'] is being abused, and consequently I translate it there as 'religion'.) A similar economic component is in play a sentence after his charge against those who strive to be rich, where he makes the famous claim that 'the love of money is the root of all evils' (6.10). In his assessment, covetousness permeates economic exchange. This is not to say that covetousness is wholly reducible to economic acquisitiveness. Nonetheless, economic acquisitiveness has a strong foothold as one form of covetousness.

to the value-laden initiatives that predominated within the benefaction system of the Graeco-Roman world.

Resourcing benefaction

We have seen that the types of benefaction often undertaken by pre-Constantinian Christian communities were much different from elite-based benefaction; moreover, the motivational basis was to be different from the norm, at least according to some canonical forms of Christian discourse. The reason why the motivational basis is to be different is articulated most clearly in the discourse of Paul. In his theological frame of reference, initiatives of beneficence on behalf of the destitute had little to do with people taking the initiative to act on behalf of others. For Paul, remembering the destitute is linked to what we might call 'Spiritful membering'. That is, in Paul's view of things, Christian giving emerges from spiritual gifting within Jesus-groups. This is why he lists generosity in his lists of the Spirit's work – both 'the fruit of the Spirit' which are given to all those in Christ (*agathōsunē* in Gal. 5.22, referencing 'generous goodness')[18] and in a more concentrated form as a 'gift of the Spirit' given to some Jesus-followers in particular (Rom. 12.8; cf. 1 Cor. 12.28).[19] Despite differences in concentration levels, generosity testifies to and enacts the inbreaking of right relationships as result of the Spirit's transforming presence within Jesus-groups.

In his best theological moments, Paul imagined the body of Christ to be the epitome of the abundant community, whose resources were supplied by an abundant Spirit, where all members had important contributions to make, regardless of their prosopographic profile, and where each incarnation of the body built its identity and mission around the indigenous resources brought to it by its mutually gifted members. In this way, Paul's vision has some overlap with what some today are calling ABCD – asset-based community development.[20] But for Paul, these were not simply community-resourced assets. They were theological capital, precisely because they were resourced by the Spirit of the self-giving Son of God. They spoke of the presence of God within the relatively unimpressive communities of Jesus-followers. Paul understood beneficent initiatives within Jesus-groups in terms much different from all other forms of benefaction of his day, not simply with regard to its type or motivation but also to its ultimate source, vibrantly active in ordinary communities of Jesus-devotion.

---

[18] So, L&N 57.109: 'the act of generous giving, with the implication of its relationship to goodness – "to be generous, generosity"'.

[19] On the relationship between these two forms of Spirit enabling, see Longenecker, *Remember*, 281–7.

[20] See the Asset-Based Community Development Institute (https://resources.depaul.edu/abcd-institute/Pages/default.aspx, accessed February 2018); John McKnight and Peter Block, *The Abundant Community: Awakening the Power of Families and Neighborhoods* (San Francisco: Berrett-Koehler, 2012); Steve Corbett and Brian Fikkert, *When Helping Hurts: How to Alleviate Poverty without Hurting the Poor . . . and Yourself* (Chicago: Moody, 2014).

Targeting benefaction in early Christianity

Were beneficent initiatives undertaken by Jesus-followers thought simply to benefit the impoverished located within Jesus-groups, or was there a broader concern? The letters of Paul provide important resources for addressing this question. From them, at least two important dimensions of this issue emerge: (1) Paul expected the focus of such initiatives to be within Jesus-groups and (2) Paul expected those initiatives to overspill beyond Jesus-groups, wherever and whenever possible.

There are two passages that bring both of these contentions together. In what is probably Paul's first extant letter, he exhorts his readers to 'do good to one another and to all' (1 Thess. 5.15), whereas he says the same in reverse order in what is probably his second extant letter: 'let us work for the good of all, and especially for those of the family of faith' (Gal. 6.10). We might want to spend time trying to figure out the relation of these two passages, but two things seem most evident.

First, Paul expected a transformed vision of relationality to result in transformed patterns of practice within Jesus-groups empowered by a transforming Spirit; after all, it was in relational practices within Christian communities that Jesus-followers were to learn both that and how 'Christ lives in me' (Gal. 2.20; cf. 3.27; 4.19).[21]

Second, Paul expected those transformed patterns of practice to overspill beyond Jesus-groups; after all, the grace that was transforming them into 'reincarnations' of the self-giving Son was unmerited by them as well as by those beyond Jesus-groups (cf. 2 Cor. 9.13). All were unworthy of the gracious gift offered by God, who resourced generosity among Jesus-followers as a natural expression of that grace within their lives. At the level of worldview, trying to restrict the flow of generosity in any form or fashion would be like trying to join an AC electricity cable to a DC electricity cable.[22] Unsurprisingly, then, as the Petrine author seems to have thought, when Christians 'do good' to those around them (1 Pet. 2.12, 20; 3.11, 16-17; 4.19), they are extending divine 'blessing' within their indigenous contexts as agents of 'the God of all grace' (1 Pet. 3.9; 5.10).

Conclusion

What we have seen regarding beneficent initiatives by pre-Constantinian Christians is a spotty, generalized portrait, not least because our resources for reconstruction

---

[21] Part of discerning how 'Christ lives in me' involves adjudicating abuses of beneficence in Jesus-groups. Pauline texts indicate that beneficent initiatives toward the needy required monitoring, lest they be abused. This is evident in the Thessalonian letters regarding those who decided not to work in order to allow the Christian community to care for them and in 1 Timothy regarding which widows are the most deserving of corporate care. This required Jesus-groups to use a hefty dose of common sense about who should and should not be recipients of 'care-full' resources. If divine grace is not to be presumed upon, neither should the beneficence empowered by that grace to be presumed upon.

[22] This is assumed in Paul's comments about 'the Lord's Supper' in 1 Cor. 11.17-34. The economic mismatch between the Corinthian practice and the Christian gospel's theology of divine grace has resulted (in Paul's view) in divine chastisement: 'For this reason many of you are weak and ill, and some have died' (1 Cor. 11.30).

on-the-ground realities are themselves spotty.[23] This overview might also err on the side of freeze-framing the more ideal moments and foregrounding the more impressive soundbites of Christian discourse of that initial period in the process of Christian self-identification. Clearly, not all Christians were living out the gold standard of beneficence in all situations; they must often have been hampered either by situation or volition, or both. As a rule of thumb, the ideal must often have transcended the reality; the discourse must have outstripped the concrete realities.

With that said, however, we cannot dispute that even the opponents of Christianity conceded that Christians (and, in Julian's discourse, Jews as well) outstripped their pagan contemporaries in undertaking initiatives for those in need. Perhaps, then, the idealisms of Christian discourse helped to foster the imagination of Jesus-followers to see the world in new ways, to imagine their place in the world to have import and to act on that perception in ways that made small differences. It was in those small and occasional differences, those gestures of doing good to others, or (in Julian's words) those moments of 'devot[ing] themselves to benevolence', that pre-Constantinian Christians testified against the Domination System of social Darwinism.

---

[23] See, though, Helen Rhee, *Loving the Poor, Saving the Rich: Wealth, Poverty, and Early Christian Formation* (Grand Rapids, MI: Baker Academic, 2012); Susan R. Holman, ed., *Wealth and Poverty in Early Church and Society* (Grand Rapids, MI: Baker Academic, 2008).

Benefaction Today?

John Coleby

Introduction

Benefaction, philanthropy and volunteering are significant activities of civil society. One could be forgiven for making the assumption that the roots for such activities are derived from a Judaeo-Christian value base; but, in fact, all the major religions place an emphasis on charitable giving.

People become benefactors and donate to charities and volunteer for different reasons both from within and without faith (i.e. secular) communities, particularly in the United Kingdom. I shall compare and contrast its activities and motivations. I am writing this essay from the perspective of a Catholic-inspired community practitioner – someone who is motivated by my own faith, inspired by the Gospels, Catholic Social Teaching and my lived experience as a leader, social worker, volunteer and someone who gives to charity. In conclusion, I shall attempt to identify the difference between contemporary faith-based and secular benefaction.

What is benefaction?

The word benefaction comes from the Latin *bene*, meaning 'well', and *facere*, 'to do' – it is the act of doing good.[1] Philanthropy, a synonym of benefaction, is the desire to promote the welfare of others, expressed especially by the generous donation of money to good causes. Other synonyms include almsgiving, offering, gift, favour, kindness, philanthropy, oblation, volunteering in kind.

On the subject of human nature, biologists say that babies are innately sociable and helpful to others. Of course, every animal must to some extent be selfish to survive, but the biologists see in humans a natural willingness to help.[2] Christians and Jews

---

[1] *Collins English Dictionary*, online (https://www.collinsdictionary.com/dictionary/english/benefaction, accessed December 2017).

[2] Nicholas Wade, 'We May Be Born with an Urge to Help', *New York Times*, 30 November 2009 (http://www.nytimes.com/2009/12/01/science/01human.html?mcubz=0, accessed December 2017).

say that our belief that we are created in God's image (Gen 1.27) shapes how we see God, the world and one another. It provides a theological foundation for ethics and engagement.

However, benefaction is a now a global industry and there are a number of world renowned, super-rich 'benefactors' or philanthropists. Among them are Bill Gates, Warren Buffet, Mark Zuckerberg, Margaret Cargill and Chris Hohn. They divest their wealth through their foundations and charitable trusts, giving to their causes and the things they believe in. In contrast to the global super-rich, there are thousands of people in the UK who give time and money to a wide range of causes. Other examples of benefaction are volunteering and participation in social action according to the annual giving report of the Charities Aid Foundation (CAF).[3] The Community Life survey – part of the Big Society initiative – conducted on behalf of the Cabinet Office includes volunteering as well as financial giving among its indicators of community life.[4] I shall follow its lead in including these as examples of benefaction.

An overview of benefaction in the UK

According to the Charity Commission, there are over 167,000 registered charities in the UK with an income of approximately £74.7 billion.[5] The breadth of special interest causes they support and the scope of their activities is hugely impressive. Some provide services or activities; some distribute funds to other charities and groups. Among the things they are dedicated to are meeting social, cultural and spiritual needs; campaigning for change in legislation and policy; sport; education, training and work reparation; medical research, health and well-being; and animal welfare. They include religious institutions or foundations, that is, different churches, synagogues, mosques, temples, grant-making trusts and foundations, research trusts, schools, universities hospitals and schools. The Commission numbers do not include those groups and associations who are not required to register because their turnover is less than £5,000 per annum. If these numbers were included, the figure is probably more than 400,000.[6]

In 2014, approximately 23 million individual people in the UK gave between £10 and £19 billion in gifts to 'good causes'. The higher number includes individuals,

---

[3] 'UK Giving 2014: An Overview of Charitable Giving in the UK during 2014', 2 (http://www.cafonline.org/docs/default-source/about-us-publications/caf-ukgiving2014, accessed December 2017).

[4] 'Community Life Survey 2014–2015: Statistical Analysis', 6–10 (https://assets.publishing.service.gov.uk/government/uploads/system/uploads/attachment_data/file/447010/Community_Life_Survey_2014-15_Bulletin.pdf, accessed December 2017); 'Community Life Survey 2016–2017', 3–4 (https://www.gov.uk/government/uploads/system/uploads/attachment_data/file/638534/Community_Life_Survey_-_Statistical_Release_2016-17_FINAL_v.2.pdf, accessed December 2017).

[5] 'Charity Commission Annual Report and Accounts 2016–17', 4 (https://www.gov.uk/government/uploads/system/uploads/attachment_data/file/628747/Charity_Commission_Annual_Report_and_Accounts_2016_17_web.pdf, accessed December 2017).

[6] David Ainsworth, 'There are More Than Twice as Many Charities in the UK as You've Been Told' (https://www.civilsociety.co.uk/voices/there-are-more-than-twice-as-many-charities-in-the-uk-as-you-ve-been-told.html, accessed December 2017).

trusts and foundation gift aid and corporate giving.[7] It appears that women are more generous than men, giving both more time and money: the statistics show that 63 per cent of women surveyed volunteer versus 53 per cent of men, and 48 per cent of women give money versus 43 per cent of men.[8] Interestingly, the least well-off give a higher proportion of their income to charity than the wealthy, no matter what their age, class or beliefs.[9]

According to the data from CAF, the majority of 'benefactors', approximately 33 per cent, donate to medical research into life-long conditions and cancer – 30 per cent to children's causes, 25 per cent to hospitals, 21 per cent to animals, 20 per cent to overseas aid and 14 per cent to religious causes. The percentage discrepancies are accounted for because many people give to more than one cause.[10]

A comparison between the scope of benefaction and total income is striking. While the majority of people give to medical research, more money is given to religious causes, which accounts for 14 per cent of all benefaction. Medical research receives 13 per cent, children 12 per cent, hospitals 11 per cent and animals 7 per cent.[11]

At this point, it is worth highlighting other types of benefaction that drive the industry. For example, corporate giving is the action of a for-profit company sharing some of its resources with a not-for-profit cause or charity. Typically, it includes financial resources and 'in kind' benefits such as volunteer time from its employees, strategic time or business development time. CAF, in its 2016 review of FTSE 100 companies, identified that a total of £2.1 billion was given through corporate giving in 2014 with almost all of the 100 companies reporting activity of this nature – this totals some 3 per cent of the total UK charitable sector.[12] Corporate social responsibility and social investment are other ways in which corporate bodies fund social enterprises or businesses set for social good.

Volunteering as benefaction

The UK government Community Life Survey identifies volunteering as formal, informal and employer-supported.[13] *Formal* volunteering is where people participate in or support an activity in or on behalf of an organization or group. *Informal* volunteering is where an individual helps or supports another person who is not a family member. *Employer-supported* volunteering is where an employer facilitates or enables volunteering by its employees.

---

[7] Cathy Pharoah, Keiran Goddard and Richard Jenkins, 'Giving Trends: Top 100 Family Foundations, 2015 Report', 3 (http://www.acf.org.uk/downloads/publications/Family_Foundation_Giving_Trends_2015_FINAL.pdf, accessed December 2017).

[8] 'UK Giving 2014', 9.

[9] Lucy Ward, 'Poor Give More Generously than the Rich', *The Guardian*, 21 December 2001 (http://theguardian.com/society/2001/dec/21/voluntarysector.fundraising, accessed February 2018).

[10] 'UK Giving 2014', 14.

[11] Ibid., 14.

[12] Charities Aid Foundation, 'Corporate Giving by the FTSE 100' (March 2016) (https://www.cafonline.org/docs/default-source/about-us-publications/1860a_caf_ftse100_report_web_hb_030316.pdf?sfvrsn=4, accessed February 2018).

[13] 'Community Life Survey 2014–2015', 6.

The 2013 data from the Community Life Survey shows that 23.1 million people volunteer formally at least once a year. At least 15.2 million people volunteer at least once per month. (Volunteers are defined as those over fifteen years of age.)[14]

Contemporary Christian benefaction

While the above data provides insights into the scope and depth of philanthropy in the UK, it does not drill down into the detail of giving within and for specific communities. The following section will explore trends in giving in contemporary Christian benefaction, but it will also refer to Jewish and Muslim benefaction.

All the major religions link worship and belief with the requirement to be generous with time and money. The research about charitable giving and religion suggests that religious causes attract the largest proportion of donations compared with other causes.[15] It also suggests people who give to religious causes also give substantially to non-religious causes. The amount of religious giving, however, is falling; this is likely to be due to the falling numbers of congregations.

In Judaism, *tzedakah* is the term that describes charitable giving. 'Doing' *tzedakah* is the act of providing for the poor in order to help restore the social balance. It is an act of justice rather than a paternalistic act of charity. Many Jews see *tzedakah* and its equivalent term for volunteering, *hitnadvoot*, as being connected with the concepts of generosity social action and giving freely. *Tikkun olam* means to mend the world and together with *tzedakah* and *hitnadvoot*, it articulates the work for social justice, which is imperative for social justice within and without Jewish communities.

As one of the five pillars of Islam, *zakat* is mandatory giving. All Muslims eligible to pay it must donate at least 2.5 per cent of their accumulated wealth for the benefit of the poor, destitute and others – classified as *mustahik*. It is one of the largest forms of wealth transfer to the poor in existence.[16] Charitable giving beyond *zakat* or reaching out to one's neighbour is articulated by the term *sadaqah*, which is similar to the Hebrew word *tzedakah* and has connotations of justice as well as charity. In the UK, many millions of pounds are raised within Muslim communities particularly for international development.

Christianity also has a long history in relation to charitable giving. It finds its roots in the Old and New Testaments, specifically in the doctrine of redemptive almsgiving. Alms given in kindness and with mercy is considered as righteous and acceptable to God and, therefore, redeeming of sin (Dan. 4.27; Tob. 12.8; Mt. 10.24; Lk. 19.8-10). It is

---

[14] 'Community Life Survey 2014–2015', 6.

[15] David P. King, 'Faith and Giving', in *Achieving Excellent in Fundraising*, ed. Eugene R. Tempel, Timothy L. Seiler and Dwight Burlingame, 4th edn (San Francisco: Jossey-Bass, 2015), 145–52, esp. 142.

[16] Zainulbahar Noor and Francine Pickup, 'Zakat Requires Muslims to Donate 2.5% of Their Wealth: Could This End Poverty?', *The Guardian*, 22 June 2017 (https://www.theguardian.com/global-development-professionals-network/2017/jun/22/zakat-requires-muslims-to-donate-25-of-their-wealth-could-this-end-poverty, accessed February 2018).

easy to see how the cultural memory of almsgiving in Christian communities survives and is reinterpreted as a contemporary imperative.

The concept of the tithe or giving one-tenth of one's disposable income to the Church is seen as part of the commitment in some Christian communities. The concept of stewardship is also widely utilized, especially in North America, to give expression to the idea that all Christians are called to respond to the generosity of God using their wealth and talents to build the kingdom of God and a better world for the good of all people.

Some would say that the Roman Catholic (RC) Church has done more than any institution or movement to raise people out of poverty. Indeed, the kingdom of God for a Catholic is encountered through faith in Jesus Christ as the Son of God and living a life of service and good works. This is reflected in the range and depth of Catholic benefaction around the world both in terms of money and services for developing, marginalized and economically vulnerable communities.

Although it is not arranged as a single corporation, 'RC plc' is the biggest, wealthiest and most influential movement on the planet. It attracts many critics because of its actual and perceived wealth, its lack of transparency and various scandals. In spite of this, Catholics continue to give funds for the causes of the Church whose social justice programmes are provided without qualification to people of all faiths and none.

In the twentieth and twenty-first centuries, many UK Catholic-inspired charities were founded to meet the needs of the community and the general population. Services and support are not reserved for Catholics or Christians, and, in general, they are offered unconditionally. Historically, leaders of religious congregations or clergy inspired many services such as the Father Hudson Society in Birmingham and Nugent Care in Liverpool. Funds are raised from the lay benefaction and philanthropy through collections and appeals in parish communities. This continues to be a popular model for raising funds for good works.

However, a large proportion of the day-to-day financial giving within Catholic – as well as other Christian and faith communities – is for housekeeping purposes. For example, the maintenance and upkeep of buildings, salaries for clergy and lay employees, the central administration of a diocese and the functions it is required to support such as education and catechesis, Caritas, sick and retired clergy, and youth ministry. All Catholic dioceses in England and Wales have charitable status – as do all religious congregations – and, as such, they attract financial support in the form of donations and philanthropy from their membership.

The RC Diocese of Westminster receives £23 million per year in voluntary donations; and, by this measure, it is the wealthiest RC diocesan trust in the UK. In contrast, the Catholic Agency for Overseas Development (CAFOD) receives £41 million per year in donations for its work in the developing world. In Germany, the Diocese of Cologne published its full balance sheet in 2014, revealing a net worth of £3.35 billion.

In the UK, the Church Commissioners – the charitable body which manages the assets of the Church of England – has an estimated value of £8 billion. In the United States, the picture is similar. While much of the value attributed to the Church is accounted for in the appreciation of assets such property and buildings as well as investments, it all ultimately comes from the benefaction of lay people.

The Bakhita Initiative is a good example of successful philanthropic engagement by the Church leading to high-profile benefaction from high net worth donors, ordinary donors, organizations and groups as well trusts and foundations. In 2014, the initiative was established to fight modern slavery and human trafficking through promoting an international partnership between the Church, police and civil society. In the case of England and Wales, Cardinal Vincent Nicholls and Sir Bernard Hogan-Howe established and informal partnership to promote progressive policy developments and joint working at the local regional and international level.

This led to the establishment of the Santa Marta Group, best described as a standing conference of bishops and heads of national police forces to promote joint working. The Santa Marta Group reports to Pope Francis. Initial funding was provided by the Catholic Bishops' Conference of England and Wales; but substantial funds were acquired from trusts and high-value donors in order to drive and extend the membership worldwide and, therefore, influence the battle against modern slavery and human trafficking.

The second strand of the Bakhita Initiative in London was to establish a refuge for women escaping from slavery and trafficking, where the Metropolitan Police and the Church could work together to restore women damaged by their experiences – but also to collect intelligence to identify and bring to justice perpetrators as well as rescue further victims. In 2015, Caritas Westminster opened Bakhita House for trafficked women. In 2014, a campaign was launched to help fund the project for five years. In this field, there are minimal public funds available and Bakhita House's remit is to work with the most vulnerable who have no recourse to public funds. Through a variety of activities and awareness-raising events and appeals, new funds were raised for this work from a donor base made up of fifty individuals and including three trusts and foundations.

The second dimension of benefaction is volunteering or the giving of time and talent to the community for the common good. There is little specific research on volunteering in the Christian community – although in 2014, the Cinnamon Network carried out an audit of faith communities (including some mosques and synagogues) to form a national picture. The findings were drawn from an audit of over 2,000 communities. The sample represented a 47 per cent response rate. The average outcomes per community were 8 projects, 1656 beneficiaries, 4 paid staff, 66 volunteers, 3319 paid hours, 9988 volunteer hours and £111,000 in volunteer hours.[17] The significance of the audit lies in the fact that it is the first time the collective contribution of faith communities for the common good has been articulated and quantified so clearly. The data serves as a standard for communities to work towards taking into consideration their size and resources.

Between 2012 and 2014, Caritas Westminster (the social action umbrella agency of the Diocese of Westminster) carried out a less ambitious survey of social action in its 215 communities. The survey identified a total of 960 individual projects at an average of four per community. Further work is being undertaken to identify numbers

---

[17] Cinnamon Network, 'Cinnamon Faith Action Audit', 7 (http://www.cinnamonnetwork.co.uk/wp-content/uploads/2015/05/Final-National-Report.pdf, accessed February 2018).

of volunteers and beneficiaries so that an accurate overview of volunteering and engagement can be maintained, grown and celebrated.

What motivates people to be philanthropists and benefactors?

It is fascinating to reflect on what motivates people to charitable giving and volunteering. Beth Breeze's research suggests that there is broad acceptance among donors that charitable giving should and is targeted at people who are needy. However, when she analysed the 'giving decisions' of her sample, she found there was a disconnect between how people thought about charitable giving and how they actually made decisions to give funds.[18] As she writes,

> [A]ll 60 interviewees were committed and methodical donors, yet their charitable decision-making did not appear to involve much precision, forethought or indeed afterthought . . . Despite popular beliefs that charitable giving should be directed primarily to those who are needy, donors often support organizations that promote their own preferences, that help people they feel some affinity with and that support causes which relate to their own life experiences.[19]

In short, Breeze's work suggests that charitable giving is largely supply driven and not demand-led. So in contrast to religious concepts of redemptive almsgiving, *tzedakah*, *zadak* and *sadaqah* are not means for the redistribution of wealth between rich and poor or a way of meeting the needs of those less well-off or marginalized but rather a means to reinforce a public identity and demonstrate success to the world.

Other research suggests there are three reasons why people give money to charity: altruism, impure altruism and non-altruism. The first is valuing good done by the charity alone; the second is deriving a feeling of self-worth or value because of the contribution; and the third is showing off to friends or competitors how wealthy a person might be.[20]

Charles Harvey suggests that what drives entrepreneurs to give is their desire to see people help themselves. So, typically, when they give resources they give them with their expertise and connections.[21] I believe none of the above is inconsistent with what motivates Christians to give. Christians do not live in an exclusive bubble. We know from Breeze's study on motivation that donors are less scientific and more intuitive

[18] Beth Breeze, 'How Donors Choose Charities: The Role of Personal Taste and Experiences in Giving Decisions', *Voluntary Sector Review* 4.2 (2013): 165–83 (www.researchgate.net/publication/272147122, accessed February 2018).
[19] Breeze, 'How Donors Choose Charities', 71, 81.
[20] Michael Sanders and Francesca Tamma, 'The Science behind Why People Give Money to Charity', *The Guardian*, 23 March 2015 (http://www.theguardian.com/voluntary-sector-network/2015/mar/23/the-science-behind-why-people-give-money-to-charity, accessed February 2018).
[21] Charles Harvey, 'Why Entrepreneurs Like Bill Gates Become Philanthropists', *The Guardian*, 22 May 2014 (http://theguardian.com/voluntary-sector-network/2013/may/09/bill-gates-warren-buffet-philanthropic, accessed February 2018).

when it comes to deciding which causes to give to. It is a reasonable assumption that a sample of Christian charitable givers would display the same traits. We also know that charitable giving and volunteering can be transformative. For example, the phrase from volunteers, 'I get more out than I put in' comes to mind. This has echoes of the Talmudic and biblical phrase, 'Love your neighbour as yourself' (Lev. 19.18; Mk 12.31). This volunteer reaction implies that this imperative of reaching out to one's neighbour is not only about respect for other people. It also suggests that it is inherently good for the self and therefore not purely altruistic in nature.

There is little research that directly examines the motivation for Christian benefaction. Some comparative work has been done in the United States on counting and measuring 'giving' in terms of numbers of donors and the amount they give compared with other denominations. In charitable giving, there appears to be an assumption that people give because they are Christian: in other words, there is an implicit imperative that Christians share their wealth precisely because they are Christian. In particular, the University of Notre Dame has published research on RC charitable giving within the United States.[22] Researchers found that, while there was vast potential for increasing the charitable giving from an increasingly wealthy community, there were significant barriers to this. Their hypothesis lies in the assertion that Roman Catholics compartmentalize their wealth when it comes to their faith. This happens as a result of there being little explicit formation given in in relation to the use of money and wealth in day-to-day Catholic thinking.[23] In addition, wealth insecurity has been identified a psychological barrier holding back generosity. This is the idea that a donor questions whether they will have enough resources left to meet their own present and future needs. The concept of comfortable guilt – where people feel they have done enough can also be seen as a challenge to philanthropy.

While there is a re-emerging emphasis on stewardship and tithing, it is not considered as an essential element of living the faith as Roman Catholic. This is of concern because, although religious giving both in the UK and the United States attracts the largest share of charitable giving overall, it is going down in value, and until the connection can be made, this trend is likely to continue given the competition from other causes and the effects of increasing secularization.

Notwithstanding the ambiguities with regard to charitable giving by Christians and non-Christians alike, the RC Church has some very clear teachings on the use of money, alms and the universal rights of all people to have access to 'goods' which help them fulfil their potential.[24] This includes the centrality of the poor in the mission of the Church and the requirement to respond to their needs in charity and justice.[25] The social doctrine of the Church is not for nothing referred to as its 'best kept secret'.

---

[22] Brian Starks and Christian Smith, *Unleashing Catholic Generosity: Explaining the Catholic Giving Gap in the United States* (Notre Dame: University of Notre Dame, 2011) (https://icl.nd.edu/assets/96494/unleashing_catholic_generosity.pdf%22%3Eunleashing_catholic_generosity.pdf, accessed February 2018).

[23] Starks and Smith, 'Unleashing Catholic Generosity', Executive Summary (5).

[24] Pontifical Council for Justice and Peace, *Compendium of the Social Doctrine of the Church*, new edn (London: Continuum, 2005), 86.

[25] Pontifical Council, *Compendium*, 91, 92.

In my mind, this further highlights the disconnection referred to by the work of the University of Notre Dame. Does the disconnection extend to service and volunteering? The answer is probably yes.

Mathew Kelly, in his book *The Four Signs of a Dynamic Catholic*, speaks about the 7 per cent of people who do 'everything'. His four signs are prayer, study, generosity and evangelization. Charitable giving and service overlap with generosity and evangelization. His theory is that the 7 per cent becomes 8 per cent, or even 10 per cent, and this is transformational. He also adds that the happiest people he knows are the most generous with their time and money.[26] The Church's teaching on benefaction, service and the common good is derived from the ultimate gift to humankind from God of his Son Jesus Christ. Jesus Christ is the exemplar for all Christians. The imperative for Christians is to share in the eucharist and to love one another. The implications of Jesus's washing of feet (Jn 13.1-17) are that to live an authentic Christian life, love, service and generosity are also a perquisite to living.

For Christians, there is plenty of doctrine that encourages generosity and service. The assumption that Christians become benefactors because they are Christians has some validity, but it is clear that by no means all worshipping Christians are generous or are actively volunteering in service of the community. It seems reasonable to assume Christians are also liable to operate using Breeze's heuristic principles.[27]

Conclusion

Benefaction in the UK and North America is alive and well. Religious causes including day-to-day housekeeping continue to attract the largest proportion of society's charitable giving. Big projects such as Caritas's Bakhita House and disaster appeals capture the need to respond by communities and individuals to both give money and time. However, this is in decline in both the UK and North America, and its efficacy is profoundly affected by the media cycle which moves on quickly.

It is not always possible to disentangle why people give money or volunteer for a particular cause. However, it is likely that they use the measures of personal connection, a notable patron or know someone in the receiving charity, as internal guidelines for giving. Alternatively, as one major Catholic donor said to me, 'I have been very lucky and I am very thankful so I want to give something back.'

I also believe that people want to give to successful causes and projects. For the wealthy, this is especially important, as this is means to extend oneself by gaining community recognition. The RC Church and other faith groups have clear teachings on charity, justice and wealth creation. While large numbers of people within these groups, especially the Catholic Church, are generous, there appears to be a disconnection between their motivations to give and the depth of their understanding of Catholic social teaching. I believe that it is this phenomenon which may account for the reduction in charitable giving to church and religious causes.

[26] Matthew Kelly, *The Four Signs of a Dynamic Catholic* (Hebron: Beacon, 2012), 109.
[27] Breeze, 'How Donors Choose Charities', 9.

8

Response to Bruce Longenecker

John Coleby

It is clear from Bruce Longenecker's paper that benefaction in the Early Church goes through two phases, pre- and post-Constantine. In the former, benefaction is at the micro level, where members of the Christian community provide for poor people, especially the widow and orphan. In the latter, benefaction is more institutionally focused, illustrated by the provision of hospitals and refuges and services. As Bruce points out, once the Roman Empire became Christianized, the wealth of the community was reflected in bigger gestures and gifts to benefit the whole community. Some of the motivation for giving reflects Graeco-Roman eugertism of rich benefactors, who are expected to give to civic projects in return for political influence and enhanced personal status.

In contemporary benefaction/philanthropy, nothing much has changed. The super-wealthy make their point and are asked to the policy table of governments and the United Nations. The church opens hospitals and schools in its name, and secular benefactors give their names to university departments, for example, the Cass Business School, London, and the Saïd Business School, Oxford. Many of the wealthiest families have their own charitable foundations, such as the Waites Foundation and Sainsbury's Trust in London. Giving at this level perpetuates the visibility and influence of such families and groups. However, in Christian communities and other faith communities, the micro level of benefaction, in direct support of human dignity and solidarity, is still very powerful. For example, the London Catholic communities collect for, work in and manage – as well as campaign against – hunger. Recent traumatic incidents see an outpouring of generosity in money and in kind. The Grenfell Tower appeal is a good example.

There are most definitely overlaps between early and contemporary Christian benefaction. In the UK and the United States, the Catholic communities were relatively poor until the mid-twentieth century. They were largely migrant working-class communities who developed and educated themselves, thus developing wealth which could then be put at the disposal of big projects, such as church- and school-building, but at the same time providing for less well-off and destitute people in the community – the modern widow and orphan. This is where Christian giving comes into its own, through the provision of outreach projects, combating loneliness, hunger, employment training and shelter. As Christian communities, we still do these things because of the deeply held imperative to 'step forward in love'. In my view, this is not exclusively altruistic or sacrificial but rather is based on the biblical axiom of 'Love your neighbour as yourself' (Lev. 19.18; Mk 12.31). This is reflected in the comments often expressed by volunteers: 'I am giving something back', or 'I get as much out of my volunteering as I give.'

So the question of motivation is a complicated one. In contemporary giving, Breeze has identified that people believe charitable giving should be and is directed to meet the needs of people considered poor;[1] yet, when scrutinized, people's giving behaviour does not necessarily reflect this. I suspect Christians are no less susceptible to such inconsistencies and there are competing voices for who is needier and, therefore, where funds should be directed. Yet, recognition, status and legacy and social expectation as well as duty all have a dimension in the act of benefaction.

---

[1] Beth Breeze, 'How Donors Choose Charities: The Role of Personal Taste and Experiences in Giving Decisions', *Voluntary Sector Review* 4.2 (2013): 165–83 (www.researchgate.net/publication/272147122, accessed February 2018).

9

Response to John Coleby

Bruce W. Longenecker

It is heartening to hear from John Coleby's stimulating essay that in our twenty-first-century world, 'all the major religions place an emphasis on charitable giving'. The first-century Roman world seems to have been much different. In this short response, then, it might be interesting to give a brief (and, therefore, slightly simplistic) overview of how religious devotion was usually configured in that distant world in relation to the poverty which had engulfed the lives of so many (an issue I do not deal with in my paper on benefaction in early Christianity).

For many people in the world that Jesus-devotees began to infiltrate, honouring the deities probably had very little to do with rectifying moral failings or acting with benevolence toward others. Often honouring the deities was essentially an exercise in pragmatic self-advancement; people offered reverence to the deities in order enhance their prospects for success in this life. According to the Roman statesman and orator Cicero (106–43 BCE), 'Jupiter is called Best and Greatest not because he makes people just or sober or wise, but because he makes them safe, secure, wealthy, and opulent' (*On the Nature of the Gods* 3.87). This statement follows on from a question Cicero had asked, 'Did anyone ever give thanks to the deities because he was a good man?' Cicero's answer is negative; the deities are worshipped, he said, only because of what they can give to a supplicant. The Roman playwright Plautus (approximately 255–185 BCE) had one of his characters explain things in this way: 'The deities put money in the hands of a man to whom they are well disposed. So now I'll attend to the business of sacrificing to them. It's my intention to look out for myself' (*Curculio* 530–32). No doubt Plautus had his character speak in an exaggeratedly crass fashion for humorous effect, but even so, exaggeration is rhetorically effective to the extent that it has some true-sounding resonances with its audience.

There were exceptions, of course, and at times we get glimpses of people who connected the dots between their religious devotion to the Roman deities and generosity toward the needy. However, in the pre-Christian world, Judaism was the religion that stood out starkly from the rest for making strong, organic connections between its deity and generosity toward the needy. Arguably, those same distinctives were what occasionally attracted gentiles to adopt a form of devotion to the Jewish deity without becoming Jewish themselves. (The author of Acts calls such people 'God-fearers'; see especially in Acts 10.2.)

In this regard, one of the things we see in the rise of Christianity from the first century onwards is the taking of Judaism's rich traditions of concern for the needy into the harsh Graeco-Roman world that could all too easily be characterized as intransigent towards the needy. Historically speaking, in the earliest forms of Jesus-devotion, we see a form of Judaism that included in its mission the concern to offset deep-rooted needs in the name of the deity of Israel and a single Galilean Jew, whose own ministry was marked by concern for the poor as one of its primary features.

I suspect that same Galilean Jew, whom the earliest Christians proclaimed as 'Lord', would have been heartened to hear that 'all the major religions [of the twenty-first-century world] place an emphasis on charitable giving'. No doubt that same Galilean Jew would have kept up the pressure on those who call him 'Lord' today, ensuring that twenty-first-century followers imitated his initial followers in doing good to all (Gal. 6.10).

10

Patronage and People:
Paul's Perspective in Philippians

Steve Walton

Introduction

Patronage was all-pervasive in the Roman Empire in the first century AD, whether in the emperor's power to appoint his preferred people to high office or, more locally, in the daily dependence of clients on their patrons for food and provision. In this essay, I shall sketch how the system of patronage worked, the impact it had on society and social relations and how the early Christians – and Paul in particular – responded to this widespread and important cultural reality. Patronage may not exist in the same form today, but relationships of power and dependence continue to be the daily experience of many of our fellow human beings. I am therefore aiming to provoke and stimulate reflection on the shape which Christian engagement and relationships might take today.

Patronage in the Roman world

The Roman Empire was home to a massive web of patronage, emanating outward from the emperor himself, so that just about every free person was someone's client and many were also someone's patron.[1] These relationships required reciprocal responsibilities: the patron provided for the client, often materially, and the client supported the patron, generally by rendering services and support for the patron in his (and it was normally *his*[2]) political and social ambitions. Such relationships were

---

[1] On patronage in general, see Gerald W. Peterman, *Paul's Gift from Philippi: Conventions of Gift-exchange and Christian Giving*, SNTSMS 92 (Cambridge: Cambridge University Press, 1997), ch. 3; Peter Lampe, 'Paul, Patrons and Clients', in *Paul in the Greco-Roman World: A Handbook*, ed. J. Paul Sampley (Harrisburg, PA: Trinity Press International, 2003), 488–523; Lynn H. Cohick, *Women in the World of the Earliest Christians: Illuminating Ancient Ways of Life* (Grand Rapids, MI: Baker Academic, 2009), 285–91; and, more fully, Richard P. Saller, *Personal Patronage under the Early Empire* (Cambridge: Cambridge University Press, 1982); Andrew Wallace-Hadrill, ed., *Patronage in Ancient Society*, Leicester-Nottingham Studies in Ancient Society 1 (London: Routledge, 1989).

[2] For examples of female patronage, see Cohick, *Women*, 288. See also the examples of female power exercised (sometimes through influencing a husband) in Margaret Y. MacDonald, *Early Christian*

described as 'giving and receiving' (cf. Phil. 4.15): the client would express obsequious thanks for the patron's provision, and such thanks would put the patron under further obligation to continue to help the client.[3]

To be the greater giver placed a person in a position of social superiority – a patron was regarded as having honour, a key value in first-century Greek and Roman societies.[4] Even to speak of 'friends' (Greek φιλοί *philoi*, Latin *amici*) – to a modern Western ear a relationship of equals – was to use a term which brought such a relationship of mutual obligation into play.[5] There was an asymmetry, an imbalance of power, in such relationships, for the client was dependent on the patron for key things. These things could be as basic as food and shelter through the daily allowance known as a *sportula*,[6] but might also include opportunities for development both individually and for the client's family, for example, through loans on favourable terms or the exercise of influence on the client's behalf.

As an example of this, Juvenal sends up the rush of patrons to be first to the morning greeting of the patron known as the *salutatio*, properly dressed in his toga:

> And besides, not to flatter ourselves, what, value is there in a poor man's serving here in Rome, even if he be at pains to hurry along in his toga before daylight, seeing that the praetor is bidding the lictor to go full speed lest his colleague should be the first to salute. (*Satires* 3.119–20)

Wealthy people's houses were designed to facilitate such social exchanges, with reception areas built so that the patron could receive his clients' greetings each morning.[7] Moreover, this area would be open to public view, so that those passing by would know of the power of the patron and the regard in which he was held by his clients.[8]

Although the relationship could be humiliating for clients, the patronage of a wealthier person could provide a route out of poverty. Juvenal goes on:

Women and Pagan Opinion: The Power of the Hysterical Woman (Cambridge: Cambridge University Press, 1996), 42–43.

[3] S. C. Mott, 'The Power of Giving and Receiving: Reciprocity in Hellenistic Benevolence', in *Current Issues in Biblical and Patristic Interpretation: Studies in Honor of Merrill C. Tenney Presented by His Former Students*, ed. Gerald F. Hawthorne (Grand Rapids, MI: Eerdmans, 1975), 60–72, here 63; Peter Marshall, *Enmity in Corinth: Social Conventions in Paul's Relations with the Corinthians*, WUNT 2/23 (Tübingen: Mohr Siebeck, 1987), 157–64.

[4] Bruce J. Malina, *The New Testament World: Insights from Cultural Anthropology*, 3rd edn (Louisville, KY: Westminster John Knox, 2001), 27–57; in relation to patronage, and with helpful analysis of gender differences in honour, see Cohick, *Women*, 288–89.

[5] Saller, *Patronage*, 11–17; Cohick, *Women*, 289 n. 13 notes that *amici* 'friends' could be qualified in the case of a client as *amici minores* 'lesser/inferior friends', *amici pauperes* 'poor friends' (i.e. friends who are poor) or *amici inferiores* '(socially) lower friends'.

[6] Lampe, 'Patrons', 491–92.

[7] Bruce W. Winter, *Seek the Welfare of the City: Christians as Benefactors and Citizens* (Carlisle: Paternoster/Grand Rapids, MI: Eerdmans, 1994), 46.

[8] Carolyn Osiek, 'Archaeological and Architectural Issues and the Question of Demographic and Urban Forms', in *Handbook of Early Christianity: Social Science Approaches*, ed. Anthony J. Blasi, Paul-André Turcotte and Jean Duhaime (Walnut Creek, CA: AltaMira, 2002), 83–103, here 89, 91, 92–93.

It is no easy matter, anywhere, for a man to rise when poverty stands the way of his merits: but nowhere is the effort harder than in Rome, where you must pay a big rent for a wretched lodging, a big sum to fill the bellies of your slaves, and buy a frugal dinner for yourself. You are ashamed to dine off delf; but you would see no shame in it if transported suddenly to a Marsian or Sabine table, where you would be pleased enough to wear a cape of coarse Venetian blue. (*Satires* 3.164–70)

Juvenal is portraying a man who gains the chance to be the client of a wealthy person and is thus able to eat and dress better in the expensive city of Rome. It is worth noting that the person Juvenal describes has his own slaves for whom he provides – the patronage system included clients who could be people of some means, but who nevertheless struggled to make financial ends meet.

Patronage was not simply about money or physical needs. The effect of patronage was to produce a hierarchical social structure, shaped by vertical divisions in which a patron would have clients who themselves might have clients, etc. There were possibilities for upward social mobility in such a situation, as a higher-up patron promoted the interests of clients by gaining preferment for them.[9]

Paul's receipt of financial support

Although Paul's general policy was to maintain financial independence,[10] he does speak of Phoebe the deacon who carries his letter to the Romans from Corinth to Rome (Rom. 16.1-2) as his 'patron'.[11] Paul says she has been a προστάτις *prostatis* 'of many and also of me myself'. The term he uses is the feminine form of the masculine προστάτης *prostatēs*, which means 'patron'; its use suggests that Paul accepted hospitality at her home in Cenchrae, the port of Corinth. This feminine form is also found in a papyrus from 142 BC which speaks of a woman who is 'patron' to her fatherless son,[12] and in a third-century AD inscription from Aphrodisias in western Anatolia (modern Turkey), which mentions a Jewish woman, Jael, who is a 'patron' of the synagogue.[13] It is thus

---

[9] Lampe, 'Patrons', 492–3.

[10] 1 Thess. 2.9; 1 Cor. 4.12; 2 Cor. 11.27; 12.14; cf. Acts 20.34. See Steve Walton, 'Paul, Patronage and Pay: What Do We Know about the Apostle's Financial Support?', in *Paul as Missionary: Identity, Activity, Theology, and Practice*, ed. Trevor J. Burke and Brian S. Rosner; LNTS 420 (London: T&T Clark, 2011), 220–33 esp. 221–5.

[11] On Phoebe, see recent discussions in Susan Mathew, *Women in the Greetings of Romans 16.1–16: A Study of Mutuality and Women's Ministry in the Letter to the Romans*, LNTS 471 (London: Bloomsbury T&T Clark, 2013), 65–85; Cohick, *Women*, 301–7; Joan Cecelia Campbell, *Phoebe: Patron and Emissary* (Collegeville, MN: Liturgical, 2009); Caroline F. Whelan, '*Amica Pauli*: The Role of Phoebe in the Early Church', *JSNT* 49 (1993): 67–85.

[12] Edwin A. Judge, 'Cultural Conformity and Innovation in Paul: Some Clues from Contemporary Documents', *TynBul* 35 (1984): 3–24, here 20–1; see further Robert Jewett, *Romans*, Hermeneia (Minneapolis: Fortress, 2007), 946 n. 47.

[13] Text and translation: Joyce Reynolds and Robert Tannenbaum, *Jews and God-fearers at Aphrodisias: Greek Inscriptions with Commentary*, Proceedings of the Cambridge Philological Society 12 (Cambridge: Cambridge Philological Society, 1987), 41. See also discussion of other examples of female patrons in Ramsay MacMullen, 'Women in Public in the Roman Empire', *Hist* 29 (1980): 208–18, here 211; Cohick, *Women*, 291–303; R. A. Kearsley, 'Women in Public Life in

surprising to find the translation 'helper' or 'help' in some English translations of Rom. 16.2 (TNIV, NRSV, NIV 1984; contrast NIV 2011, RSV); it is more likely that Phoebe is a woman of substance who contributed in cash and kind to Paul's ministry[14] and perhaps helped Paul with tricky relationships with city authorities (cf. his experience in Corinth, Acts 18.12-17). Paul is thus following in the footsteps of Jesus, who accepts financial support for his ministry and his band of followers from wealthy women (Lk. 8.1-3).

In Acts, when Paul is in Corinth, his style of activity changes when Silas and Timothy arrive: he is able to give himself fully to preaching and teaching (18.5),[15] rather than 'arguing in the synagogue' only on sabbath days (18.4), and this implies that they arrive bearing gifts which free Paul from the necessity of working to support himself (18.2-3). Luke states that they arrived 'from Macedonia' (18.5). Paul had left them in Beroea when he had to flee to Athens (17.14). It is probable that these gifts are those mentioned in 2 Cor. 11.9 and Phil. 4.15, where Paul indicates that only the Philippian church helped him financially in his ministry in Corinth. If so, Paul's letter to the Philippians would be expected to be a 'thank you' letter for their support, and we shall reflect on that letter shortly.

The point to notice here, in the light of these examples, is that the earliest Christians did not reject patronage outright; instead, they used the terminology and some of the practices associated with patronage in the service of Paul's evangelistic and pastoral ministry. Paul was not entirely dependent on gifts from others, for he could and did work with his hands when necessary, as in the early part of his time in Corinth when he worked alongside Priscilla and Aquila (Acts 18.2-3). Indeed, Ronald Hock makes a cogent case that we should consider this Paul's *normal* practice, suggesting that it lies behind Paul's statements about his work and his calls to others to work (e.g. 1 Thess. 2.9; 1 Cor. 4.12; 2 Cor. 11.27; cf. 1 Thess. 5.14; 2 Thess. 3.6-13; Acts 20.34-35).[16]

Reading Philippians in the light of ancient patronage

Let us now return to Philippians and consider this letter, which some call a 'thankless thanks'.[17] As we noted earlier, there is clear evidence that Paul received gifts from the Philippian believers (4.15-16, 19), and yet the 'I thank' word group (εὐχαριστέω *eucharisteō*, etc.) is found only in this letter in thanks to *God* (1.3; 4.6). This surprises us,

---

the Roman East: Iulia Theodora, Claudia Metrodora and Phoebe, Benefactress of Paul', *TynBul* 50 (1999): 189–211.

[14] Jewett, *Romans*, 7; Joseph A. Fitzmyer, *Romans: A New Translation with Introduction and Commentary*, AB 33 (London: Geoffrey Chapman, 1993), 731; Gerd Theissen, *The Social Setting of Pauline Christianity*, SNTW (Edinburgh: T&T Clark, 1982), 73–96 esp. 94–5.

[15] The imperfect συνείχετο *suneicheto* 'devoted himself' may well be inceptive, implying that Paul became fully occupied with proclamation and continued to do that (Richard N. Longenecker, *Acts*, The Expositor's Bible Commentary (Grand Rapids, MI: Zondervan, 1995), 278–9).

[16] Ronald F. Hock, *The Social Context of Paul's Ministry: Tentmaking and Apostleship* (Philadelphia: Fortress, 1980).

[17] Gerald W. Peterman, '"Thankless Thanks." The Social-Epistolary Convention in Philippians 4.10–20', *TynBul* 42 (1991): 261–70.

as modern people, but would be particularly surprising to Paul's first readers because of the conventions surrounding gift-giving and receiving which we noted earlier. For instance, Seneca writes,

> Listen to the words of petitioners. No one of them fails to say that the memory of the benefit will live for ever in his heart; no one of them fails to declare himself your submissive and devoted slave, and, if he can find any more abject language in which to express his obligation, he uses it. (*Ben.* 3.5.2)

However, Gerald Peterman notes a letter from the physician Chairas, dated 29 August AD 58.[18] He writes,

> I may dispense with writing to you with a great show of thanks; for it is to those who are not friends that we must give thanks in words.
>
> Γράφειν δὲ σοι μεγάλας εὐχαριστίας παρετέο(ν)· δεῖ γὰρ τοῖς μὴ φίλοις οὖσι διὰ λόγων εὐχαρτιστεῖν.

This suggests that Paul may be deliberately subverting the usual social conventions in the way he portrays his relationship with the Philippian believers. Let us examine Philippians further to see if we can learn more about this different perspective.

Early in the letter, Paul mentions the Philippians' 'partnership (κοινωνία *koinōnia*) in the gospel from the first day until now' (1.5), and this is something for which he thanks God (1.3). 'Partnership' is a Pauline favourite word and refers to sharing in a common feature.[19] Here, it very probably includes a reference to the converts' financial support of Paul's gospel mission,[20] especially because of the similar language and idea in 1.5-11 and 4.10-20,[21] which show Paul 'bookending' the letter with the key theme of partnership in the gospel:[22]

Philippians 1	Philippians 4
v. 3 'I give thanks to God' Εὐχαριστῶ τῷ θεῷ	v. 10a 'I rejoiced in the Lord' Ἐχάρην δὲ ἐν κυρίῳ
v. 3 'remembrance of you' μνείᾳ ὑμῶν	v. 10a 'you renewed' ἀνεθάλετε
v. 4 'joy' χαρᾶς	v. 10a 'I rejoiced' Ἐχάρην

[18] P. Mert. 12 lines 6–9; text and translation from H. Idris Bell and Colin H. Roberts, *A Descriptive Catalogue of the Greek Papyri in the Collection of Wilfred Merton* (London: Emery Walker, 1948), 50–52 (lines 5–9), cited in Peterman, *Gift*, 74–5, with discussion on 75–7.
[19] BDAG 555 s.v.
[20] See fuller discussion in Walton, 'Patronage', 225–30.
[21] The table is adapted from Peterman, *Gift*, 91–2; English translations are mine.
[22] Gordon D. Fee, *Paul's Letter to the Philippians*, NICNT (Grand Rapids, MI: Eerdmans, 1995), 423.

Philippians 1	Philippians 4
v. 4 'request for you all' (understood of past habits) δεήσει μου ὑπὲρ πάντων ὑμῶν	v. 10c 'because you were concerned' ἐφ᾽ ᾧ καὶ ἐφρονεῖτε
v. 5 'fellowship, participation' κοινωνίᾳ	v. 15 '[the church] participated' ἐκοινώνησεν
v. 5 'gospel' εὐαγγέλιον	v. 15 '[of the] gospel' εὐαγγελίου
v. 5b 'from . . . until now' ἀπὸ . . . ἄχρι τοῦ νῦν	v. 15 'in the beginning' ἐν ἀρχῇ
v. 6 'the one who began a work in you' ὁ ἐναρξάμενος ἐν ὑμῖν ἔργον	v. 13 'the one who strengthens me' τῷ ἐνδυναμοῦντί με
v. 7a 'to be concerned concerning you all' φρονεῖν ὑπὲρ πάντων ὑμῶν	v. 10b 'to be concerned about me' τὸ ὑπὲρ ἐμοῦ φρονεῖν
v. 7b 'fellow-participants' συγκοινωνούς	v. 14 'being fellow-participants' συγκοινωνήσαντες
v. 7b 'chains' δεσμοῖς	v. 14 'suffering' θλίψει
v. 9 'overflow' περισσεύῃ	vv. 12, 18 '[to] overflow' περισσεύειν, περισσεύω
v. 11 'having been filled' πεπληρωμένοι	vv. 18, 19 'I have been filled', 'may [God] fill' πεπλήρωμαι, πληρώσει
v. 11a 'fruit' καρπόν	v. 17 'fruit' καρπόν
v. 11b 'Jesus Christ' Ἰησοῦ Χριστοῦ	v. 19 'Christ Jesus' Χριστῷ Ἰησοῦ
v. 11c 'glory. . .of God' δόξαν. . .θεοῦ	v. 20 'the glory to God' τῷ. . .θεῷ. . .ἡ δόξα

Interestingly, Paul is very diplomatic in the way he speaks, not explicitly mentioning money to a church of varied socio-economic status.[23]

---

[23] See the superb imaginative reconstruction of how different people in Philippi would 'hear' Paul's letter on this theme in Peter Oakes, 'Jason and Penelope Hear Philippians 1.1–11', in *Understanding, Studying and Reading: New Testament Essays in Honour of John Ashton*, ed. Christopher Rowland and Crispin H. T. Fletcher-Louis, JSNTSup 153 (Sheffield: Sheffield Academic, 1998), 155–64. Oakes provides the theoretical underpinning of his reconstruction in Peter Oakes, *Philippians: From People to Letter*, SNTSMS 110 (Cambridge: Cambridge University Press, 2001), 55–76.

Turning to 4.10-20, we find several relevant points.[24] First, Paul three times expresses his pleasure at their gifts:[25] he rejoices in their concern which has been revived (v. 10a); he acknowledges their partnership with him 'in the matter of giving and receiving' (v. 15); and he is 'fully satisfied' (v. 18, NRSV) with their gifts. Thus, it is mistaken to present Philippians as a 'thankless thanks'. However, each of these points is qualified in ways which subvert the common cultural understanding of relationships involving financial gifts, as we shall see.

Secondly, there is language here which is commonly used in the context of patronage relationships.[26] The language used appears regularly in discussions of friendship, which we noted earlier can denote patronage relationships. Friendship is about social relationships, and not just about money, of course.[27] Paul, however, uses this language in a way which undermines the usual asymmetrical view of patronage relationships. He qualifies his joy at their renewed concern by stating that he is not in need of their help, for he has learned contentment with what he has (vv. 11–13), thus correcting any view that life is about possessions and money – a corrective which would be important both for Philippian believers who had not been able to contribute to the gift for him because of their poverty and also for those who were well-off among the community.

Paul goes on to qualify his gratitude by placing himself and the Philippians in a relationship of 'partnership', using the verb 'partner' or 'share' (κοινωνέω *koinōneō*, v. 15), echoing the use of the cognate noun in 1.5. Paul does not stand in their debt as a client, but they are his partners in mission – they stand on level ground.[28] Their gifts to Paul are *God's* provision for him, for through them Paul is strengthened by God to 'do all things' (v. 13), that is, to face all kinds of circumstances, whether good or bad (v. 12).

Paul then rules out the possible suggestion that he is hinting that he needs further help (v. 17) – bear in mind that thanksgiving in Paul's culture(s) could be a moral lever to draw further gifts from the giver. Rather, he wants the Philippians to accumulate 'profit' for their 'account' (v. 17),[29] namely, experiencing God providing for them (v. 19).

Paul's third statement of gratitude (v. 18) is qualified by a theocentric interpretation of their gifts. For sure they are 'the things you sent' (τὰ παρ' ὑμῶν), but Paul receives them as a 'sacrifice to *God*'. Thus, Paul is not in their debt, but rather, *the God to whom they have given* will satisfy their needs (v. 19). The glory therefore goes to God (v. 20). Paul is portraying himself and the Philippians as fellow clients of God, the supreme patron – so perhaps his description of God as 'father' is a deliberate choice, for the *paterfamilias* ('father of the household') was the patron of his own extended family.[30]

---

[24] For what follows, see Peterman, *Gift*, 121–61; Peterman, 'Thanks'; Stephen E. Fowl, 'Know Your Context: Giving and Receiving Money in Philippians', *Int* 56 (2002): 45–58; Stephen E. Fowl, *Philippians*, THNTC (Grand Rapids, MI: Eerdmans, 2005), 189–201.

[25] With Fee, *Philippians*, 425.

[26] Some also see it as 'accountancy' or business language: see Peter T. O'Brien, *The Epistle to the Philippians: A Commentary on the Greek Text*, NIGTC (Grand Rapids, MI: Eerdmans, 1991), 533–34, 538–40.

[27] See Peterman, *Gift*, 53–65, 125, 147; Marshall, *Enmity*, 157–64.

[28] Peterman, *Gift*, 159.

[29] καρπός *karpos* is used in the sense of 'profit' (BDAG 510 s.v §2) and λόγος *logos* in the sense of 'account' (BDAG 601 s.v §2.b).

[30] See L. Michael White, 'Paul and *Pater Familias*', in *Paul in the Greco-Roman World: A Handbook*, ed. J. Paul Sampley (Harrisburg, PA: Trinity Press International, 2003), 457–87.

The 'riches' of God come to the believers 'in Christ Jesus' (v. 19). Such a picture of the relationships of Paul and the Philippians with each other and with God is rooted in Jewish thought and Scripture.[31] It is striking that Paul ends the letter by invoking the generous love ('grace', χάρις *charis*) of the Lord Jesus Christ for them (v. 23), a love which Paul has portrayed fully in the 'hymn' of 2.5-11.

The theocentric theme echoes the teaching of the Jewish Scriptures that giving to the needy pleases God (Prov. 19.17; cf. Sir. 35.2-3; 3.14-15; Heb. 13.16), and thus locates compassion and honouring God as motives for helping those in need (in this case, Paul). In the Greek and Roman worlds, helping the needy was motivated by gaining honour for oneself.[32] By contrast here, the honour goes to God the giver, not God's human agents.

To sum up our discoveries from Philippians, we have seen Paul reimagining the nature of human relationships of giving and receiving in the light of God's generous love in Christ. This God provides for his people through each other – but Paul is clear that God is the source of what is given and should receive the glory for what is given and received.

Other evidence

To this brief study of Philippians, we can add a few other points more briefly.

Paul is in tune with his Jewish heritage in regarding material things and money as being held in stewardship by humans – they belong first and foremost to God, and humans have them on loan to use in service of God, humanity and God's world.[33] Paul thus writes, 'What do you have that you did not receive? And if you received it, why do you boast as if it were not a gift?' (1 Cor. 4.7), and that in a context where he is critiquing the Corinthian culture of competition for honour which the believers have bought into by having a hierarchy of Christian teachers and leaders (1 Cor. 3.1–4.7). Paul calls on them to stand out from that culture as different.

We have already noticed that Phoebe the deacon is presented as Paul's patron (Rom. 16.1-2). However, there is an ambiguity about the nature of the relationship, for Paul's mention of Phoebe is a commendation of her to the Roman believers, typically the action of a patron for a client. Hence, Lynn Cohick comments, 'Paul commends Phoebe's actions so that the Roman church might act similarly towards her. She is not to be their benefactor, even as Paul is not their benefactor. Rather the goal is reciprocity.'[34]

Paul's little letter to Philemon sheds further light on our theme, for Paul asks Philemon to be ready to provide hospitality for him when he visits (v. 22), and such a request would place Paul in debt to Philemon. Paul speaks of Philemon in 'friendship'

---

[31] See Peterman, *Gift*, 149, 152, 155–6; Lampe, 'Patrons', 505–7.
[32] See Fiona J. R. Gregson, *Everything in Common? The Theology and Practice of the Sharing of Possessions in Community in the New Testament* (Eugene, OR: Wipf & Stock, 2017), 93–6, 106–8, 120, 191–2, 195.
[33] E.g. Gen. 1.26-28; Ps. 24.1; see Steve Walton, 'Primitive Communism in Acts? Does Acts Present the Community of Goods (2:44–45; 4:32–35) as Mistaken?', *EvQ* 80 (2008): 99–111, here 105.
[34] Cohick, *Women*, 305.

terms as 'our beloved and co-worker' (v. 1), language which is consistent with
Philemon being patron to Paul's client. Paul similarly asks that Philemon would 'give
[me] benefit' (ὀνίνημι *oninēmi*, a patronage term, v. 20). However, Paul writes strongly
and boldly to Philemon about his slave Onesimus, claiming that he could command
Philemon, but chooses not to (vv. 8–9), and he writes of Philemon's 'obedience' over
this matter (ὑπακοή *hupakoē*, v. 21). Further, Paul claims that Philemon owes Paul
his very life, again using patronage language, 'you *owe* your very self to me' (σεαυτόν
μοι *προσοφείλεις*, v. 19). There is thus a mixture of language which sometimes places
Philemon in the place of patron and sometimes Paul.

As with Philippians, God is placed at the centre of the relationship – notice the eight
references to Jesus or Christ in this short letter (vv. 1, 3, 5, 6, 8, 20, 23, 25) – and Paul is
Philemon's 'partner' (κοινωνός *koinōnos*, v. 17). Paul and Philemon – and Onesimus –
are on level ground before God-in-Christ. That is why Paul does not *command*
Philemon to accept Onesimus back, although he uses powerful rhetorical tools to
persuade him to do so, for he is addressing a brother in Christ, not a subordinate.

Conclusion

We began by reflecting on patronage in the ancient world, which created and maintained
asymmetrical power relationships of dependency. Having read Paul through this lens,
we have seen an impressive shift of emphasis from cultural expectations of competing
for honour and seeking one's own interests. In their place, Paul puts both the example
of Jesus, who gave himself to the point of death for needy humanity (Phil. 2.5-11; cf.
2 Cor. 8.9), and his own determination to be satisfied with what he has (Phil. 4.11-
13) before the believing communities. Paul locates himself and the believers on a
social map without human hierarchy, where humble dependence on the grace of God
through Christ enables people to have different attitudes and thoughts concerning each
other, and thus to act differently as the Spirit enables them to reproduce the humility of
Christ in their relationships.

Patronage Today

Helen Hekel

Introduction

How does patronage, as seen in the Roman world and described by the apostle Paul in Philippians, challenge us to reflect on today's model of responding to poverty? As Steve Walton has shown, patronage in the Roman world was pervasive, embedded in the culture, creating a system of social interactions, ruled by the interdependency between clients and patrons.[1] Thousands of years later, we too have a model of patronage which exists in an organized system between global actors. Our world today is different to what Paul and New Testament (NT) Christians faced in their time. Yet, the characteristics of interdependency and power dynamics are similar. In this essay, I will reflect on some of my experiences working in the field of development and humanitarian aid, and the ways in which I have encountered dependency and power imbalances in our modern-day model of patronage. I will also outline some emerging models moving towards the idea of partnership and how Christians have a key role to play in changing the discourse and mindset of how we can approach a global response to poverty.

Our world today

Each day, as we turn on our TV, listen to the radio or open up the newspaper, we read of more tragedies unfolding around the world: poverty, hunger, war, violence, outbreak of diseases and environmental disasters. We see the effects of these events on communities and individuals, in a variety of countries: Ethiopia, Syria, Nepal, South Sudan, the Democratic Republic of Congo (DRC), Colombia and more – while closer to home we see a rise in terrorist attacks in France, Germany, Belgium, Turkey and Tunisia.[2] We live in a time where news travels across the globe in the space of minutes, where we can see live images of the faces of men, women and children who are thousands of kilometres from where we are.

---

[1]   See Steve Walton, 'Patronage and People: Paul's Perspective in Philippians', in this book.
[2]   This section reflects the news at the time of writing (July 2016).

Most of us are shaken by these events and want to find a way to respond to the needs we see. Those in leadership positions in governments engage in such responses: they sign treaties, pledge resources to other countries, raise money on appeals, look for partners and implementing agencies to do the work on the ground. The United Nations (UN) and international non-governmental organizations (NGOs) also provide support to these communities. It is this web of relationships that I look to in this reflection on patronage as we can relate these institutions as patrons to the local communities who are, for the purpose of this essay, the clients.

The complex nature of modern-day aid

I have worked in countries overseas with various NGOs, both on emergency-aid projects and on development issues, funded by government foreign aid departments and the UN. I have worked in projects working with displaced communities, supporting families and individuals who have fled their homes and villages because of conflict or natural disasters and are now living in 'borrowed homes', with little stability and sense of ownership, as they have lost their land and belongings as well as their livelihoods. For many such families, they fall into the category of 'recipient of aid', from their own or a foreign government, or from local or international NGOs. Like many before me, I have worked in these situations and been confronted with the many challenges of these contexts – discussions and decisions over lack of continued funding for projects; concerning projects' efficiency and effectiveness; regarding the challenges of delivering quality to the standards set internationally; engaging with the issue of security and access to areas; concerning corruption and fraud; about adhering to local and international governments' agendas; regarding concepts of impartiality and beneficiary accountability; and much more. In all of this, I have been torn between responding to the needs of the people I was there to serve and following the guidelines of the system in place, the requirements of the governments and of the donors funding our projects.

The issue of patronage today is complex. The relationship between client and patron is a lot less personal than in the NT: given today's global scale, the rising needs across the globe, the international dimension and the multitude of actors engaged in aid and development, it is hard to keep a face and a name to each individual. In NT days, patronage would have enabled the receiver (client) to fulfil a career or a trade: in theory, it could have balanced out some inequalities of those who had much and those who had less. The reality in today's context of development and aid – like the ancient context – is that the relationship between those giving aid and those receiving it is unequal: one side holds the financial means and resources; the other competes for them in a demanding context. In many cases, recipients of aid rarely have the luxury of choosing who they will receive aid from, so when the donor attaches conditions to the funding, the receiver or client will comply.

The process of receiving aid from 'patrons' is extremely competitive. Charities and NGOs compete to secure funding from governments to implement projects in other countries. National organizations and civil society organizations also compete for funding from UN agencies or embassy offices in their countries. Governments are competing with each other to secure the best projects and results. Churches and grass-roots organizations compete for the attention of benefactors to fund their community projects. In such a competitive environment, patrons lay out conditions for clients: the receiver or client needs to deliver identified outcomes, use a chosen approach, in specified geographical areas, for a particular target group, and all with some financial restrictions. With such conditions, it is difficult for local NGOs to receive funding from international donors: a recent report from the International Federation of the Red Cross and Red Crescent societies estimated that of the total humanitarian assistance funding given directly to NGOs (international, regional, national and local), only 1.6 per cent went directly to local and national NGOs,[3] despite these actors being ideally positioned to respond to disasters in local communities, well before international agencies will reach these.

So, how does this context of accessing funding affect the targeted communities? Despite the competition, are the communities receiving the ways and means to 'come out of poverty'? What strings come attached to the patron/client relationship in modern-day aid?

This imbalance of power and reliance on aid presents a real challenge in the relationship. In an attempt to secure funding, this reliance on donors can lead to *designing projects which do not necessarily meet the expressed needs of the communities.* To give an example, in one particular project on which I was working in the Horn of Africa, we were looking to secure funding for activities in the communities for the year to come, as our current cycle of funding was coming to an end. Up to that point, our projects had been fully funded by an international donor, providing safe and clean water to displaced communities, improving food security in the community and providing health centres where infants were screened for malnutrition and treated, among other activities. We were also seeking to meet some of the psychosocial needs of the community, particularly for children: this was done by setting up safe play areas for children, called Child-Friendly Spaces (CFS). As we looked to approach our then-current donor, we were informed that due to the decrease of available funds, they would only be funding emergency and life-saving activities, which did not include psychosocial activities. Of course, I understand the complexity of responding to rising and multiple needs in the world and that a greater focus on life-saving activities should be prioritized. Nevertheless, I also felt the need for these families and their children to have a sense of stability, safety and 'normalcy'. So despite the demand from parents and children for these safe spaces, we had to stop these activities temporarily while we looked for another donor willing to fund the safe spaces. Thankfully, volunteers in the community continued to run the CFS until we were able to find another source of

---

[3]   International Federation of Red Cross and Red Crescent Societies, 'World Disasters Report 2015', 105 (https://ifrc-media.org/interactive/wp-content/uploads/2015/09/1293600-World-Disasters-Report-2015_en.pdf, accessed May 2017); Bibi van der Zee, 'Less than 2% of Humanitarian Funds "Go Directly to Local NGOs"', *The Guardian*, 16 October 2015 (https://www.theguardian.com/global-development-professionals-network/2015/oct/16/less-than-2-of-humanitarian-funds-go-directly-to-local-ngos, accessed May 2017).

funding. This example illustrates the complexities of this environment, when there is a finite amount of funding available and a multitude of rising needs.

Part of the problem we encounter in our modern times is the drive for *immediate or short-term results*. Whereas in the past, a patron would have supported a client for many years, or until the training for a trade was completed, modern-day institutions are more likely to fund projects which will provide quick gains or results and look to achieve this at minimal cost.[4] We can all understand the need to show value for money and evidence for the impact of projects on local communities. The trouble is that this trend creates an environment which prioritizes 'quick fixes' and short-term solutions over long-term investments in projects which seek to tackle deep-rooted and complex issues, and where results may only appear over generations, but could have a lasting, sustainable impact.

I paint this picture to demonstrate the complex and global environment which these relationships bring into play. However, there is a fundamental question: Does this model help to save lives? It seems like the obvious question, but I have wondered time and time again about how flawed our model is, especially when I continue to see the symptoms of poverty and injustice on the news each day. Like many others, I have had my share of doubt. In one of my most difficult moments, I asked myself, 'What difference is this making? Regardless of what we do, villages and civilians are still attacked, the country is still at war – this is useless! We are never going to make a real difference, things are not going to get any better!' Sharing these thoughts with a colleague, he told me something I will always remember. He said, 'If we were not here, if we were not screening these children for malnutrition and supplying these families with extra food, if we were not installing clean water sources and distributing seeds to farmers, do you not see that more people and children would have died? Perhaps we are not seeing an improved situation as you would like to see it, but by the work we are doing through the local communities, we are stopping the number of deaths from increasing.'

Yes, that is at the heart of the issue: there are flaws in the current system in place, but lives are restored and deaths are minimized. However, we can look to a new model and, particularly, a new discourse, which could have greater impact and lasting change.

Looking to a new discourse

It is interesting to look at the origin of the word *patronage*, from the Latin *patronus*, which means 'protector of clients' or 'defender', and from *pater* meaning 'father'. The concept of 'patron' as a protector or defender brings a lot to think about in the light of modern-day practice. Can we see examples of this attitude in the donors of today

---

[4] On the complexities of and imbalances of power in our current humanitarian system and the trends in project funding, see Dhananjayan Sriskandarajah, 'Five Reasons Donors Give for not Funding Local NGOs directly', *The Guardian* 9 November 2015 (https://www.theguardian.com/global-development-professionals-network/2015/nov/09/five-reasons-donors-give-for-not-funding-local-ngos-directly, accessed May 2017).

such as governments and development organizations, seeing themselves as defenders or protectors?

What implications does this discourse hold for Christians, following the reflections of Steve Walton on the Apostle Paul's *thankless letter*?[5] Looking at our own attitude, do we not see the same impact of this discourse of the 'helper': when I choose to give money to charity or to sponsor a child, am I not making some conditions in my mind about how this money should be used? What expectations do I have of the charity, of the child or student I am sponsoring? Am I willing to allow that child to make their own decisions, even when these go in a different way to what I had hoped for?

What about the impact on local communities targeted? How much input do they have in the decisions made for them by external agents? Is our current system not a *patronizing* system disguised under contractual agreements and the label of 'partnership'?

How can we begin to speak of true and equal partnerships? Models of participatory development have gradually taken importance in developmental discourse and practice over the past decade, in the hope, perhaps, of turning the tables from a top-down approach to a bottom-up approach to development.[6] Examples of this type of approach to development can be found in village-saving groups, farmer field schools and community-led total sanitation initiatives, among others.[7] Church and community transformation approaches, such as those supported by Tearfund and other international NGOs, seek to envision and empower local churches and communities to identify their own needs and the resources they have at hand to help meet them. These approaches provide reflective tools, including Bible studies to encourage churches to reflect on their role in their communities, and practical approaches and techniques including 'community description', information gathering, analysis and assessment and local decision-making.[8] One common local response to poverty is the establishment of small savings or 'self-help' groups, in which small community groups (often female-led)

---

5   See Walton, 'Patronage', in this book.

6   Grassroots, bottom-up, and localization are key terms and approaches in contemporary aid and development. Localization means taking local, subnational contexts into account in the setting of goals and targets as well as in the development of programmes and projects that seek to achieve those goals. Sustainable development. The UN regards members of groups in these contexts such as women, children, indigenous people, farmers and local authorities as major stakeholders in the SDGs (https://sustainabledevelopment.un.org/mgos, accessed January 2018), while 'Adapting to new challenges through local, inclusive, and context specific responses' was a key issue discussed at the 2016 World Humanitarian Summit (https://www.agendaforhumanity.org/summit, accessed January 2018).

7   To read more about the approaches given, see 'Integrated Production and Pest Management Programme in Africa' (http://www.fao.org/agriculture/ippm/programme/ffs-approach/en/, accessed May 2017); and 'Overcoming Challenges in Community-led Total Sanitation' (https://learn.tearfund.org/resources/publications/footsteps/footsteps_91-100/footsteps_97/overcoming_challenges_in_community_led_total_sanitation/, accessed January 2018).

8   Tearfund, 'Church and Community Mobilisation in Africa' (Teddington: Tearfund, 2017) describes the history and process of church and community mobilization (CCM), a church and community transformation approach; pp. 15–16 focus on the steps of the approach (https://learn.tearfund.org/~/media/files/tilz/churches/ccm/2017-tearfund-ccm-in-africa-en.pdf?la=en, accessed January 2018). This 2014 report provides an evidence-based study of the impact of CCM in Tanzania: https://learn.tearfund.org/~/media/files/tilz/churches/church_and_community_mobilisation__tanzania_research_summarymay2014.pdf?la=en (accessed January 2018).

save together, each member putting a very small amount each week into a shared fund. As the fund grows, the members are able to take out first small, and then, later (as the fund grows further), larger loans that are repaid with interest over an agreed time period.[9] Loans are made to cover education, healthcare costs and income-generation projects. Each group is self-governing and self-sustaining, but facilitation-intensive, as they require support to learn more about financial and business management and skills in order to flourish.[10]

These approaches are seen as an alternative to top-down approaches and seek to bring local communities and individuals to the decision-making process, driving the process of change and development in their communities themselves, analysing their own problems, deciding on priority actions and designing the activities they want to carry out. These movements seek to counteract the dependence on external entities and give back ownership of projects to local communities. Greater change in communities can also be found in supporting and developing civil society organizations (local and national NGOs), who have a drive to see transformation and change in their communities and are part of these.

During my years of work at Tearfund, I have seen a model of development which builds on this participatory, community-led development but goes further: Tearfund's model, essentially, is a model centred on relationships. This is a model centred on the gospel – where love and compassion is at the centre of what we do,[11] where second chances are possible and where local action with the right level of support and input can spark up change in communities.[12] Tearfund's 'Bridging the Gap' report describes the way in which the combination of a church and community mobilization (CCM) approach and advocacy training has begun to equip three churches and communities to solve their own problems and advocate for themselves.[13] One community member described her own transformation in the following terms:

> Before CCM, I was a 'nobody'. Today, I am a councillor representing my parish at the sub-county. After the CCM training, I felt empowered to approach people and discuss issues that affected us in our villages, and people asked me to represent them at the sub-county. now everybody in the parish knows me, and it's because of CCM. CCM has transformed our lives as women in these communities in

---

[9] Tearfund, 'Partnerships for Change: A Cost Benefit Analysis of Self-help Groups in Ethiopia' (Teddington: Tearfund, 2013), 3 (https://learn.tearfund.org/~/media/files/tilz/research/tfund_ethiopia_self_help_executive_sum_web.pdf, accessed January 2018).

[10] Tearfund, 'Saving for a Very Dry Day' (Teddington: Tearfund, 2017), 7, evaluates the contribution of self-help groups to resilience in East Africa and looks at those supported by Tearfund and other NGOs (https://www.tearfund.org/~/media/files/tilz/churches/self_help_groups/2017-tearfund-tearnetherland-saving-for-a-very-dry-day-en.pdf?la=en, accessed January 2018).

[11] On Tearfund's faith-based response, see https://learn.tearfund.org/themes/church/tearfunds_faith-based_approach/ (accessed December 2017).

[12] See, e.g., the story from Recife cited by Katie Harrison earlier in this book, reported in Tearfund, 'Why Advocate on Waste and a Circular Economy' (Teddington: Tearfund, 2017), 8 (https://learn.tearfund.org/~/media/files/tilz/circular_economy/2017-tearfund-why-advocate-on-waste-and-a-circular-economy-en.pdf?la=en, accessed January 2018).

[13] Tearfund, 'Bridging the Gap' (2016) (https://learn.tearfund.org/~/media/files/tilz/topics/advocacy/2016-tearfund-bridging-the-gap-en.pdf, accessed January 2018).

many ways. CCM has improved gender balance, hygiene, support of widows, and education. Through CCM advocacy, we have been able to get services in our community: for example, we now have four boreholes in our parish, a functional health centre, and we facilitate community monitors for pregnant women.[14]

Churches and communities overseas are being empowered to find their own solutions to their local problems: they are equipped with resources, advice, training, learning from other projects and financial backing to see their communities flourish.

There are still conditions to be met, such as certain financial parameters and organizational structure to be in place. At the centre of this model is the willingness to build a genuine partnership and see local churches and communities flourish. This word *partnership*, today, as it was during NT times, refers to sharing in a common feature. In Tearfund's work, the common features are our faith, as Tearfund works with local churches and Christian NGOs, and a shared passion for eradicating poverty by bringing whole-life transformation to individuals in the world. This is built on trust and underlying values of human flourishing and the desire to support and empower local churches and communities to shape and drive their own transformation.

We all look to see good things come from the people, projects and charities we invest in. We give to families or projects overseas or charities because we believe in what they are trying to achieve and we want to be a part of the solution. Aid is not only about finances; it can also be about taking part in the journey with an individual or a community and be a part of their lives. Supporting a project financially enables people to create connections in this global world. It helps each person to be part of a global community and journey with others. I am excited when I read about the impact of projects I support. I feel privileged to have played a small part.

Let us then consider entering the relationship of patron-client, of giver-receiver, as one of mutual learning, despite the obvious inequalities and imbalances of power. Let us consider how each one can approach giving with humility. Even in the overwhelming contexts, when you might meet countless number of individuals in need every day, where you cannot put a name to a face – even then, there are precious moments, when you connect with that one individual who will remind you that all these nameless faces and hands are unique and all have something to teach you.

It is so easy in the field I have been working in to develop a 'saviour' mentality about oneself, in which I consider myself 'selfless' and 'good' for putting my safety in peril, setting aside the comforts of my home country, putting up with the heat, the mosquitos, the bitter cold, the repetitive food, the lack of a warm shower and so forth. You can also start to think you have all the answers and stop listening to local knowledge. I have been surprised time and time again by the courage and generosity of the people I have served. In fact, I have probably learned more because of them and remember them more than they will remember me – just one foreigner among many who come to their country and leave, never staying long enough to learn the names of their children or learn the local language.

---

[14] Tearfund, 'Bridging the Gap', 15.

Despite our differences across the globe and the inequalities that we see, there is a great element that we share as humans, and that is that we work as communities, not as islands. We might think of the response from the world to the attacks in Paris in 2016, the generosity of the public towards the earthquake in Nepal in 2015, the response of the world in light of the shootings and hostage situation in a shopping mall in Nairobi in 2013. We are moved, inspired, outraged and, ultimately, connected in seeking justice for all – and this brings us back full circle to the start of this essay: ultimately, as a society we are moved by the plight of others and we seek ways to help. We just need to consider which model to follow and be aware of our intentions and aware of our own prejudices.

Conclusion

In this short study, we have reflected on the dynamics of power and dependence that exist in our model of development and international aid today. We have also looked at a different discourse which compels us to respond to the needs of others in a different way, in an equal partnership, where each party can give and receive in turn. As the church of today, we can do so, acknowledging that all that we have has been given to us by God.

In preparing this essay, I have been challenged to think about my own attitude towards the 'other' and also on my own attitude to giving and receiving. I was challenged by my own selfishness when I worked in the humanitarian field: like many others, I was stunned by the generosity and hospitality of the people I encountered as they would lavish their best food and bring out their best tea set for me. It put me to shame as I protected my things and only gave away gifts on my terms. I have been challenged by the words of the apostle Paul in his letter to the church in Corinth:

> You will be enriched in every way so that you can be generous on every occasion, and through us your generosity will result in thanksgiving to God. This service that you perform is not only supplying the needs of the Lord's people but is also overflowing in many expressions of thanks to God. Because of the service by which you have proved yourselves, others will praise God for the obedience that accompanies your confession of the gospel of Christ, and for your generosity in sharing with them and with everyone else. And in their prayers for you their hearts will go out to you, because of the surpassing grace God has given you. Thanks be to God for his indescribable gift! (2 Cor. 9.11-15, NIV 2011)

Let us consider what the world might be like if we all gave freely, with no expectations in return, no conditions attached, no restraint and no complaint, but instead, gave freely in recognition that God has given to us first, as a symbol and outpouring of his love for us. Just as the Christians in those early days, and as Paul instructed in his letter to the Philippians, we can all thank God for the gifts we give to and receive from each other. Perhaps in this spirit of thankfulness and generosity we will begin a journey of whole-life transformation and restored relationships across this world.

12

Response to Steve Walton

Helen Hekel

I really enjoyed Steve Walton's paper, and in preparing my own, I have found the way that he has drawn out the distinction between patronage and partnership particularly helpful. I suspect – as I hope came through in my paper – that if those of us working in aid and development are really honest with ourselves, we have not often clearly thought through the distinctions between them. Without this kind of clarity in articulating what we think we are doing and want to do, it is quite easy to be confused in our behaviour and practice – meaning that what we *want* to be partnership continues to contain elements of patronage, perhaps especially as we pursue 'best practices' that place demands on those with whom we are in the kind of partnership that is not mutual.

On Steve's second question about the training of future church leaders, I think there is scope for stronger mutual relationships between academics and practitioners and trainee church leaders. Practitioners have much to say about the reality of the experience of seeking to serving those living in poverty in ways that honour people's God-given dignity and agency. Equally, academically trained theologians can help practitioners to reflect on, critique and – where necessary – develop their practice so that their work more closely reflects their aspirations. In the case of Christian development organizations, such as Tearfund, this aspiration is for *koinonia*, *true* partnership, rather than partnership in name only.

A further challenge to both 'parties' in dealing with the reality of practical service is the demand of other 'patrons' – such as a charity's donors or supporters. Charities such as non-governmental organizations (NGOs) are often mediators between a wide range of benefactors and beneficiaries. Often we find that while these patrons value partnership as a model, they do have a variety of assumptions or demands which make it harder to become a true partner, rather than a patron to those with whom we work in communities around the world.

We have to navigate this not only in our work with those living in poverty whom we seek to serve but also in the ways we talk about our work to those we want to serve by stewarding their financial gifts well. In his paper, Steve discussed some of the ways that Paul challenged and subverted the common contemporary understandings of patronage as he aimed to shape the giving-relationships in the early church. What can charitable organizations learn from Paul's rhetoric and ideas as we tell the story of the work we of which we are a part, so that our supporters can become partners too?

13

Response to Helen Hekel

Steve Walton

I found reading Helen Hekel's essay very moving, as she conveys graphically the difficulties and frustrations of providing resources which actually make a difference in situations of poverty, rather than perpetuating a situation of dependence on 'charity' from those with greater means. She speaks from experience in the field, and that means her words and examples carry weight.

In both of our essays, the issue of inequality is very significant. I argue that Paul addresses this by calling his churches to think differently and, in consequence, to act differently. The challenge which Helen presents us is how to carry this transformation of thinking through into real participatory development, where the people receiving 'aid' are making real decisions about what receives aid and how the money is used – rather than the wealthy donors controlling the use made of their money. I am heartened to read of Tearfund's relational approach to this delicate negotiation, engaging deeply with local churches and their needs and concerns. This connection raises a couple of questions for me.

First, how do we in the Western church pursue what it means for us to see ourselves as neither superior nor inferior, but genuine partners with Christian people in the majority world? My Anglican Church near Cambridge had the privilege of a partnership with a church in Rwanda through our diocesan link with the Diocese of Kigali, and we learned a great deal both from a team from the church in Rwanda visiting us and a team from our church visiting Rwanda. Having our Rwandan sisters and brothers visit meant we learned of the painful realities of the murder of many of their families and neighbours during the Rwanda Holocaust. Their response of generous forgiveness – in the midst of great pain – taught us Westerners much and challenged the easy way in which we hold grudges over minor matters. They gave us a sense of proportion and of reality about what it means to live as Christians.

Secondly, how can Christian development organizations better communicate to their donors that partnership is the key feature of the relationship with the recipients of 'aid'? Tearfund's website and their magazine are good examples of doing this well, in my view. What I wonder further is how they can inform and educate future church leaders about the realities and principles of such Christian development work – those training in the theological colleges and courses of the churches. I cannot recall such issues ever being raised in my own training, back in the 1970s, and am not aware that things have changed much in that regard. Yet, convincing the church's leaders about partnership as the prime model of Christian development work is critical to convincing the churches they will lead. So how can this be done better?

14

Paul and the Gift to Jerusalem: Overcoming the Problems of the Long-Distance Gift

John M. G. Barclay

Introduction

Paul undertook many challenging tasks, but one of the hardest was his effort to get as many of his churches as possible to contribute to a collection for the 'saints' in Jerusalem. He spoke of this in a number of places in his extant letters (1 Cor. 16.1-2; 2 Cor. 8–9; Rom. 15.25-28) and devoted much time both to the practical organization of this long-distance gift and to its theological explanation. In this chapter, we will explore, first, how gifts worked in the ancient world, and why they were difficult across a distance, and then the special problematics of the Jerusalem gift. The rest of the chapter will examine the rhetorical and theological dynamics of 2 Corinthians 8–9, in order to draw out Paul's notion that both giver and receiver, in their reciprocity, participate in the divine gift that flows through each to the other.

Gifts in antiquity

Gifts broadly defined (i.e. gifts as benefits and favours as well as material things) circulated everywhere in the Graeco-Roman world, at all social levels and in all social domains. They constituted one pattern of exchange (alongside trade and pay) but were distinguished from other systems of reciprocal exchange by being voluntary, personal and non-calculable (i.e. not subject to legal regulation or precise monetary evaluation). They were *not* distinguished from reciprocal exchange, as modern Westerners might think, by being unilateral, one-way, with no strings attached. On the contrary, gifts were designed to create or sustain relationships, and those relationships were two-way, with expectation of return.[1] The return could be of a different kind to the gift and at a different time, such that the return for a material favour could be non-material.

---

[1]   For ancient gift-giving, and its expectations of reciprocity, see John M. G. Barclay, *Paul and the Gift* (Grand Rapids, MI: Eerdmans, 2015), 11–65.

This was especially the case when the wealthy gave benefactions to their cities or to voluntary associations, in the ancient system of benefaction we call 'euergetism'.[2] In famine relief, in the construction of civic amenities or in carrying out official duties without pay, the elite were eager to give and to be known as givers. They could afford to give without material return, and in any case the return most precious to them was gratitude and honour, social acceptance and an enduring fame.[3]

Lower down the social scale, and even among those struggling to survive from day to day, gifts circulated in patterns of return that were both material and non-material. Swapping, sharing and lending assistance, giving money or goods was a crucial form of survival among those at or near subsistence level (who constituted the majority of the population in the ancient world). It was astute to gain a reputation for generosity even if that was never going to be inscribed on stone or known outside a small social circle. From early in Greek history (700 BCE?) Hesiod gives advice that makes good sense among economically vulnerable members of society:

> Invite your friend, but not your enemy, to dine; especially be cordial to your neighbour, for if trouble comes at home, a neighbour's there, at hand . . . Measure carefully when you must borrow from your neighbour, then pay back the same, or more, if possible, and you will have a friend in time of need . . . We give to a generous person, but no-one gives to someone who is stingy. (Hesiod, *Works and Days*, 342–56)

What is evident here is that gifts invite, indeed expect, a return, and are in this sense hardly distinguishable from a loan (except that a legally contracted loan can be recovered by action in law). For those with little surplus and with constant exposure to the vagaries of ill health, accident and failed crops, it was prudent, indeed necessary, to be generous because you never knew when you might need something in return: to be stingy was to cut yourself out of the circles of reciprocity that were the main insurance system of the poor. When we ask why the poor gave (and still give) generously, beyond what they can afford, here is at least part of the answer: because their lives depend on participating in a system of gift-and-return in which they are likely to need, one day, the liberality of others.

This is the informal, regular, face-to-face system of gift that operates locally among neighbours, family and friends; indeed, by entering into this system of give-and-take, strangers became friends. An anonymous gift would make no sense here and is very rare in antiquity: the whole point of gifts is to form and sustain relationships, and anonymity would defeat that aim. Gifts are carefully placed. There is no point in giving to those hostile to you, to those known to be stingy, as they would be *unwilling* to give any return; and there is little point in giving anything substantial to the totally indigent (like the Prodigal Son, a destitute migrant to whom 'no one gave anything', Lk.

[2] Famously described by Paul Veyne, *Bread and Circuses: Historical Sociology and Political Pluralism*, abridged and trans. Brian Pearce (London: Penguin, 1990).
[3] For a full survey of the evidence, see James R. Harrison, *Paul's Language of Grace in its Graeco-Roman Context*, WUNT 2/172 (Tübingen: Mohr Siebeck, 2003).

15.16), since they would be *unable* to give a return. (Of course, if they prayed for God's blessing on you, or if you thought that *God* would give a return, there might be value in this.[4]) And it was hazardous to give to anyone at a distance, unless you already had a tie of mutual commitment by which to maintain the system of reciprocal benefit, even without the pressure of physical presence. Otherwise, to give 'over the horizon' would create no relationship, and without such mutuality, it would hardly constitute a gift.

Long-distance gifts are, in fact, a rare phenomenon in antiquity. Rulers and emperors might grant money to cities or populations at a distance. Helena of Adiabene sent famine relief to the inhabitants of Judaea when she herself became, through conversion, a Jewess;[5] the Roman emperor might send famine relief to a loyal city in a province, or money for the reconstruction of a city devastated by an earthquake.[6] In such cases, the gift would be well advertised, and the gratitude and political loyalty of the recipients would be all that the donors needed and wanted. Long-distance ethnic or religious ties might evoke gifts, such as the donations from the Diaspora made to the Jerusalem temple (alongside the tax that adult male Jews paid every year): since the wealthy typically gave money and furniture to local temples, it made sense for Jews or proselytes in the Diaspora to give gifts to 'the one Temple for the one God'.[7] Voluntary associations might support one another in different locations in accordance with ties of common commercial interest or ethnic connections.[8] Friends and family sent money and material gifts via intermediaries to their friends or kin at a distance, continuing previously established face-to-face relations despite the interval of space. All of these recognize or affirm existing relationships, ties of politics, friendship, ethnicity or kinship; one would hardly venture a gift at a distance to someone to whom one was not already connected. And, besides the obvious dangers in long-distance transfer of money or goods (given the frequency of highway theft), one needed high levels of trust that gifts sent over a distance would reach their intended destination and would be used for the purposes intended. When giving to a neighbour you could always call in the debt; when giving at a distance, the gift, the relationship and its returns were far more liable to loss.

The Jerusalem collection: A hazardous gift

At the height of his mission in the Mediterranean world, Paul devised a project to collect money from churches in Galatia (central or western Turkey), Achaia (southern

---

[4] For Jewish ideologies of gift, in which God is invoked both as giver and as the one who will recompense a generous gift, see Barclay, *Paul and the Gift*, 39–45.

[5] Josephus, *Ant.* 20.49–50; *J.W.* 4.567; 5.55.

[6] For examples of imperial benefactions, see Frederick Danker, *Benefactor: Epigraphic Study of a Graeco-Roman and New Testament Semantic Field* (St Louis: Clayton, 1982). See further the discussion of benefactions by Lynn Cohick in this volume.

[7] For the 'half-shekel' tax (Exod. 30.11-16) and its collection in the Diaspora, together with other donations from the Diaspora to the Temple, see John M. G. Barclay, *Jews in the Mediterranean Diaspora from Alexander to Trajan (323 BCE–117 CE)* (Edinburgh: T&T Clark, 1996), 417–21.

[8] See David J. Downs, *The Offering of the Gentiles: Paul's Collection for Jerusalem in its Chronological, Cultural, and Cultic Contexts*, WUNT 2/248 (Tübingen: Mohr Siebeck, 2008), 112–18.

Greece) and Macedonia for 'the saints' in the Jerusalem church, people hundreds of miles away and mostly of different ethnicity.[9] At one point, he describes this collection as for 'the poor among the saints at Jerusalem' (Rom. 15.26), a commitment perhaps identical with, or more likely a subset, or an imitation, of the agreement at the Jerusalem conference to 'remember the poor' (Gal. 2.10).[10] This suggests that material relief is an important aspect of this gift, and in 2 Corinthians 8–9, the longest piece of exhortation about this collection, Paul speaks of the 'lack' among the saints which the gift is meant to fill (2 Cor. 8.14; 9.12). The fact that the collection took several years to gather – begun perhaps in 53 CE and not delivered until 57 CE – indicates that it was not designed to meet a short-term emergency, unlike the famine relief sent from Antioch to Jerusalem (described in Acts 11.27-30). In fact, this elongated timescale, and the way that Paul describes the collection in Romans 15, as the Gentiles' material return for Jerusalem's 'spiritual' gifts (15.26-27), suggest that the collection had a symbolic and not just a material value. In Romans 15, Paul figures the collection as the fruit of his Gentile mission and is anxious lest, after all, it be refused in Jerusalem. It seems it signified for him the tie between the Jerusalem church, with its largely Jewish membership, and the churches he had founded, from largely non-Jewish inhabitants of Graeco-Roman cities. Since gifts create or represent reciprocal relations, Paul intended this gift to tie the churches together across geographical, cultural and political divides. Whether it succeeded in that task is uncertain – and the fact that Acts makes no clear reference to this collection has been taken by some to indicate its failure.[11]

The gathering of this monetary collection was obviously far more problematic than Paul had expected. Although it was not the same as the temple tax, which was collected annually from adult male Jews both in the homeland and in the Diaspora, Paul may have expected that his collection would be an equally routine affair. The instructions in 1 Cor. 16.1-4 suggest regular tiny deposits of money which would add up to something substantial enough for Corinthian delegates to take to Jerusalem, perhaps accompanied by Paul. But unlike the temple tax, this collection had no scriptural warrant, no support from tradition, no cultural parallel and no atoning significance ('ransom for the soul', Exod. 30.12, 16 LXX). It represented no pre-existent ethnic bond, and it attempted to span a distance shortened by few if any bonds of acquaintance. Paul himself knew Jerusalem well, and it is possible that Cephas/Peter had visited Corinth, but even if so, he was not universally acclaimed there (1 Cor. 1.10-12). Otherwise it is not clear if any of Paul's converts had any familiarity with Jerusalem or with the church members

---

[9] For recent full-length treatments of this phenomenon, see Downs, *Offering of the Gentiles*, and Stephan Joubert, *Paul as Benefactor: Reciprocity, Strategy, and Theological Reflection in Paul's Collection*, WUNT 2/124 (Tübingen: Mohr Siebeck, 2000).

[10] For argument that Gal. 2.10 indicates a general commitment to the poor, not a specific reference to any collection, see Bruce W. Longenecker, *Remember the Poor: Paul, Poverty, and the Graeco-Roman World* (Grand Rapids, MI: Eerdmans, 2010), 157–219. For argument that it reflects the earlier collection from the church in Antioch (Acts 11.27-30), a model for the later collection reflected in 1 Cor. 16.1-4, 2 Cor. 8–9 and Rom. 15.14-32, see Downs, *Offering of the Gentiles*, 33–9.

[11] The reference to Paul bringing 'almsgiving' in Acts 24.17 has been read by some as an oblique reference to the collection; for an argument that Acts makes no reference at all to this collection, see Downs, *Offering of the Gentiles*, 60–70. Of course, silence can be read in more than one way, but Acts 21 suggests that Paul was not well received by the church in Jerusalem, as Paul himself had feared (Rom. 15.31).

there. The most Paul can offer as a mark of their common identity is to depict the Jerusalem recipients as 'saints' (1 Cor. 16.1; 2 Cor. 8.4; 9.1, 12).

Paul's somewhat desperate pleas in 2 Corinthians 8–9 reflect the fact that the Corinthian church had lost interest in this collection (8.6, 10-11).[12] It is possible that they had become positively hostile to it, out of increasing hostility to Paul himself. There are indications that they have lost confidence in Paul and suspect him of intending to pocket this money, after refusing to take pay for his work as an apostle (2 Cor. 11.16-17). Perhaps for that reason, Paul sends Titus ahead to get the Corinthians back on board, and he goes to some lengths to assure them of the probity of the emissaries chosen to take the money to Jerusalem alongside himself (2 Cor. 8.16-24). A local gift one can deliver oneself, certain that it has reached its destination; a long-distance gift disappears over the horizon, and one needs high levels of trust that it will go where one intends. A local gift is part of a face-to-face relationship; a long-distance gift such as this, to unknown recipients, lacks an otherwise essential quality of gift, a personal connection. This impersonality makes the gift feel, in ancient terms, more like a tax, an exaction, than a gift – a feeling Paul tries hard to dispel with his insistence that he wants this gift to be voluntary, not from compulsion (2 Cor. 9.5-7). And because of this distance and impersonality, it would be hard for the Corinthians to imagine any kind of reciprocal relationship with the saints in Jerusalem. What sort of relationship can this gift create, and how will it benefit the Corinthians, either in material or in non-material terms? What will the gratitude of the Jerusalem saints mean to them, assuming that it is gratefully received and that Corinth gets to hear that? What sort of honour can Jerusalem provide, and what would it be worth? And what sort of exchange could develop between Gentile believers in southern Greece and 'the saints' in Jerusalem? There were justified grounds for fearing that this gift would disappear into a black hole without any ensuing friendly relationship – which would make it, in ancient terms, not a good but a bad gift.

Paul's attempts to enable a long-distance gift

Paul's attempts to rescue the situation, to revive the Corinthian commitment to the Jerusalem collection, and to motivate this long-distance gift can be found in the extraordinary and highly rhetorical arguments of 2 Corinthians 8–9.[13] It is worth noting first what he does *not* do here. We might have expected him to play on the Corinthians' emotions with graphic descriptions of the poverty of the Jerusalem saints, evoking pity by reference to their hunger, their homelessness or their social marginalization. Paul knows how to describe such conditions in relation to himself (e.g. 2 Cor. 6.4-10; 11.23-29) but makes no attempt to do so in relation to the Jerusalem believers. He refers here

---

[12] Hans Dieter Betz finds two separate letters in 2 Corinthians 8–9, with the second (chapter 9) introducing the topic afresh, *2 Corinthians 8 and 9: A Commentary on Two Administrative Letters of the Apostle Paul*, Hermeneia (Philadelphia: Fortress, 1985). Most, however, take the two chapters to be part of a single letter.

[13] For an analysis of its rhetoric, see Kieran J. O'Mahony, *Pauline Persuasion: A Sounding in 2 Corinthians 8–9*, JSNTSup 199 (Sheffield: Sheffield Academic, 2000). For an earlier treatment of one part of the argumentation (2 Cor. 8.12-15), see John M. G. Barclay, 'Manna and the Circulation

in general terms to their 'lack' (*hysterēma*, 8.4) or 'lacks' (*hysterēmata*, 9.12), but he does not in these chapters refer to the saints as 'poor' (cf. Rom. 15.26), and he offers no depiction of their poverty. Perhaps Paul simply did not know enough about their material condition to give any description of it (it was some time since he had been in Jerusalem), perhaps he could take for granted that they knew what 'lack' meant, or perhaps it would have been hard to make the case that they were any poorer than the Macedonian believers, whom Paul praises for giving generously out of their own deep poverty (8.1-5). This does not mean that the relief of material poverty has fallen out of the picture – filling up the 'lack' of others is a significant part of the argumentation here (8.14). Nor does it mean that Paul eschews any appeal to emotion, preferring to keep on the level of cool, logical argumentation. In fact, these chapters are full of emotional appeal, but the emotions Paul wishes to evoke circle less around the needs of others and more around the motivations to give, motivations internal to the Corinthians and to their relationship to God (and to Paul).

In fact, the bulk of these chapters is spent on manoeuvring the Corinthians into a willingness to give, rhetoric being deployed in antiquity (as today) not to override the will but to make the will willing to do what the persuader would wish. (We are apt to find here arm-twisting, even 'manipulation', but that is a reflection of our modern ideal of 'autonomy' and our naivety about the ways in which we ourselves are influenced by the persuasive techniques of politicians or advertisements.) Paul wants the gift to be voluntary, not an exaction or necessity – in fact, it would not count as a gift at all were it involuntary (9.5, 7). 'Voluntary' may not mean 'spontaneous': Paul approves the way the Macedonians had given 'spontaneously' (8.3), but a willing decision to give may arise from the encouragement of others (cf. 8.17), and Paul, who is careful here not to *order* the Corinthians to give (8.8), is perfectly happy to persuade them, by many available means, to do the right thing (8.8-10). Some of this persuasion concerns the honour of the Corinthians – or their shame, if they were to fail to carry out what Paul says they have promised. As we have seen, honour is a major element of gift-giving in antiquity, typically as the currency returned to the wealthy when they distribute material benefits to those lower down the social scale. But even at a lowlier level, as we glimpse in Hesiod, there is honour in being known as generous – as a giver and not as a Scrooge. In this case, Paul reminds the Corinthians of the honour or shame that will circulate among the churches who are taking part in this collection, and especially of their reputation in the eyes of the Macedonian believers. He holds up before them the level of Macedonian generosity (8.1-5), whose 'abundant joy and extreme poverty have overflowed in a wealth of generosity on their part' (8.2). And he makes them shudder at the thought that, having boasted of the Corinthians' willingness to give, the Macedonian delegates might arrive in Corinth to find no contribution at all. 'I am sending the brothers in order that our boasting about you may not prove to have been empty in this case, so that you may be ready, as I said you would be; otherwise, if some Macedonians come with me and find that you are not ready, we would be

of Grace: A Study of 2 Corinthians 8:1–15', in *The Word Leaps the Gap: Essays on Scripture and Theology in Honor of Richard B. Hays*, ed. J. Ross Wagner, C. Kavin Rowe and A. Katherine Grieb (Grand Rapids, MI: Eerdmans, 2008), 409–26.

humiliated – to say nothing of you – in this undertaking' (9.3-4). Here the shame in not keeping one's promises, in not matching your reputation or fulfilling others' hopes, is a key part of Paul's emotive appeal.[14] In a local, face-to-face gift the shame of not carrying through on a promise would be acute in the relationship between benefactor and potential beneficiary. Here, in a long-distance gift, all the work of honour and shame has to be done at the giver's end of the transaction, and it is those who are watching the giver – that is, the fellow givers and Paul the organizer of the gift – who are depicted as the audience before whom the honour of the giving is displayed. As we shall see, however, the *gratitude* for the gift, the thanks that are the normal return for a benefit or favour, is to be given *not* to the Corinthians (or Macedonians) but to God (9.11, 12), the ultimate source and owner of the gift. In this respect, one key element of the honour-reward for giving will not materialize, which places all the more weight on other factors that will motivate the Corinthians to give.

In fact, there are several other, and deeper, motivations at play here, in the *theological* impetus of the gift. To read this passage in Greek is to be struck by the many ways in which Paul turns the term *charis* – which means favour or privilege (the privilege of taking part in this collection, 8.4), the gift of the collection itself (8.7), and the gift or grace of God in Christ, which has set the whole momentum of this collection in motion. When he begins by speaking of the Macedonian churches, we expect Paul to say, 'We want you to know, brothers and sisters, about the generosity of the churches in Macedonia.' Actually what he says is, 'We want you to know, brothers and sisters, about the grace (*charis*) *of God* that has been granted to the churches of Macedonia' (8.1). Behind and before human generosity stands the generosity of God, which enables and impels the human momentum of grace. The whole discussion finishes with the resounding 'thanks be to God for his inexpressible gift' (9.15, a reference to Christ) and this echoes the Christological statement that stands at the centre of chapter 8: 'for you know the *charis* of our Lord Jesus Christ that, because he was rich, for your sakes he became poor, so that by his poverty you might become rich' (8.9).

This verse is usually translated another way, that Jesus, '*although* he was rich, yet for your sakes he became poor', with Jesus's richness understood as a possession or status which he renounced in becoming poor. But I am inclined to think that Paul is playing here on different senses of wealth and poverty, since he has just described the Macedonians' giving as a 'wealth of generosity' (8.2). In other words, Jesus's poverty (his becoming human) is not a renunciation of his wealth, but an expression of it, his 'richness' being not something he once had and gave up, but his wealth of generosity. Hence, it was *because of* his richness (*plousios ōn*) that he became poor (in the incarnation) so that by his poverty we might become rich – that is, rich in the same way, in gift and generosity.[15] In any case, what is clear is

---

[14] We may compare the appeal to the Corinthians' reputation for excelling ('abounding') in all things (8.7; cf. 1 Cor. 1.7), a form of 'holy flattery' as Luther would have said.
[15] For this reading, see John M. G. Barclay, '"Because He was Rich He Became Poor": Translation, Exegesis and Hermeneutics in the Reading of 2 Cor. 8.9', in *Theologizing in the Corinthian Conflict: Studies in the Exegesis and Theology of 2 Corinthians*, ed. R. Bieringer, M. M. S. Ibita, D. A. Kurek-Chomycz and T. A. Vollmer (Leuven: Peeters, 2013), 331–44; cf. Kathryn Tanner, *Economy of Grace* (Minneapolis: Fortress, 2005), 79–85.

that Paul figures believers as channels or conduits of divine grace, given grace in order to 'pay it forward' in generosity to others. This is what he refers to later as their 'obedience to the confession of the gospel of Christ' (9.13): it is because they stand in the path of this grace that they are swept up into its momentum, their wills reshaped in voluntary obedience to its trajectory. 'Voluntary obedience' may sound like an oxymoron to us, with our peculiarly modern antithesis between obligation and (autonomous) freedom. But Paul wants a cheerful and a willing gift (9.5-7) which is also a form of submission to the grace of the gospel, because he knows that wills can be both directed and free.

Placing the Corinthians within the flow of divine grace ensures that their relationship to Jerusalem is 'triangulated' by reference to God. The gift of God in Christ is not just an example they are to imitate; it is a force by which they are enabled and empowered, in fact, transformed. It is as they participate in this gift, allowing it to become both the moral and ontological basis of their action, that they will embody it in their giving, extending the momentum of divine grace received into divine grace passed on. Paul's main work here is to reposition the Corinthians within this flow of grace, making it clear that what they pass on is not truly their own but only what they themselves have received. As conduits of this grace, they can block or unblock this flow, but they are not its source. And for this reason, he can assure them that by giving to Jerusalem they are not putting in jeopardy their own security or well-being. It is God who gives seed to the sower and gifts to the giver (9.10), and against the natural inclination of givers (then and now) to limit their giving before it bites into their future security, Paul assures the Corinthians that 'God is able to provide you with every blessing in abundance, so that by always having enough of everything you may share abundantly in every good work' (9.8). As is even more evident in the Greek, it would have been hard for Paul to pile up more 'alls' and 'everythings' in the course of one sentence![16]

Thus, all the heavy lifting in these chapters is performed in motivating the giver, focused on the 'push factors' in energizing the wills of givers rather than on the 'pull factors' in the needs of the recipients. This is partly to do with the problem of the long-distance gift in the ancient conditions of communication. Knowing exactly what Jerusalem needed, depicting it accurately, explaining it to people who lived in different circumstances at a considerable distance – all of that was next to impossible in relation to this long-range gift. Better to work on the real sticking point – their unwillingness to give at all. And better to work within the one frame that really did unite the believers in Corinth and the believers in Jerusalem – not their common humanity as such, and certainly not common ethnicity or citizenship, but their common status as 'saints', in shared allegiance to Jesus Christ. It is by framing the Corinthians repeatedly as part of the God-sourced cascade of grace that this gift might have the momentum to travel the distance between Corinth and Jerusalem. A long-distance gift needs a lot of power to get airborne: participating in the *charis* of God unleashed in Christ is just the energy required.

---

[16] For a broad theology of giving in this connection, see Miroslav Volf, *Free of Charge: Giving and Forgiving in a Culture Stripped of Grace* (Grand Rapids, MI: Zondervan, 2005).

Even long-distance gifts aim at reciprocity

So will this gift be one-way, and would it be all the better for being so? For reasons deep in the theology of the Reformation, in the philosophy of the Enlightenment and in the economic and political developments of the modern West, we have come to idealize the notion of the one-way gift, 'pure altruism', the gift without strings, creating no obligation on the recipient, and expecting no return.[17] The anonymous gift enables and enacts exactly that. And certain Gospel passages, which advocate the strategic giving of gifts to those who cannot or will not return (while expecting, indeed guaranteeing, a return from God) have entered into the impression that reciprocity and exchange is commercial and sordid, while gifts live in a purer world of non-circular relations.[18]

One might think that a long-distance gift would enable precisely this sort of unilateral charity. So it is all the more striking that Paul does *not* endorse that idealization of the gift, but imagines and expects, even across distance, a form of reciprocity between givers and receivers, between Corinth and Jerusalem. 'I do not mean that there should be relief for others and pressure on you, but it is a question of a fair balance between your present abundance and their need, so that their abundance may be for your need, in order that there may be a fair balance. As it is written, "The one who had much did not have too much, and the one who had little did not have too little" [Exod. 16.18]' (8.13-15). The 'fair balance' (*isotēs*, 'equality') is expected to run in both directions: the surplus of one will go to meet the deficit of the other, *each way*. The terms are abstract and broad: it is not at all clear what Jerusalem will have in surplus (material or non-material) or when it will be given to the Corinthians. But it is striking that Paul imagines and insists on this, even in this schematic fashion. He does not settle for, far less idealize, the one-way gift. He figures the Corinthians, for all their surplus in knowledge, speech, eagerness, and so on (8.7), as also vulnerable to lack, needing something from others, even Jerusalem; he does not figure them as the all-sufficient patron.

The quotation about the manna does not spell out how it came to be that the one with much did not have too much and the one with little did not have too little. But it is here interpreted as an expression of a *sharing of surplus*, a redistribution of God-given excess; and it is taken to apply in both directions by a process of continual rebalancing.[19] Rather than one side being permanently the patron, and the other the ever-grateful client, each is a patron to the other or, better, each is equally the client of a surplus-providing patron (God), who gives in order that grace be circulated between them.[20] What Paul means by 'equality' or 'fair balance' is that process of equalization by

---

[17] See Barclay, *Paul and the Gift*, 51–63.

[18] Passages such as Mt. 6.1-5 and Lk. 6.27-38 are often cited here: they warn against the desire for a human reward and work for the creation of new relationships even when a return cannot be expected or guaranteed. But such texts make very clear that there will be a return – only it will come *from God*. Thus, these texts do not idealize non-reciprocity as such; they simply enable creative and extreme forms of giving that do not depend on human reciprocity.

[19] See Barclay, 'Manna and the Circulation of Grace'.

[20] The problematics of one-way charity, reinforcing power differentials, crushing the dignity of the recipient, and creating dependencies that reduce rather than enable the agency of the poor, are well

which giving in one direction is continually, though perhaps differentially, equalized by giving in the other. Even the long-distance gift is expected to be, in some fashion and at some time, bilateral. Each can expect, at some time and in some respect, to be in surplus, with enough to give to others, *and* at some other time or in some other respect, to be in deficit, requiring others to fill up that lack. If the long-distance gift was difficult to motivate, precisely because it made the possibility of such reciprocity remote, Paul does not give up on this expectation, but underlines it, even if he is not precise as to its means. The mutuality in gift and need is integral to his vision of social relations, as in the repeated instruction to love, serve and build up 'one another' (Gal. 5.14; 6.2; Rom. 14.19, etc.). It is also his vision of the body, whose varied members give to one another and depend on one another in equal measure (1 Cor. 12.12-31; Rom. 12.4-8). It is striking that this vision is not abandoned, even in the case of the long-distance gift.

There are other examples of long-distance gift in the Pauline letters, not least the material support that the Philippians send to Paul in prison (in Ephesus or Rome; Phil. 4.10-21). There are also gifts and favours of a different kind at play between Paul and Philemon, in their long-distance conversation over what to do with Onesimus. In such cases, a similar dynamic applies: Paul places the gift within a larger theological frame, and figures the parties within a *koinōnia* in which each has something to give to the other. This pattern of 'giving and taking' (Phil. 4.15) is not a corruption or diminishment of the gift but its proper expression, since the relationships that Paul intends to build are of two-way benefit, triangulated by the endless and sufficient giving of God in Christ.

Indeed, it is this theological frame which shapes all Paul's construals of gift-giving. God is the superabundant giver who gives through each party to the other. Thanksgiving for the gift goes first and foremost to God, its ultimate source. By giving and by receiving, each party is therefore taken deeper into the 'inexpressible gift' of God in Christ, giving to and receiving from God precisely as they give on to others and receive from them. This triangulation relieves the pressure on the human relationship. The power of the givers is softened if they are merely the brokers of a God-given gift. The obligations of the receivers are first and foremost to God, rather than to the human giver. And if the intended return never in fact materializes, God will give sufficient return in some other way. Even in a long-distance gift, the creation and sustenance of human relations of reciprocity are not secondary but primary goals. But these relations are subsumed into a theological dynamic which demonstrates that the purpose of this gift-giving goes further than the mutual satisfaction of human wants, directing all parties towards their true human fulfilment, in vulnerability and abundance, in drawing from and responding to the gifts and grace of God.

known. For a popular critique, see Robert D. Lupton, *Toxic Charity: How Churches and Charities Hurt Those They Help (and How to Reverse It)* (New York: HarperOne, 2011).

Raising Funds in One Place, Giving to Another: Gift Distribution Today

Virginia Luckett

Introduction

In the previous essay, John Barclay discussed the ways in which Paul encouraged churches in Greece and Rome to give to fellow believers a great distance from them; in Jerusalem, a city that few of them would have visited or – before coming to faith – had much commonality. The purpose of this paper is to think about modern giving and benefaction, in the light of 2 Corinthians 8–9. It is a modern-day contextual approach, which draws on the passage as if readers were the first hearers of Paul's message, being asked to think about those living in poverty today.

The passages from 2 Corinthians 8–9 that form the basis of Professor Barclay's contribution are good ones to be looking at, because they have great relevance to those fundraising for church and development work internationally. I have great joy and privilege of being a fundraiser for Tearfund. We aim to inspire Christians and churches in the UK to join with us in the mission and vision of Tearfund – to mobilize local churches all over the world to alleviate global poverty. So much of what Paul describes and which Professor Barclay has unpacked, in practical terms, is our experience of fundraising now, in the present day here in the UK for often unseen and quite hard-to-know churches and partners overseas.

In fact, it is so much my world that I am basing my contribution on this passage of Scripture too, but I will be taking the liberty of giving it a bit of a modern-day twist. So, as you read this passage again, imagine yourselves as one of the first hearers of this letter – not from Paul, but from a charity like Tearfund – but in the present day:

> Now, brothers and sisters, good reader, we, Tearfund want you to know about the grace that God has given the Ugandan and Peruvian churches, so many churches. In the midst of a very severe trial, their overflowing joy and their extreme poverty welled up in rich generosity. For I testify, because I have seen with my own eyes that they gave as much as they were able, and even beyond their ability. Entirely on their own, they urgently pleaded with us for the privilege of sharing in this service to the Lord's people. And they exceeded our expectations. (2 Cor. 8.1-5)

The extraordinary generosity of people in poverty

The primary way we in Tearfund do our long-term, life-transforming developmental work of teaching people to help themselves out of poverty is through Bible stories. That should not come as a surprise because in Heb. 4.12 we are told, 'The word of God is living and active, sharper than a double-edged sword.' It was Martin Luther, the sixteenth-century church reformer, who said, 'The Bible is alive, it speaks to me; it has feet, it runs after me; it has hands, it lays hold of me.' We know from our own experience that the Bible is unlike any other book because it is the living words of God; when you wrestle with its meaning, you are changed. We also know that belief is a driver of behaviour, so if your work involves facilitating behaviour change, then it is important to engage people's beliefs.

So let me now take you to Uganda, to meet Betty. Betty lives in rural Uganda; she attends a village church that is part of the Pentecostal Assemblies of God, one of Tearfund's partners. She is living in close to absolute poverty with an income of around a dollar a day. She lives in a small mud hut that she and her husband built with their own hands. She has a pit latrine, which is basically a hole in the ground, to use as a toilet, and which she has been taught to dig by the church. She has to walk miles to collect water, there is no electricity, very little fuel, her food is totally dependent on successful harvests and the changing climate is affecting that. Life, by anyone's standards, is extremely hard for Betty and to add to her struggles, she is grieving because she is recently bereaved; her mother died about six months ago. She is a woman who appears to have *nothing to give* and is in desperate need to receive.

She was at her church and she heard the story of the feeding of the five thousand (Mt. 14.14-21), a very familiar story to many. After the teaching from the pastor, who is also one the Tearfund-trained facilitators working in the Pentecostal Assemblies of God, they had a discussion under the community tree. They discussed what this story might mean for them. They marvelled at how Jesus took the loaves and fishes and fed so many people; they sympathized with the disciples and how they struggled to have faith and to trust God to provide. They recognized that Jesus only took a small thing, what was in his hands, and multiplied it up; they remembered how many other stories they had heard from the Bible that also communicated that God often takes very small things, given with a faithful heart, and multiplies them up. They discussed what 'loaves and fishes' they might have – what they might have in their hands – however small, that they could offer to God and use creatively to bring something of God's kingdom here on earth.

After the discussion, Betty went home – and when she woke the next morning she said, 'Husband, I think I have a "loaves and fishes" under our bed.' She got down on her knees and she took out a small box from under their small truckle bed and revealed what was inside: a single item – a ball of wool. This ball of wool was precious to Betty, as it was the only thing her mother had left her when she died.

Despite the way that she treasured the wool, Betty said to her husband, 'I am going to sell it and use it for God's kingdom here in our village.' With the few coins she made from selling the ball of wool she was able to buy some cassava seeds, which she planted and nurtured. When the cassava had grown she had enough to feed her family and to save for seeds. She planted again, and in the second year and she was able to grow enough cassava to feed her family *and* to give to some to her neighbours. The year after that, she was able to grow enough to feed her family and neighbours *and* some to sell. With the money she made from selling the spare cassava, she bought a cow, which now provides milk for her family and the village. Betty, the woman who had nothing, used her 'loaves and fishes' – the ball of wool her mother left her – offered it to God and used her God-given entrepreneurial creativity to help feed her whole village.

This amazing truth is deeply challenging to us all, because Betty had learnt something that not many of us grasp: she had become convinced of something so deep down that, despite having nothing, *she was able to give*. Indeed, she was able to give to the work of the kingdom in a way that many of those of us in the West, in our heart of hearts, would regard as foolhardy and beyond expectations.

So, let's go back to our fresh reading of 2 Cor. 8.8-9:

> So I am not commanding you, but I want to test the sincerity of your love by comparing it with the earnestness of others' like Betty. For you know the grace of our Lord Jesus Christ, that though he was rich, yet for your sake he became poor, so that you through his poverty might become rich.

Jesus's generosity

The journey to become convinced of something deep down, as Betty was, can take a very long time. I've been a Christian for half of my life now and I still find it utterly amazing that Jesus, as it says in Phil. 2.6-8,

> being in very nature God [meaning he *is* God], did not consider equality with God something to be used to his own advantage; rather, he made himself nothing by taking the very nature of a servant, being made in human likeness. And being found in appearance as a man, he humbled himself by becoming obedient to death – even death on a cross!

Our God became human: the one through whom all things were made became human. God with us.

I think it is only through my work with Tearfund that I have come to understand a something of the life lived by a person being born in Bethlehem 2,000 years ago into circumstances that, we would say today, were impoverished. To be born into such poverty means you are born into a life of acute vulnerability. Jesus's family, with Joseph as a carpenter, were unlikely to experience the absolute poverty experienced by too many people around the world today – but they were not a part of the Roman, or even Jewish, 1 per cent.

About three years ago, I went to visit one of Tearfund's partners in a very isolated part of the Andes in Peru, where I met a wonderful couple, Muma Julia and her husband Fernando, who was a shepherd. They lived in a hut made of mud and straw, on the side of mountain, at a high-enough altitude that those of us visiting had to take altitude sickness tablets. While the men went to look at the sheep, Muma Julia chatted with the women of the group about her life. One of the topics of discussion involved the way that she gave birth to her nine children, not all of whom survived, by hanging on to some leather straps that Fernando had tied to the roof of their hut so she could she could hang in a semi-squat upright position to cope with the labour and birth. She had no medical pain relief or assistance, just lavender tea and her husband, who – at least – knew something about helping sheep to give birth. It was a reminder to us of how many women still give birth and of how Mary might have given birth to Jesus.

The reality, that we in the West often fail to understand, is that the fact that both Jesus and Mary, his teenaged mother, actually survived the birth experience is quite extraordinary. Estimates of the infant mortality rate at that time of Jesus, suggest that a person had a 30–50 per cent chance of dying before reaching maturity.[1] At any time during Jesus's life, there might have been failed harvests and mass starvation, unexpected disease or injury or political unrest and war. Life, for the vast majority of the population, at the time of Jesus would have been brutal, painful and short. Nevertheless, this is where God chose to be with us.

Jesus's incarnation shows us how closely he aligns himself with the poor. It shows us that he chose a life of deep human intensity, raw, naked and utterly vulnerable – at the mercy of the Roman Empire and everything that it could throw against him. He truly made himself nothing, by taking on the likeness of a human, at that time, in that place. It shows us just through thinking about the life he would have led, which I can guess at through the countless stories I have heard and people I have met who are living in absolute poverty today, just how far he was prepared to go to save us. It shows me again, just how much he *loves*, when our God could have led any other life, but he chose life in a marginal corner of a great empire.

His life and example is one of deep generosity and sacrifice rooted in immense love, that self-emptying *kenosis* that would culminate in the Godhead's ultimate act of love and generosity, Jesus's sacrifice on the cross. The cross is an unrepeatable, a once-and-for-all act of redemption for the whole of creation, but so much of the hallmark of Jesus's life is his generosity. It is a generosity expressed in empathy, compassion and care. We see this in the way that he had compassion for people, how he gave of his time, care and love, how he prayed with and for people. One example that really sums this up is Mk 5.21-35, the story of the woman with bleeding. She was a woman with an illness that would have separated her from her community, and she had few resources left, having, as Mark says, 'spent all she had' (v. 26). It seems that she did not want to interrupt Jesus on his way to the house of the synagogue leader Jairus, and was happy to try her luck – to try to touch Jesus's clothes – and melt away in the crowd. Yet Jesus, feeling the effect of her touch stopped, sought her out, and affirmed her action and

[1] M. Bar-Ilan, 'Infant Mortality in the Land of Israel in Late Antiquity', in *Essays in the Social Scientific Study of Judaism and Jewish Society*, ed. S. Fishbane and J. N. Lightstone (Montreal: Concordia University, 1990), 3–25.

her faith (v. 34), an acknowledgement that let the crowd know that he regarded her as someone acceptable, touchable and worth his time.

On some occasions, the moment was small, or taking place in passing: a drink of water at a well, a momentary pause in a journey to heal a person with leprosy or a man who was blind.[2] On other occasions, it was dramatic tremendous, lavish – and life-transforming, like the changing of water into wine at a wedding, saving a huge social drama or the feeding of five thousand people on a fairly remote hillside.[3]

Now, let's return to our updated letter, and think about what Jesus's example means for those of us who follow him.

Generosity encouraged

Because just remember this, good reader: Whoever sows sparingly will also reap sparingly, and whoever sows generously will also reap generously. Each of you should give what you have decided in your heart to give, not reluctantly or under compulsion, for God loves a cheerful giver. (2 Cor. 9.6-7)

In my department at Tearfund, we put a good deal of effort and time into increasing our understanding of our supporters and potential supporters. This is in part because we really value our supporters, but also because we want to learn what might encourage them in their faith – and in their support of Tearfund.

One of the approaches taken over the past decade is an occasional longitudinal survey, a piece of market research that reaches thousands of the general public in the UK. Through it, we have been able to track growth and decline in church size, regular church attendance and people's perception of Tearfund. From the insights it provides, we can learn more about what people know and understand about Tearfund and our fellow Christian development agencies, what motivates people to give and how to reach our target audience, both in terms of media and messaging.

For example, Figure 15.1 shows that regular church attendance was 6.3 million people in 2013 and that there was an underlying downward trend, meaning that by 2018, there could be just 5 million regular churchgoers. The regular churchgoers (those who attend once a month or more) are split up across the denominations (Figure 15.2).

As well as being identifiable by denomination, regular churchgoers can also be split up into 'tribes' that have particular theological beliefs, behaviours, styles and approaches to worship and liturgy. This can be seen in Figure 15.3, which also shows that the only tribe seeing ongoing growth are the charismatics.

We use the information we can draw from these surveys, along with other research and conversations, to develop our fundraising communications with the UK church. At the same time, one thing remains true as we seek to engage every tribe and denomination in the church: we are seeking to inspire *true generosity*. Such generosity

---

[2] E.g. Jn 4.7; Mt. 8.1-4; Lk. 17.11-19; Jn 9.1-7; Mk 10.46-52.
[3] Jn 2.1-12; Mt. 14.13-21.

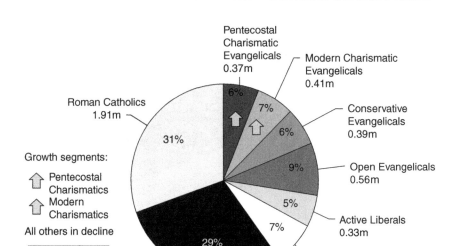

UK Regular Churchgoers (6.3m)

Pentecostal Charismatic Evangelicals 0.37m

Modern Charismatic Evangelicals 0.41m

Roman Catholics 1.91m

Conservative Evangelicals 0.39m

Growth segments:

⇧ Pentecostal Charismatics

⇧ Modern Charismatics

All others in decline

Open Evangelicals 0.56m

Active Liberals 0.33m

Total of all 4 Evangelical Groups = 1.7m

Traditional Moderates 1.84m

Less Active Liberals 0.46m

6% 7% 6% 9% 5% 7% 29% 31%

Base = UK Regular churchgoers: (N=1361 adults 16yrs plus) attending church at least once monthly, TAM 2013

Figure 15.1. UK church attendance, February 2005–February 2013

is a response rooted in a life giving stream of gratitude – gratitude towards a generous God who gives us everything. Henri Nouwen describes it in the following terms:

> Asking people for money is giving them the opportunity to put their resources at the disposal of the kingdom. It's offering people the chance to invest what they have in the work of God. When Jesus fed five thousand people with only five loaves and two fishes, he showed us how God's love can multiply the effects of our generosity. God's kingdom is the place of abundance where every generous act overflows its original bounds and becomes part of the unbounded grace of God at work in the world.[4]

This is also the subject of the Archbishop of Canterbury's Lent book for 2016, *Dethroning Mammon*, which argues that learning to see correctly is a spiritual discipline through which we can remember the identity of things of that are of true value – which are not the things of mammon.[5]

---

[4] Henri Nouwen, *The Spirituality of Fundraising* (Nashville, TN: Upper Room Ministries and the Estate of Henri Nouwen, 2004), 25.

[5] Justin Welby, *Dethroning Mammon* (London: Bloomsbury Continuum, 2016).

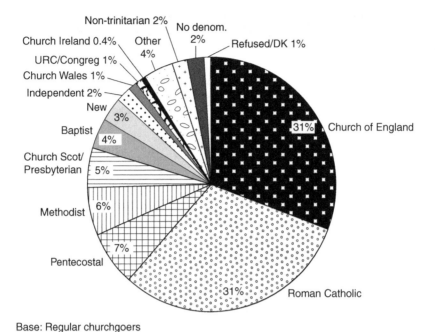

Base: Regular churchgoers

Figure 15.2. Denominations of regular UK churchgoers

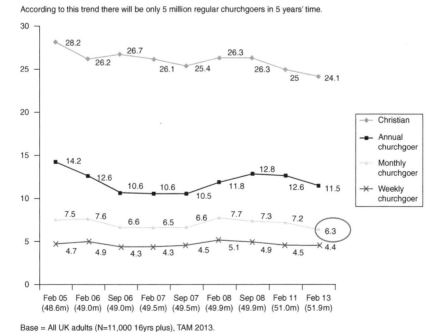

Base = All UK adults (N=11,000 16yrs plus), TAM 2013.

Figure 15.3. Christian traditions of UK regular churchgoers

True generosity is about conversion: a conversion away from the worldly things that we place our hope and security in, however good and right they may appear to be – our families, our savings, our house, our job – that ultimately are not God. It is about denying the god Mammon the domination that it desires over our lives. This means stepping away from the false hope of security and abundance that tempts us to pursue our own gains at the expense of others', to work and earn to a point of exhaustion. Doing this involves cultivating deep prayer, including the prayer of a listening heart that hears God's compassion over the suffering in our world – suffering that he has called all Christians, and organizations like Tearfund, to help alleviate. From this root, becoming truly generous involves stepping bravely into a space of recognizing the *truth* of our lives – that we are totally dependent on God and trusting that God will indeed provide all that we need. This is what Betty did, as we saw at the beginning of this paper.

What an amazing vision Nouwen describes: every generous act becoming part of the unbounded grace of God at work in the world! This is what Betty, in her extreme poverty, understood as she gave away her excess cassava to her neighbours *before* selling it at the market, and this is what we need to understand as givers. This understanding and attitude challenges the distance gap between the giver in the minority world and the recipient in the majority world and can prevent it from becoming an empathy or relationship gap.

Conclusions

So let us return to 2 Corinthians one last time:

> This service of giving that you perform is not only supplying the needs of the Lord's people but is also overflowing in many expressions of thanks to God. Because of the service by which you have proved yourselves, others will praise God for the obedience that accompanies your confession of the gospel of Christ, and for your generosity in sharing with them and with everyone else. And in their prayers for you their hearts will go out to you, because of the surpassing grace God has given you. Thanks be to God for his indescribable gift! Praise God! (2 Cor. 9.12-15)

In this essay, we have witnessed the extraordinary generosity of people living in poverty through the example of Betty, who gave up the last gift she had from her mother in order to serve her family and community, and who gave away the abundance of her second crop before selling it. We have also looked at Jesus's generosity, rooted in his love and compassion and expressed in his sharing of the human experience, living life on the margins of his world, and giving his time, energy and power to serve. Finally, we looked at encouraging generosity in the church in the UK to give to those living in poverty around the world. I suggest that while communications skills and messaging are hugely important in this work, without a deeper understanding of the existence of the roots of a deep generosity in a person's relationship with

God, fundraisers in Christian organizations will struggle to overcome the distance in geography and understanding that lies between rich and poor across the globe today. However, if we can follow Paul's example and recognize both the existence of this deeper generosity and encourage Christians to realize it, we may be able to bridge this gap.

Response to John Barclay

Virginia Luckett

In my experience as a fundraiser, there is no such thing as pure altruism, and it is refreshing to hear from John Barclay that gifts in ancient antiquity were never understood as or meant to be a one-way exchange. Their purpose was to build relationship. This is the best type of giving, where there is a fuzzy line, a blur, between the donor and recipient because there is a deep recognition that both benefit in mutual reciprocity. As a Christian organization, this reciprocity is at the heart of Tearfund's fundraising, but it is a multi-faceted relationship our organization looks to foster with each other, ourselves, the Triune God and creation. Generosity is the driving motivation for this, rooted in our whole Christian life response to a God who gave everything and continues to give us all things. We Christians today, like the Corinthians, as John describes, should consider our faith and our faith-filled response recognizing everything we think, do or own comes from God.

Long-distance gifts are still a challenge today – I should know! It is hard to give financially into a seemingly unknown situation to an unknown, hard-to-get-to-know people, and that is before we consider the complex sociopolitical situations country by country and the changing climate that besets the world's poorest. This is why stories are so important. They humanize a complex problem as so much can be communicated heart to heart in a simple true story of a poor woman who sells her most precious possession because she is captivated by a future, yet unrealized hope, for herself and her community.

Just as John suggests, extraordinary examples of generosity like this and the Macedonians can inspire and at the same time challenge us; but I know through my work, there is divine grace in giving. Time and time again, we in Tearfund hear from our supporters how much joy they find in their giving – to say it is a privilege to hear their stories cannot fully capture the reverence with which we hear them. As John discusses in relation to Paul's call to the Corinthians, I can say that each and every giver is a blessing to the kingdom, part of our modern day God-sourced cascade of grace.

Response to Virginia Luckett

John M. G. Barclay

I find Virginia's story of Betty in Uganda inspiring. It is a story of how gift-giving, trust and community operate among the relatively poor, breaking down the assumption that rich Western Christians are always the givers and the rest of the world the receivers. Although Paul does not use stories from the poor in Jerusalem, he does use the example of the poor Macedonians (2 Cor. 8.1-5) to activate the Corinthians' giving, but what Virginia provides richly complements that. If all giving is part of the 'cascade of grace', the purpose of our giving is to enable others to give, in which they will in some cases be paying it 'back' but, in many cases, rather, paying it 'forward' to others.

Paul's model of giving generally involves some form of reciprocity, and he imagines gifts going two ways between Corinth and Jerusalem. But the reciprocity does not have to be as simple as this kind of bilateral arrangement. Very often, gifts circulate in what anthropologists call 'generalized reciprocity': a gift from one person gets passed on, in substance or in spirit, to other people in the community and, thus, circulated around the wider society in a way that certainly benefits the original giver, but not in a direct or immediate way. (You let someone into the traffic, in a way that will not benefit you directly, but it does set a tone of considerate behaviour among drivers that will benefit you when you need someone to let you into the traffic.) Thus, it exactly fits the biblical picture that Betty in Uganda (and others like her) should not be just the recipient of benefaction from richer countries but should be enabled to become herself a giver, thus enabling others to become givers, and so on *ad infinitum*. And the more we hear such encouraging stories, the more we are inspired to give, because we are not sinking money into a bottomless pit of 'receipt' but investing it into a system of generosity, collaboration and hard work (a mixture of business and charity), which will itself be productive, for the benefit of all.

Thus, when we hear such stories, we do not sit back and say, 'They can do it for themselves', but we are inspired to get on board with such creative processes of gift and development. And in and behind it all, inspiring, directing and funding such generosity, is the 'grace of God in Betty' (cf. 2 Cor. 8.1), a momentum Paul would want us to be part of, both for Betty's sake and for ours.

Wealth and Dehumanization:
Ezekiel's Oracles against Tyre

Myrto Theocharous

Introduction

The author of the book of Revelation, aiming to level a fierce economic critique against Rome as the prevailing empire of his time, makes use of Old Testament (OT) images and forms, one of which is Ezekiel's oracle against Tyre. As Richard Bauckham has shown in his study on the economic critique of Rome, Tyre was infamous enough for its excessive trade and economic exploitations to serve as an ideal prototype for the author of Revelation to use.[1]

It is not the purpose of this paper to elucidate Revelation's use of the Tyrian descriptions but to go back to Ezekiel and explore Tyre in the prophet's imagination. What is particularly intriguing about Ezekiel's oracles against Tyre, specifically chapter 28, is that he does not hesitate to rewrite the primeval story of the creation, sin and fall of Adam in economic terms, in order to address the problems of his day. Humanity's creation and its fall is known from Genesis 2–3, it is briefly commented on in Job 15 and it is fully described again in Ezekiel 28 with the king of Tyre in the role of Adam.[2] Ezekiel presents us with what he views as proper Adam (i.e. human) vs profane Adam and the process of devolving from the first state to the last, that is, the dehumanization or de-Adamization process.[3] As Andrew Mein notes, 'There has

---

[1] Richard Bauckham, 'The Economic Critique of Rome in Revelation 18', in *Images of Empire*, ed. Loveday Alexander, JSOTSup 122 (Sheffield: Sheffield Academic, 1991), 47–90. Apparently, Tyre was useful not only for John's critique against Rome but also in a similar way for the author of the Sibylline Oracles (4.90, 5.455, 7.62). Strom finds the oracle against the king of Tyre serving as the background of Acts 12.20-23, Mark R. Strom, 'An Old Testament Background to Acts 12:20–23', *NTS* 32 (1986): 289–92.

[2] Williams states, 'In the Old Testament it does seem to be the only general parallel to Gen. 2–3.' Anthony J. Williams, 'The Mythological Background of Ezekiel 28:12–19', *BTB* 6 (1976): 49–61, here 53.

[3] The term 'dehumanization' used here is not derived from any philosophical discussions on ontology. It is simply a way of describing how the biblical author views the role of humans within his religious framework or, rather, the failure of fulfilling that expected role. I often use the neologism 'de-Adamization' in order to keep the focus of the discussion within the boundaries of the biblical text.

been widespread agreement that Ezekiel represents an important milestone in the development of Israelite ethics.'[4] Ezekiel's attack on Tyre is merely a glimpse into his ethics, but an important one since he locates it in the foundations of world history.

The book of Ezekiel

Ezekiel is a prophet of the exile. The book talks about him and his prophetic activity taking place in Babylon among the community of Judaean exiles in the year 597 BC. Mein alerts us to the importance of this context in examining the ethics represented in the book and notes that

> as exiles these people belonged to two different moral worlds – two different realms of moral possibility. On the one hand, they were drawn from Judah's ruling élite, and, before their deportation, would have participated in decisions affecting major communal institutions like the temple and the army. But, on the other hand, their new status as a dominated minority within the huge Babylonian empire brought little or no political autonomy and posed serious threats to their communal identity. They were no longer able to participate in the main areas of political and religious life. Their moral world was sharply circumscribed, and it was really only in the spheres of family, business and immediate community that they could take moral decisions.[5]

However, the fact that they were members of Judah's ruling elite means that the message about Tyre's affluence and power was indirectly referring to the attitudes they once held in Jerusalem, their former aspirations. After all, a lot of the wording used against Tyre is similar to the wording used against Jerusalem in Ezek. 16 and elsewhere.[6] Moreover, there are recognized allusions to Jerusalem's high priest in the oracle against the Tyrian ruler.[7] At the same time, since the Judaean exiles are now in the position of the dominated minority, they need to hear that God is just, not only in the way that he dealt with them, but also in how he will deal with anyone who appears unconquerable, even deified, and rejoicing at Jerusalem's demise (Ezek. 26.2).[8]

---

[4] Andrew Mein, *Ezekiel and the Ethics of Exile* (Oxford: Oxford University Press, 2001), 1.
[5] Mein, *Ezekiel*, 1.
[6] See, e.g., the connections noted on being enamoured with one's beauty in John T. Willis, 'National "Beauty" and Yahweh's "Glory" as a Dialectical Key to Ezekielian Theology', *HBT* 34 (2012): 1–18.
[7] Although some argue that Phoenician kings adorned themselves with precious stones like the high priest (Michael D. Coogan, *A Brief Introduction to the Old Testament: The Hebrew Bible in Its Context*, 2nd edn [Oxford: Oxford University Press, 2012], 328).
[8] See Carly L. Crouch, 'Ezekiel's Oracles against the Nations in Light of a Royal Ideology of Warfare', *JBL* 130 (2011): 473–92. Crouch argues that the defeat of the human king was tantamount to the defeat of the divine king in ancient Near Eastern ideology. So, the defeat of the king of Jerusalem posed a theological threat to those espousing the royal military ideology, that is, the deported elites. The use of oracles against the nations by Ezekiel is meant to reassert Yahweh's claims of divine kingship. The concern is that Yahweh's name is vindicated (478).

The literary context

From all the oracles given by prophets, Ezekiel's critique of Tyre is the longest since he dedicates three whole chapters to this city, four oracles in total. In the first oracle, in chapter 26, Tyre rejoices that the 'gateway of the peoples' is open to her, after the fall of Jerusalem, which calls for Yahweh's response and imminent manifestation of his poetic justice. God is stirring Nebuchadnezzar's armies, to bring destruction on the city of Tyre.[9] In chapter 27, the second oracle is cast in the form of a 'dirge' (קינה *qynh*, 27.2). In this lamentation, Tyre is portrayed as a beautiful ship in the heart of the seas made up of a variety of materials from different nations, followed by a long list of merchandise Tyre traded in. This ship was so heavy that it sank in the heart of the seas and caused a great wailing to everyone watching from their shores. Ezekiel 28 begins the third oracle which is addressed to the prince of Tyre in the second person. The prince is portrayed as transgressing the boundaries of 'humanness' and assuming the status of a god by amassing great wealth. The punishment is similar to the first oracle: strangers will come against the king and he will die violently in the heart of the seas. Finally, the fourth oracle is again a lamentation (*qynh*, 28.12) for the king of Tyre, another title for the prince of Tyre of the previous oracle,[10] only here the king is described as the perfect primal human in the garden of Eden, full of wisdom and beauty, who ended up corrupting his sanctuaries through his trading activities and was cast out as profane by God himself. He is annihilated by fire and returns to dust.

The wealth and dehumanization of Tyre

The oracles against Tyre focus on the city's trade, which is obvious from the uniquely high concentration of commercial terms in Ezekiel 26–28.[11] We shall concentrate on chapter 28 (two clear parts [vv. 1–10 and 11–19], brought together into a unitary composition),[12] where the word against Tyre climaxes and because nowhere else is the dehumanization of Tyre more evident. Chapter 28 zooms in on the king as the collective representative of Tyre.[13] As Cooke says, 'In both passages [28.1-10, 11-19]

---

[9] For the discussion concerning the date and the number of the neo-Babylonian sieges of Tyre see, Norman K. Gottwald, *All the Kingdoms of the Earth: Israelite Prophecy and International Relations in the Ancient Near East* (Philadelphia: Fortress, 2007), 311–16.

[10] For an explanation of the two different titles, see Daniel I. Block, *The Book of Ezekiel: Chapters 25–48*, NICOT (Grand Rapids, MI: Eerdmans, 1998), 93–96.

[11] Out of the seventeen times that the word רֹכְלִים *rōkĕlîm* ('merchants') occurs in the OT, eleven are found in Ezekiel and ten of these are found in his words against Tyre. The feminine noun רְכֻלָּה *rĕkullâ* ('trade, merchandise') occurs four times in the OT and all of these are found in Ezekiel's words against Tyre. Moreover, the highest concentration of the noun מַעֲרָב *maʿărāb* ('merchandise, imports') is found in Ezekiel 27 (nine times out of twenty-three in the OT), and the word עִזָּבוֹן *ʿizzābôn* ('goods, wares') occurs seven times in the OT, all of which are in Ezek. 27 (vv. 12, 14, 16, 19, 22, 27, 33). This concentration of terms shows that Tyre's commerce is the primary theme in these oracles.

[12] Block, *Ezekiel 25–48*, 88.

[13] In the first part, the leader of Tyre is addressed as 'prince' (נָגִיד *nāgîd*) and in the second part as a 'king' (מֶלֶךְ *melek*). There are no strong grounds, however, in regarding these two as distinct individuals (see note 11). They are both references to the head of Tyre, the collective representative of the city.

the prophet is thinking, not so much of any particular individual, as of the nation whose character is embodied in the person of its chief.'[14] The city is thus personified in its leader.

The first part of the chapter begins and ends with a significant discourse marker involving the transgression of human boundaries. The phrase functioning as a bracket is 'you are but a mortal (אָדָם *'ādām*), and no god (אֵל *'ēl*)' repeated in vv. 2 and 9.[15] This statement by God acts as a corrective to the blurring of boundaries of identity taking place in the king's heart (לֵב *lb*) or self-perception ('I am a god; I sit in the seat of the gods, in the heart of the seas', v. 2).

This part of the chapter is an insight into the arrogant heart and mind of the Tyrian king, but the text goes further to unpack what it is that generates and sustains this hubris. Of course, the author does not have access to the king's psychological state, but it is *external* observations of Tyre and its king by the author, probably shared with his audience, that stir his imagination in assuming the king's internal state of being. What is observable is a vast increase in wealth brought about by great wisdom or skill in trade (28.4-5). The Greek OT (LXX) actually translates the king's 'wisdom' (חָכְמָה *ḥokmâ*) as scientific knowledge (ἐπιστήμη *epistēmē*), thus distinguishing it from the 'god-fearing' wisdom (σοφία *sophia*, e.g. Prov. 1.7). The author recognizes that the king's arrogance and pride is actually derived from the success in his commercial endeavours (28.5). It is economic success that led him to value his own wisdom as extraordinary, even divine (28.2, 6). In other words, wealth accumulation and control over international trade function as external indicators of the state of the king's heart. As 26.2 clarifies ('Mortal, because Tyre said concerning Jerusalem, "Aha, broken is the gateway of the peoples; it has swung open to me; I shall be replenished, now that it is wasted"', NRSV), this wealth accumulation is competitive in nature and benefits from the demise of economic rivals. For Ezekiel, the wealth accumulation of the king of Tyre signifies overstepping human boundaries. It is reminiscent of Deuteronomy's warnings on the self-perception wealth accumulation may bring:

> When you have eaten your fill and have built fine houses and live in them, and
> when your herds and flocks have multiplied, and your silver and gold is multiplied,
> and all that you have is multiplied, then do not exalt yourself, forgetting the LORD

[14] G. A. Cooke, *The Book of Ezekiel*, ICC (Edinburgh: T&T Clark, 1936), 313. Similarly, Block links chapter 28 thematically with the attack against the entire city of Tyre:

> Tyre's trade and the manner in which she pursued it constitute the major thematic link with the prophet's words against the city. The pairing of *rĕkullâ* and *ḥayil* in 28:5 echoes 26:12 and summarizes the long commercial list in 27:12–25. Since the king of Tyre embodies the collective spirit of the city, the references to his commercial ventures are not as unexpected in this chapter as some would imagine. On the contrary, his hubris is fed by his mercantile success. (Block, *Ezekiel 25–48*, 89)

Others think that Ezekiel had a specific king in mind, Ithobaal (or Ethbaal) II, who ruled over Tyre between 887 and 856 BC, although lack of personal details may indicate that this is aimed at any Tyrian king. Hector Michael Patmore, *Adam, Satan, and the King of Tyre: The Interpretation of Ezekiel 28:11–19 in Late Antiquity* (Leiden: Brill, 2012), 4.

[15] The prince of Tyre claims to be god in a generic sense (28.2), although the claim may also be taken to state equality with the head of the pantheon, El (Block, *Ezekiel 25–48*, 97).

your God, who brought you out of the land of Egypt, out of the house of slavery . . .
Do not say to yourself, 'My power and the might of my own hand have gotten me
this wealth.' But remember the LORD your God, for it is he who gives you power to
get wealth. (Deut. 8.12-18 NRSV)

The morality of the king's trade will be commented on later.

The king assumes full control over seafaring,[16] which, for the prophet, is essentially
the same as claiming to 'sit in the seat of the gods, in the heart of the seas' (v. 2). This
hubris, brought about by economic success, calls for a talionic form of response by
God, making the punishment fit the crime: bringing the king down to the pit and
handing him over to destruction by brutal nations. The realm over which he presided
will become his burying place 'you shall die a violent death *in the heart of the seas*' (v.
8, my italics).[17]

The second section of chapter 28, which is a lamentation (*qynh*), mirrors the first
section, only here, the description of the king's rise and fall is cast in primeval terms. It
is pushed back to creation and, in a sense, is a rewritten story of creation and the fall.

Ezekiel's purpose is not to replace the 'master' primeval story of Genesis by
promoting a variant tradition. As Kvanvig writes,

Alternative stories . . . deviate from master narratives, but they do not contest
them. They can add, move, and remove features from the master narrative in order
to make new accents in it, but not to dissolve its communicative force. Alternative
narratives can live together and lend authority to each other.[18]

Ezekiel's point is not to tell us that the king of Tyre is *like* the primal human; for Ezekiel,
he *is* the primal human.[19] It is as if Ezekiel has acquired new insight on how the world
operates. Cosmic instability witnessed in the present was usually attributed by the
ancients to a rebellious primeval act. For Ezekiel, this cosmic trauma that throws the
world in disarray, primarily in the fall of Jerusalem, is no longer emphasized to have
been brought about by a serpent's allurements or a woman's enticements. It is not even
because this Adam desires the wisdom of the gods. This Adam *already* possessed this
divine gifting, but it was self-referential. It was used to generate economic power with
narcissistic results. It is this king, his actions and his coming demise that informs us of
how humanity falls. It is the Tyrian king who shows us the significance of the creation

---

[16] Maritime knowledge was a famous Phoenician trait attested in various sources of antiquity. Philo
of Byblos and other classical writers say that the city of Tyre 'invented' ship-building. H. Jacob
Katzenstein, *The History of Tyre: From the Beginning of the Second Millennium B.C.E. until the Fall
of the Neo-Babylonian Empire in 538 B.C.E.* (Jerusalem: Schocken Institute for Jewish Research,
1973), 24.

[17] The city of Tyre was situated on an island before Alexander the Great connected it to the mainland
by a dyke. It literally lay 'in the midst of the sea' (Ezek. 27.32) (Katzenstein, *History*, 9).

[18] Helge S. Kvanvig, *Primeval History: Babylonian, Biblical and Enochic: An Intertextual Reading*
(Boston: Brill, 2011), 8.

[19] See these distinctions made by Dexter E. Callender, Jr, *Adam in Myth and History: Ancient Israelite
Perspectives on the Primal Human*, Harvard Semitic Studies 48 (Winona Lake, IN: Eisenbrauns,
2000), 87.

and fall story. By being presented as God's primal being, he is potentially *every* human and he becomes the paradigm of how Adam is de-Adamized. As Zimmerli puts it, this is 'Everyman's story'.[20] Ezekiel is redefining primeval sin in commercial terms. The controlling factor here is the Tyrian situation, and this is what motivates the author to adopt, perhaps, a sarcastic terminology in order to respond to Tyre's pride. But, while this creation language may be employed sarcastically to attack the Tyrian king, it functions at the same time as a commentary on the fall of Adam, perhaps seeking to deepen our understanding of its cause or even to redefine it. It gives economic ambition a primary place in explaining human corruption and makes economic greed and oppression to be the ground of dehumanization, that is, the fall of Adam.

The transition to this section is not at all unnatural since the language of the first section, about Adam wanting to be God (*'El*), brings to mind Adam's sin in the garden of Eden. The Genesis creation story does not mention elements such as the abundance of trade or violence. These are features taken from human history (Tyrian and possibly Israelite) and projected, although awkwardly, to the events in the garden of Eden (v. 13). The fame of Tyre's fauna may have also triggered Ezekiel's Eden language. Phoenicia's cedar forests were very famous. Amenhotep III admiringly calls this area the 'Land of Gardens' or the 'Land of the God' (cf. 28.13 and the 'mountain of God' in 28.16).[21]

The unfamiliar elements led many scholars to suppose a variant tradition of creation or borrowed mythological language from Mesopotamian myths.[22] However, the text cannot be used safely to inform us of pre-existent ancient Near Eastern myths.[23]

Some think that the text was once intended against Jerusalem's high priest due to the precious stones mentioned that match those on his breastplate. Whatever the text's prehistory, the chapter as it now stands is clearly against the Tyrian king, but the presence of these elements may very well indicate that the prophet is *indirectly* attacking his own religious leaders.[24]

The king of Tyre is Adam, the primal human, because he was created (בָּרָא *bārā'*, cf. Ezek. 28.13) by God, a verb used of the creation of Adam in Gen. 1.27-28 and an indication that Ezekiel is adapting a well-known biblical tradition.[25] This Adam was created as a representative of God, in his image and likeness, as the characterization 'signet of perfection' communicates in v. 12. To be God's signet ring means that he was assigned a role to represent the divinity, authorized by God himself. We could say that the seal represents or signifies the 'essence' of a person. Joseph, for example, practically becomes the essence or avatar of Pharaoh as the bearer of Pharaoh's seal (Gen. 41.40-44).[26] Indeed, the LXX seems to have seen some identification with the 'image and likeness' language of Gen. 1.26 and translates 'seal of likeness' (ἀποσφράγισμα ὁμοιώσεως *aposphragisma homoiōseōs*). The 'signet' metaphor has strong associations

[20] Walther Zimmerli, *Ezekiel 2*, Hermeneia; trans. James D. Martin (Philadelphia: Fortress, 1983), 95.
[21] Katzenstein, *History*, 8–9, 47–8.
[22] For an overview see Williams, 'Mythological Background', 49–61.
[23] See the primeval language employed against Egypt and Assyria in Ezek. 29.3 and 31.2-9 (Williams, 'Mythological Background', 59).
[24] Block, *Ezekiel 25–48*, 106–7, 111.
[25] Ibid., 106.
[26] Callender, *Adam*, 93–4.

with royal imagery, and kings in Mesopotamia did consider themselves as vice regents of their god.[27] What is striking, here, is that Tyre's god is not mentioned, but the king of Tyre is presented as YHWH's regent. Such characterization was used of Judahite kings Jehoiachin and Zerubbabel in Jer. 22.24 and Hag. 2.23,[28] thus a further indication that Ezekiel may be *indirectly* speaking of his own people's downfall.

Wealth, wisdom and beauty are presented as God's endowment on the king of Tyre, which he will eventually defile.[29] Beauty strongly suggests physical beauty as it is used physically of Jerusalem (16.14, 15, 25) and also in ancient Near Eastern descriptions of the creation of the king.[30] Corral says that in the context of the oracle, beauty refers to the magnificence and opulence that Tyre manifested to the beholder. It is Tyre's prosperity, since it says that it was 'builders who perfected your beauty' (27.4).[31] Even as early as in the letters of Rib-addi, king of Byblos, Tyre's beauty is compared to that of Ugarit. The king of Tyre himself, in his correspondence with Akhenaton, refers to his city as 'a great city'. But also, classical writers share this view of Tyre. Curtius, for example, says that Tyre excelled all the cities of Syria and Phoenicia in size and glory.[32]

The king is covered in precious stones, enhancing his beauty, but the significance of the stones lies in the list as a totality.[33] The enumeration of the stones in v. 13 is set up to recall the high priestly breastpiece and reveal the priestly orientation of the primal human.[34] This element emphasizes the sacredness of this state of Adamhood.

In v. 14, the king is portrayed as a cherub or as being *with* a cherub. The Masoretic pointing suggests quite clearly that the cherub and the first human figure are one and the same, despite the fact that in Gen. 3.24 there is a distinction between human and cherub.[35] Of course, this phrase may also be taken metaphorically meaning 'you were *like* a cherub'. The Greek and Syriac versions suggest that one should read 'you were *with* the cherub' rather than 'you *were* the cherub'.[36] This lack of clarity has sparked a variety of interpretations. In Second Temple times and after Origen, people associated this text with the fall of Satan.[37] The rabbis, however, thought that this text speaks of

---

[27] Callender, *Adam*, 96–7.

[28] Block, *Ezekiel 25–48*, 105.

[29] See also Callender, *Adam*, 105.

[30] Callender, *Adam*, 97–100.

[31] Martin Alonso Corral, *Ezekiel's Oracles against Tyre: Historical Reality and Motivations* (Rome: Editrice Pontificio Istituto Biblico, 2002), 158.

[32] Katzenstein, *History*, 15–17, 31.

[33] The list in MT Ezekiel 28 does not contain all the precious stones from the priest's breastpiece. The LXX lists the twelve stones, instead of the MT's nine, in agreement with LXX Exod. 28 (Callender, *Adam*, 102).

[34] Block, *Ezekiel 25–48*, 106–7; Block, however, believes the connection with primeval stones (cf. Gen. 2.12) is stronger (111). He thinks that the connection with the high priest should not be exaggerated. The imagery simply functions as evidence to the wealth and splendour of the king (112). See also Callender, *Adam*, 103–4.

[35] Callender, *Adam*, 109.

[36] Block takes the king as a cherub and notes that it reminds us of the cherubim guarding the entrance to the tree of life. However, he notes that this cherub is not two but only one, and it walks about in the garden. It is not stationed, so this departs from what we know from Genesis about cherubim (Block, *Ezekiel 25–48*, 112–13).

[37] See James Barr, '"Thou art the Cherub": Ezekiel 28.14 and the Post-Ezekiel Understanding of Genesis 2–3', in *Priests, Prophets and Scribes: Essays on the Formation and Heritage of Second Temple Judaism in Honour of Joseph Blenkinsopp*, ed. E. Ulrich, J. W. Wright, R. P. Carroll and P. R. Davies, JSOTSup 149 (Sheffield: Sheffield Academic, 1992), 213–23. This interpretation arose in the context

Adam.[38] What we certainly know about cherubim is that they are closely associated with YHWH's presence and that they are also associated with kings in ancient Near Eastern iconography.[39] In other words, the text communicates that the Tyrian king, as Adam, is in the closest proximity possible to the divine, where cherubs are, and is nearly identified with God, especially given the fact that he is a human in the divine habitation, the holy mountain of God, and walks among stones of fire (v. 14). These stones enhance the brilliance and magnificence of the picture[40] as well as the sense of proximity to the divine presence and glory, which is usually manifested through fire.[41] Identification with YHWH is possibly further enhanced by the verb 'to walk' in the hiphil stem (הִתְהַלָּכְתָּ *hithallāktā*), for the hiphil participle of this verb is used of God himself in the garden of Eden in Gen. 3.8.

In v. 15, Ezekiel locates the moment when 'malice' (עַוְלָתָה *ʿawlātâ*)[42] was found in God's perfectly created being.[43] This word is the opposite of perfection or completeness (תָּמִים *tāmîm*), and its presence within the king marks the end of his period of perfection and the beginning of his dehumanization/de-Adamization.

How did 'malice' find its way into the king? Verses 16 to 18 show the way the king had gradually corrupted his perfect nature through the use of the preposition בְּ/*b* (because, in or through): '*because of* the abundance of your trade they filled your midst with violence, and you sinned', where the more common root for 'sin' (חטא *ḥṭ*) is used.[44] A second בְּ/*b* preposition stating the cause of profanation or acquiring a proud heart is found in v. 17: 'because of your "beauty" or "splendour" (יְפִי *yāpî*)'.[45] Beauty, that is, Tyre's prosperity and luxury, became another ground for hubris giving the illusion of power and self-accomplishment. It is worth noting the repetition of 'multitude' or 'abundance' in v. 16 (בְּרֹב *bĕrōb*) and v. 18 (מֵרֹב *mērōb*). Excess seems to be a key component in the dehumanization process and excess fills with 'violence'.

---

of anti-Marcionite apologetics. Marcion said that since the devil is the one who beguiled Adam into sinning and the devil is created by God, then God is the one to blame for the existence of evil. Tertullian agrees that the devil is culpable, but traces the origins of evil in the devil himself. Taking Ezekiel 28 to be prophetic of the devil, he argues that he was initially created pure. He resists reading Adam or the king of Tyre in the text since that would not harmonize with what he knew from the Genesis creation story (Patmore, *Adam*, 43–8).

[38] Patmore, *Adam*, 43–8.
[39] Callender, *Adam*, 111.
[40] Block, *Ezekiel 25–48*, 114.
[41] Callender, *Adam*, 119.
[42] The word עֹלָה *ʿawlâ* has a broad range of meaning, but it is usually defined as 'badness, malice or injustice' (*HALOT* s.v.).
[43] In his original state, the king of Tyre was blameless; cf. Noah (Gen. 6.9) and Abraham (Gen. 17.1) (Block, *Ezekiel 25–48*, 116).
[44] Also, Zimmerli renders the בְּ/b prepositions with 'through' (Zimmerli, *Ezekiel 2*, 86). Greenberg stresses the causal nature of this בְּ/b preposition rendering it as 'because' in 28.16 and 28.18 (Moshe Greenberg, *Ezekiel 21–37*, AB 22A (New York: Doubleday, 1997), 579–80). I think the so-called *causal beth* is the most appropriate category for the use of the preposition here; see Bruce K. Waltke and M. O'Connor, *An Introduction to Biblical Hebrew Syntax* (Winona Lake, IN: Eisenbrauns, 1990), 198; and Bill T. Arnold and John H. Choi, *A Guide to Biblical Hebrew Syntax* (Cambridge: Cambridge University Press, 2003), 105.
[45] The same language is used of Jerusalem's beauty which was perfect and bestowed by God himself (Ezek. 16.14-25).

The Hebrew word for violence, חָמָס *ḥāmās*, is reminiscent of eighth-century prophets,[46] who similarly pointed out the oppressive practices of the rich (e.g. Amos 3.10; 6.3; Mic. 6.12). Classical, biblical and other ancient Near Eastern sources are unanimous concerning Tyre's unjust practices such as tricking people into exchanging items of high value, like silver, for very cheap goods and participation in the slave trade.[47] The biblical record mentions Tyre's involvement in slave trade in Amos 1.9, Joel 4.6 and Ezek. 27.13.[48] Classical authors considered the Phoenicians to be greedy and oppressive pirates (Homer, *Odyssey*, 14.288–90; 15.415–16; Herodotus, *Histories*, 1.1; 2.54.).[49] They obtained their slaves through kidnapping or raiding and they treated them as any other commodity.[50] Moreover, after the destruction of Jerusalem, Tyrian merchants were selling Judaean exiles to Edom and the Greeks.[51]

Verse 18 is also a testimony to the immoral practices involved in Tyre's trade: 'Because of the multitude of your iniquities (עֲוֹנֶיךָ *'ăwōnêkā*), in the unrighteousness (בְּעָוֶל *bĕ'ewel*) of your trade.' The first word עָוֹן *'āwōn* is more generally used for 'sin', but the next word עָוֶל *'āwel* is more specific to dishonesty and injustice and regularly used of economic transactions (e.g. Ezek. 18.8; 33.15; Lev. 19.15, 35; Deut. 25.16).[52]

Practices connected with עָוֶל *'āwel* elsewhere in the OT include usury: the extraction of high interest and extra demands on loans given to people in financial need (Ezek. 18.8). Also, withholding pledge taken from debtors or seizing the debtors' possessions (Ezek. 33.15).[53] For Ezekiel, at least in some oracles (e.g. chapters 11, 22 and 34), injustice is also responsible for the fall of Jerusalem. In particular, 'the leaders of society, the king and ruling classes, are attacked for their greed and violence.'[54] Ezekiel 45.9 is representative: 'Thus says the Lord god: Enough, O princes of Israel! Put away violence and oppression, and do what is just and right. Cease your evictions of my people, says the Lord god' (NRSV). As already mentioned, although the oracles we are examining are levelled against Tyre, they are indirectly to be heard by the deported Judahites. Thomas Renz says that 'the picture of Old Israel is hidden in the oracles against Tyre and Egypt. Old Israel is no longer "Israel," it is "Tyre" and "Egypt".'[55] The profanation of beauty and splendour was after all primarily an accusation against Jerusalem (cf. Ezek. 16).

Although trade is absent from Genesis 2–3, by seeing the oppressive dimensions of excessive unjust trade, Ezekiel does not hesitate to read it in the creation story and

---

[46] Paul M. Joyce, *Ezekiel: A Commentary* (London: T&T Clark, 2008), 180.
[47] For examples from the classical sources, see Corral, *Ezekiel's Oracles*, 71–2.
[48] See also Patricia J. Berlyn, 'The Biblical View of Tyre', *JBQ* 34 (2006): 73–82, here 73.
[49] As early as the thirteenth century BC, there are traces of Phoenician slave trade, and in the first millennium it is documented everywhere in Northern Mesopotamia (Corral, *Ezekiel's Oracles*, 67).
[50] The Phoenicians of Sidon, especially, were very successful in combining trade with kidnapping (Homer, *Odyssey*, 14.287–98; 15.403–84l; Corral, *Ezekiel's Oracles*, 125).
[51] Corral, *Ezekiel's Oracles*, 127.
[52] Similarly Mein, *Ezekiel*, 197.
[53] For some of these practices see, Samuel L. Adams, 'The Justice Imperative in Scripture', *Int* 69 (2015): 399–414.
[54] Mein, *Ezekiel*, 94.
[55] Thomas Renz, *The Rhetorical Function of the Book of Ezekiel*, VTSup 76 (Leiden: Brill, 1999), 177.

assign to it the place of 'primal sin', the sin of humanity's fall that is able to turn a proper Adam into a profane Adam.

The language of profanation is telling of Ezekiel's priestly background. The root חלל *ḥll* permeates the entire book and it is used three times in this chapter (vv. 7, 16 and 18). By using the symbolic language of the Jerusalem temple beyond the priestly sphere, Ezekiel achieves the 'ritualization of ethics'.[56] In the context of exile where there is no temple, the values of purity and the danger of profanity which once made sense only within the context provided by the temple are still valid and extended beyond a localized Jerusalemite context.[57] Where is the sanctuary now and how does one profane it? Are the words to the Tyrian king 'you profaned your sanctuaries' (v. 18) to be taken literally?[58] Or are people warned against greed and economic injustice as equivalent to ritual uncleanness?

Finally, the fall of the king involves his casting on the ground and turning into ashes on the earth (vv. 17-18). Ashes on the ground is an indication that this primal human will return to where he was created from. It is a statement highlighting his fallen humanity, as in Gen. 3.19.[59]

Conclusions

The focus of this essay was the city of Tyre, its trade and unjust practices. We have examined Ezekiel's oracle against Tyre, focusing particularly on chapter 28 where the king of Tyre is addressed. We saw how Ezekiel casts the sin of Tyre in primeval language, portraying the Tyrian king as the primal human in the garden of Eden and explaining how he came to be 'de-Adamized', losing his proper humanity and returning to the ground. Through this oracle, Ezekiel effectually makes wealth accumulation through unjust means the primal sin of the fall of humanity. He gives sin an economic value.

Naturally, the question arises whether all accumulation of wealth is critiqued or only that which results from unjust means. First, we need to keep in mind that the responsibility of a ruler in the ancient Near East was to use his power to alleviate the suffering of the poor, the widow and the orphan.[60] The king is not the primary beneficiary of his wealth and power, and is therefore judged by whether he has used it for justice and equity or not. Therefore, we could say that the presence of injustice and unalleviated suffering in a king's realm would be enough to trigger the critique of his wealth. Second, Ezekiel goes deeper than that, prior to the observation of unjust means or oppression. The first of the two parts of chapter 28 does not hint on immoral

[56] Mein, *Ezekiel*, 261.
[57] Ibid.
[58] Corral thinks that the sanctuaries refer to the temples of the Tyrian god Melkart (Corral, *Ezekiel's Oracles*, 162–63). Callender, though, wonders why a Yahwistic prophet would care about the ritual correctness of a foreign ruler with respect to his foreign god. He thinks that 'sanctuary' can be understood as homologous with the concept of garden (Callender, *Adam*, 127). See also 5.11, 23.38–39.
[59] Callender, *Adam*, 130.
[60] H. G. M. Williamson, *He Has Shown You What is Good: Old Testament Justice Here and Now*, Trinity Lectures, Singapore, 2011 (Eugene, OR: Wipf & Stock, 2012), 25–32.

practices, but what is presented as problematic with wealth is the elevated self-perception it generates (cf. Deut. 8.11-18), what one says in his 'heart'. Greed and the 'isolating' autonomy brought about by one's wealth is critiqued in the New Testament as well, even where immorality is not the cause of wealth abundance (e.g. the rich fool in Lk. 12.13-21). What is at stake is the maintenance of the boundaries between a contingent human and his God.

Callender says, 'We are not faced only with the task of discerning the essential boundaries between humanity and the divine but ultimately the very task of *defining* humanity and the divine.'[61] Ezekiel, through this oracle, does exactly that. He defines for us what Adam is and what *El* is – what it means to be human and how one is dehumanized. The irony is that being proper Adam means having the closest proximity possible to God and behaving just like him. It means *already* having access to divine presence, sitting in 'the seat of the gods', being the authorized representative of the deity and possessing all the wisdom and knowledge necessary for ruling. Being Adam is actually an existence in sacred space, a 'transcendent' existence. It means leading a life of maintaining the world as sacred space. But it is simultaneously a dangerous space where 'Adamhood' is always at stake. In this oracle, wealth accumulation together with its unjust inner workings is what places humanity in immediate danger of profanation and jeopardizes our identity as humans. Attempting to supersede one's humanity economically is precisely how one loses one's humanity and ends up as good as dead.[62]

Gary Anderson said, 'How we talk about sin, philosophers would argue, influences what we will *do* about it.'[63] So, in attributing humanity's fall to such wealth accumulation, Ezekiel calls us to imagine what the *reversal* of the fall would look like.

---

[61] Williamson, *He Has Shown You*, 17.
[62] Zimmerli juxtaposes the story of the king of Tyre to the counterstory of Jesus as proclaimed in Phil. 2.5-11 who did not regard his 'giftedness' and 'nobility' as 'a thing to be grasped' (Zimmerli, *Ezekiel 2*, 95).
[63] Gary A. Anderson, *Sin: A History* (New Haven: Yale University Press, 2009), 13.

Poverty and Dehumanization

Ellie Hughes

Introduction

In the Spring of 2010, I had just finished my first year as a child protection social worker in South East London. In this role, I had met families torn apart by substance addiction, women fleeing and in many cases still living with domestic abuse, heard countless stories of young people involved in gang-related crime and worked constantly with women either parenting alone or in dysfunctional relationships, often in desperate and vulnerable situations. Many of these issues are the devastating impact and consequences of poverty in the UK today. However, despite the unique nature of every issue and family I found myself working with, a continuous and similar theme ran through the centre of each situation. Surrounding every family I knew and worked with was an expanse of gaping social isolation.

Looking around me, it appeared that the plethora of services available to vulnerable children and families at the time (which we should celebrate) still seemed to lack something in being able to meet the entirety of the needs presented by an individual or a family. Change often appeared to be short term, crisis was frequent, and many of the women I met seemed marooned on islands of low self-esteem, unable to form healthy and secure attachments in any form of relationships. Hopelessness abounded, and cycles of seemingly self-sabotaging behaviour often led to intervention by statutory services.

Perhaps most disconcertingly, for those working within statutory services, expectation of change seemed limited, if not non-existent. Katie Harrison's essay in this book touches upon the culture of fatalism that can grip those living in poverty, and I would also argue that it can also grip those working in services aimed at addressing the impact of poverty and vulnerability – an experience that I have known only too well, and to which I have often fallen prey. There so often seems to be an inevitability to the cycles of generational abuse, unemployment and deprivation in many families whom have become used to statutory involvement; it can be easy to lose hope.

The importance of secure and consistent relationships, built on trust and love, are often a missing ingredient in the fight for transformation and change. I sadly confess that I am one of the many social workers who have come and gone in the lives of the young people and adults who come into contact with social services, a sadness that I imagine is shared by many of my former colleagues. We expect the most vulnerable people in our society to open up their homes, their lives, their deepest trauma's and abuses to person after person who actually cannot, for often quite justifiable reasons, call themselves a friend. I do not know about you, but the deepest secrets of my life are not known by a professional I only see every few weeks. They are known by the closest and most trusted to me, and they make those relationships all the more valuable because of that. They are the relationships where I often feel most fully alive and loved – sharing deeply human experiences with other people. In this essay, I will explore how poverty, and the isolation which it often creates, can contribute to people feeling less than human, and often being treated in ways that do not engage with their full humanity. I will also explore, how a gospel-centred approach to support and intervention can enable communities to embrace and welcome those experiencing poverty and its wide-ranging consequences.

The dehumanization of people in poverty

The social isolation or marginalization of those living with the impact of poverty is not a new phenomenon. Indeed, in the Scriptures we see the lame, the leper, those suffering with poor mental health and women in various vulnerable situations, to name a few, cast out of mainstream society. Their interactions with society are often limited to those seemingly in authority – the priest, the Pharisee, the physician. The closeness of human compassion and companionship is denied them and the expectation is that somehow they will work themselves out of the position in which they find themselves. The cripple by the healing pool has no one to take him to the water (Jn 5.5-9), the woman caught in adultery has no defender to stand between her and the religious mob who seek to stone her (Jn 7.53–8.11). Yet, time and time again in these situations, it is Jesus whom we see stand in the gap between the desperate place of shame and isolation, and a future of hope and reconciliation.

Riverbank Trust, which I founded and worked at for eight years, works with a small handful of the three million households in the UK that are parenting alone. Based in South West London, our mission is to support, love and befriend vulnerable single mums and their families for the long term. We predominantly work with a small fraction of the 92 per cent of lone parent households with dependent children that are headed by mothers. Through our work in local primary schools, we also work with a small number (again) of the one million children growing up in the UK with no meaningful relationship with their fathers.[1] This is an issue linked to poverty – almost half of all children aged zero to five years old in low-income households are not

---

[1] Centre for Social Justice, 'Fractured Families: Why Stability Matters', 2013, executive summary, 12–13 (https://www.centreforsocialjustice.org.uk/library/fractured-families-stability-matters, accessed February 2018).

living with both their parents; that is seven times the number of those in the richest households.[2] Among some of the very young mothers that we work with are women who have grown up within the care system who contribute to the approximately 10,000 young care leavers, who, to quote recent research from the Centre for Social Justice, 'having experienced the most challenging and traumatic childhoods of any of our society, make this journey [from childhood to adulthood] largely alone'.[3] Furthermore, the research comments, 'Despite making up less than one percent of the population, care leavers are disproportionately represented in almost every vulnerable group, from prisoners to sex workers and problem alcohol users'.[4]

This is a deeply disturbing picture, made all the more poignant by research that suggests the consequences of such broken relationships points to a rise in teenage pregnancy, low educational outcomes, low unemployment, poor mental health and emotional problems that stem into adulthood. One study shows that those who have suffered family breakdown as children will still suffer the emotional trauma into their sixties.[5]

Such statistics and research provide us with a snapshot of some of the experiences of those living with the consequences of poverty in Great Britain today. Furthermore, this is to a large degree an accurate portrayal of what we see in Richmond and a reflection of the stories that we hear in our work with vulnerable single mums and their families. However, if our only understanding of the lives of the women and families we know comes in the context of statistics, and if we only view them through the prism of their vulnerabilities and difficulties, our only aim will be to address a perceived problem, rather than engage with a whole person. The result of this view is that we end up creating programmes and projects which are overwhelmingly outcomes-driven rather than seeking to understand and love the human being. This fallen worldview disengages the human being from the creation they were made to be and, in turn, what they were made *for*. When we lose sight of our *true* humanity within the framework of God's creation, our view and understanding of people becomes fractured and distorted.

I was talking recently with a young and very vulnerable single mum whom we have known for several years. I was sharing with her some of my thoughts for the conference on poverty at which this essay was first presented, and in our discussion, the term 'service user', which she has heard too many times throughout her childhood and young adult life, came up. She wrinkled up her face: 'I hate that word.' She hates it because my friend has a name. She has 'used services' (thankfully available to her) because she has a story, and within that story, sadly, are pains and trials and unjust abuses. But there is also much, much more to her life, more to understand of who she was created to be and what she is created for. She has a name, hopes and dreams and

---

[2]   Centre for Social Justice, 'Fully Committed: How Government Could Reverse Family Breakdown', 2014, 15 (https://www.centreforsocialjustice.org.uk/library/fully-committed-government-reverse-family-breakdown, accessed February 2018).

[3]   Centre for Social Justice, '"I Never Left Care, Care Left Me": Ensuring Good Corporate Parenting into Adulthood', 2013, 6 (https://www.centreforsocialjustice.org.uk/library/i-never-left-care-care-left-ensuring-good-corporate-parenting-adulthood, accessed February 2018).

[4]   'I Never Left Care', 6.

[5]   'Fully Committed', 17.

opinions and a personality, and many, many gifts to offer those around her. She is a wonderful person and I am honoured to call her my friend.

The very language we often use to define those who need care and support and nurture often give the message that they are defined by the needs that they have and worth nothing more – an incredibly dangerous message to send to those who, more than most, have received messages through their life experiences that they are worthless or worth very little. Labelling such as this facilitates dehumanization not only of the vulnerable but also of those in the position of 'helper' or 'service provider'. It creates a chasm between benefactor and beneficiary, between service provider and service user. This is not to say that those providing services which counsel, support and equip the poor and vulnerable lack compassion. I have first-hand experience of social workers, health professionals and those in the charitable sector who go above and beyond for those in their care. However, often even such dedicated services fail to bridge the gap of isolation between the service provision and the day-to-day lived experience of the beneficiaries of their support.

The uncomfortable truth is that it is actually much easier to deal with the label we create for those in poverty than the human beings themselves. The very language that we use denotes them as a consumer of services, where there is an expected input and outcome. This framework enables us as a society to excuse ourselves from entering into someone's lived experience and sharing in the reality of their story, which therefore isolates them from the very community they so desperately need to be a part of. The consequent danger of this is it is very easy to invent our own narratives and assumptions about who the human being really is. It is easy for the community around them to create their own false narrative and story about who these people really are, what they need and what they deserve.

In my eight years of working at Riverbank, I had countless conversations with people who simply cannot believe there are vulnerable single mothers and those living in poverty in the London Borough of Richmond, where we work. They cannot believe Richmond has a foodbank. They cannot believe we work with teenage mothers who have been kicked out of their homes. People who have lived here their entire lives, caring and kind people, are shocked when we share the scale of the difficulties we encounter. I believe this is because one of the impacts of poverty is that it disconnects and isolates people from their community, rending vulnerable people of a voice and a platform to share their difficulties and needs. It hides them and their stories behind doors and reduces them to newspaper headlines and television documentaries. One of the reasons that we run a specific mother and baby group for vulnerable single mothers is because a lot of our mums struggle to attend mainstream mums and baby groups. While the narrative created for them might suggest that they are lazy or uncaring, the stories many of our mums share with us tell a very different story which understandably explains why they may struggle to attend mainstream services. They often feel that they do not fit in and they expect that they will be judged. Often, they are experiencing environments and situations that are completely alien to them, or that have not been modelled to them as young children. Furthermore, many face a complexity of issues which may create barriers to them engaging in social situations.

The dehumanization of those living with the consequences of poverty not only limits the extent to which the fullness of their story is able to be understood but also can lead to solutions that only address the presenting perceived problem, while the underlying issues are often far more complex. In 2014, it was reported that 30 per cent of the cases before family courts in England involved birth mothers who have already been in care proceedings with previous children. It is increasingly recognized that a significant lack of support for often extremely damaged and vulnerable mothers who fall out of the 'system' once their children have been taken into long-term care or are adopted contributes to this heartbreaking statistic and the reality for vulnerable mothers who, time and time again, experience the trauma of their children being removed and placed into state care.[6] Often, the timescales that we create for vulnerable people to change, transform, indeed, to heal from gaping wounds often caused by deep childhood trauma, are completely unrealistic, and once they haven't been met, we give up – on the person, on their life, on their dreams.

We have increasingly become a society that treats things as disposable; if a piece of technology is no longer fit for purpose we throw it out and trade up for a new version. In the same way, our dehumanized view of vulnerability, dependency, brokenness and pain will never know what to do with human failure. We might not 'throw away' the vulnerable and the struggling, but far too often our frameworks for offering support and care are limited to expectations and timescales which do not appropriately or realistically account for the fragility, complexity and needs of the human soul. Much in the same way that the city of Tyre became dehumanized through her desire to be equal to or greater than God,[7] to gain economic success and strength at any cost, it may be suggested that our modern-day society dehumanizes the poor and those living with the impact of poverty as we determine the worth of one another by our perceived strength, by whether we appear to be winning, achieving and meeting the expectations of those around us. Do we want to become a society and, indeed, a church, who only value those who are working hard providing for the community? That is the dehumanization that our understanding of poverty creates, and it is a view that has forgotten the image in which we were made and the One who made us.

Being truly human

As Myrto Theocharous reminds us in her essay, the true essence of our humanity is found in the story of Eden, and particularly in Gen. 1.27: 'So God created humankind in his own image, in the image of God he created them; male and female he created them. God blessed them' (NRSV). We are made in God's image. Our humanity is found in our relationship with the creator, with our dwelling in God and God in us. For Riverbank, this belief has been formational in our ministry to vulnerable women.

---

[6] James Meikle, 'Thousands of Mothers Have Multiple Children Taken into Care', *The Guardian*, 23 June 2014 (https://www.theguardian.com/society/2014/jun/23/mothers-multiple-children-care, accessed February 2018).

[7] See Myrto Theocharous, 'Wealth and Dehumanization: Ezekiel's Oracles against Tyre', in this book.

As Christians, we believe that in order to restore humanity, we have to show first what it looks like, in its purest form. One of my favourite verses in the Bible is the one that precedes verse 27: 'Then God said, "Let us make humankind in our image"' (Gen. 1.26). 'Let us': without delving too deeply into triune theology, I think we should remind ourselves that God exists within community and that we are made in the image of that community. In her book, *The Promise of Blessing*, Kate Patterson writes, 'The Father, the Son and the Holy Spirit are an eternally perfect and satisfied community of love.'[8]

As we are made in the image of this communal God, so our humanity requires us to live in relationship, in community, to be loved and to love others. Not only do we bear the image of a holy and perfect God, which means that as human beings, we are, just as a creation, of infinite worth and value, but we do not and are not meant to exist in a vacuum from one another. This means that the message for those enduring the impact of poverty is that no matter what the world says you have or do not have to offer, no matter what your perceived failure, no matter how long it takes or what the journey looks like, you are loved. In Jesus, you are invited to a relationship and community that places great value and worth upon you.

As a twenty-two-year-old History graduate, before retraining as a social worker, I spent a year working for a Christian ministry serving vulnerable adults on the outskirts of Leeds. This organization cares for some of the most vulnerable adults in our society, many whom would struggle to maintain a tenancy without support and many of whom, were it not for their long-term residential homes, would spend a lifetime moving from one supported housing association to another, or who would have remained in abusive and dangerous situations. Its staff care for men and women who would struggle to maintain employment. They love and care for people who often display antisocial behaviour, who can be difficult and violent and some of whom have taken years and years to begin to trust those trying to help them. In one of the gardens on their farm, they have a stone with this inscription:

> For I was hungry and you gave me food, I was thirsty and you gave me drink, I was a stranger and you welcomed me, I was naked and you clothed me. I was sick and you visited me, I was in prison and you came to me . . . Truly I say to you, as you did it to one of the least of these my brothers, you did it to me. (Mt. 25.35-40)

This is a well-known passage and, like many people, I can remember singing songs based on it in Sunday School! Nevertheless, its profound message is not just that we serve, not just that we do good works, but that the restoration of humanity in the kingdom of God is honouring and doing good to those least honoured in our society, through loving relationships. We are called to love abundantly where it has not been earned. We are required to show grace upon grace, and often it will look scandalous to the world. Jesus does not tell us that if we love people we will see immediate change, or that it will result in a stronger society with a robust economy, or that problems will be instantly fixed. He tells us that it will bring honour to *him*, that it will bless *him* and that we will be living in the fullness of our humanity and all that we are created for.

---

[8]   Kate Patterson, *The Promise of Blessing* (Edinburgh: Muddy Pearl, 2015), 172.

The result of our fall is that through our 'dehumanized' eyes, we will only see the dehumanized person in front of us, and as mentioned at the beginning of this essay, our view is often fraught with frustration. Understanding our humanity in the context of our creation, and who God made us to be, restores the vision we have for the lives of those trapped in cycles of poverty. When we begin to grasp that all men and women are made in God's image, even though that image has been marred by our sin, we are able to see potential and hope even in the middle of despair and hopelessness.

One of the ways that we have tried to understand this more at Riverbank is by spending time in prayer asking God how he sees the women whom we care for. Interestingly, we often sense that God is showing us the exact opposite traits in them than those we have often inadvertently labelled them with. We are learning how to see the women we meet as women of joy, hope and healing, women who have the potential to bring peace and healing to those around them, women whom God has made as leaders, women whom God has called to break bonds of oppression. Sometimes I look at the mess in their lives and I wonder how these things could possibly come true, but we stand on the promise of Scripture, as Paul writes of God, '[God] gives life to the dead and calls into existence the things that do not exist' (Rom. 4.17). As we find our true humanity in relationship with Jesus, we are also able to see the potential for all human beings, and as those who care for the vulnerable and poor, we are able to believe wholeheartedly that God has a plan a full purpose for their lives.

Alice's story – transforming humanity

About six years ago, just a few months after Riverbank started work, I met Alice, a young woman who had recently become a single mum after separating from her husband. Forced to leave a privately rented family home, she became homeless and spent a year being moved from cockroach-infested bed and breakfasts to freezing cold temporary homes with broken boilers in the dead of winter. She had some family, also battling difficulties, but few friends or positive support structure. Over those first few years, our relationship largely existed around cups of tea in various forms of accommodation, driving round Richmond in the rain, looking at different properties, sitting in council waiting rooms and, more often than not, praying together for miracles to happen. As our relationship developed, Alice shared some of the difficulties of her childhood, of addiction, abuse and broken relationships. She also showed an interest in the God whom we prayed to together and the church that had opened its doors and arms to her and her children. She did an Alpha Course and committed her life to Jesus. Her husband continued to see his children and came to church when they were baptized, several years ago. I can remember the first time I met him. I was scared of him, he was a tough nut and would not even look me in the eye. He struggled with significant addiction issues, but Alice asked us to continue to pray for him. More recently, he too was baptized and is now drug-free and volunteering in our church. Their marriage has been restored, and it is a joy and pleasure to see them parenting together their now four children!

I love this story. It is probably one of my favourite stories in the whole world. But what it probably does not properly reflect is that Alice, her husband and their beautiful family are not clients who have passed through the Riverbank programme. They are our friends. They are part of our family. They are valuable and precious members of the church we are linked with. Indeed, despite the fact that Alice is now flourishing both at work and within her family, despite her life being largely solid and secure, we still meet occasionally for a coffee and to pray. We meet because she is my friend. She is not now – nor ever has been – my client or a 'service user' of Riverbank. Rather, she gave us the privilege of allowing us into her life, and now, for however long she wants us, we will continue to walk alongside the Riverbank with her. I remember a Christmas when I spent an evening with her family sharing in an Advent party. I was so blessed by their company, by our shared community that they are willing to share with those around them, just as community and friendship was extended to them all those years ago. Love and grace and mercy has been poured into their family, but as is discussed in other essays, the fruit of that investment is in seeing them live fully, productively, creatively, offering community to others out of the blessing that they have received.

One of the key underlying principles of Riverbank is that we care for vulnerable women and their families for as long as they want to have that relationship with us. As I have explored in this essay, relationships with people who have suffered significant rejection and abandonment are often difficult to build and trust does not come easily. Caring and supporting people who we understand to be those who deserve honour, as described in Matthew 25, make us the caregiver in the humble position of having to earn trust with ongoing love and care. These verses also help us commit to be those who come to serve, much like Jesus, with a towel around our waist, ready to wash the feet of those who have walked a long time in the dust and the dirt (Jn 13.3-17). It is the position in which we find our truest sense of what it means to be human, as we reflect most radically the character of Jesus.

Within the context of relationships with our families that are allowed time to grow and develop over the long term, we have seen and continue to see transformation occur within individual lives. This does not always look as dramatic as Alice's story, nor does it necessarily mean that those we support have all become Christians. However, I believe that as we choose to see the women we meet as our equals, as precious creations of God, and as we choose to see them through the eyes of Jesus, we will see the impact of the love of Jesus on those around us. We have seen hostile and frightened women call us their family and invite us into their homes, call us their friends and begin to find ways that they too might serve their community or help out others in need. I always find it incredibly moving when I see the families we care for comfort one another, encourage one another or try and find a way that they can help in an hour of need.

It is important to recognize the valuable role played by statutory services and other resources that address the specific issues that we have looked at in the course of this paper. However, as we have seen, the most vital ingredient in the journey toward change is that no one should ever be expected to do it alone. Riverbank exists to equip the church to be a bridge, to be family that walks alongside broken and vulnerable women, friends that go with them to the overwhelming appointments, a family that will learn and grow together and try new things but most importantly, people who will be there.

Facing the future

I have shared several stories of just a few ways in which Riverbank is seeking to share the love of Jesus with vulnerable women in our care and how these approaches restore a humanity that has been lost. It is always exciting to think of new ways in which the church can respond, to ask God how he wants to work through us and to be creative in our response to the variety of needs that we are faced with. For Riverbank, this will mean looking at how we can more intensively support very young, first-time single mums; it means addressing the needs of young fathers and helping to restore fractured and broken families. We have hopes and dreams for the ways in which we can reach out and care for those in our community. Ultimately though, in considering how the church can respond to the dehumanization of the poor and as I reflect on the lessons we have been learning through the ministry of Riverbank, it is that the stories I have shared are stories that have and are being grafted into the far bigger story of our Christian faith. It is only in the truth of the gospel that I and the team at Riverbank have any hope to offer those stripped of their humanity by the world because it is only through the cross of Jesus that any of us have been offered a way to be restored to a God who loves us and to a life that he always intended for us.

I believe through the ages that the church has constantly been awakened to this truth, from the believers caring for the poor in the early church, to the mission of Wilberforce, to the work of Jackie Pullinger in the 1970s within the walled city in Hong Kong and countless places in between; the Spirit of God will always seek to move among the poorest in our society, to bring blessing and hope to those living in darkness. I believe this is at the heart of God, to bless the poor and bring his kingdom among them. Our passion at Riverbank is to see the church step into this calling. We believe God has charged the church with the mission to preach good news to the poor, to bind up the broken-hearted, to set the captive free. Therefore, we believe that those entrusted to our care are a gift to us – to serve the least and the lost restores our humanity, and to allow others to be blessed in order that they may then go on to be a blessing makes them fully alive, fully human, creatively living in community.

Isaiah 61 has much to say about the mission of Jesus, about the promise of his kingdom. However, it is the words from verse 3 that excite me the most, that drive me to my knees in prayer and that I believe are a beautiful promise to restore those whose humanity has been stolen from them, whose light has been oppressed and voice has been silenced: 'They will be called oaks of righteousness, the planting of the Lord, to display his glory' (NRSV). God calls to life things that are not yet. God grows oaks out of acorns, and his plan is to display the broken, the mourning, the shamed, the distressed and the cast-aside as the glorious display of his splendour, fully human, fully alive, in relationship with him.

20

Response to Myrto Theocharous

Ellie Hughes

Myrto Theocharous presents a fascinating picture in her paper examining the king of Tyre, reimagined by Ezekiel as the original Adam, reframing the fall of humanity in economic terms. Perhaps the most moving – and in some ways disturbing – impact of her essay on me, were the distinctions which could be drawn between her description of the process of dehumanization experienced by the king of Tyre as he 'blurred the boundaries of identity taking place in his heart' and our own modern day society. Living in a predominantly secularized western society, I am in no doubt that God utters to us also, 'You are but a mortal and no god' (Ezek. 28.2). In exposing the idols of wealth and power which the king of Tyre sought and ultimately left him destroyed and returned to dust, this paper also compels us to consider the similar idols of our age which would tempt us to believe that we, too, individually or nationalistically are, '. . . god[s]; sitting in the seats of the gods in the heart of the seas' (Ezek. 28.2).

Holding this in mind, I found it helpful and an interesting correlation with my thoughts on the dehumanization of the poor, to consider Myrto's thoughts on the king of Tyre's story as 'everyman's story'. As we place our own fall as human beings within the King's story – one of idolatry and a misunderstanding of who we are created to be – it helpfully explains not only how we become dehumanized by our own idolatry and greed, but furthermore how this then impacts how we view the poor. When we misconstrue the gifts that God has graced us with (such as wealth or wisdom, as Myrto identifies) as benefits of our own making, the work of human hands, our view of not just ourselves but the rest of humanity becomes warped and defiled. I find it interesting that in the king's desire for excess, and his pride in this accumulation of power and wealth, he loses the God-given ability to see people as they really are: his desire to be a god actually prohibits him from being able to love and display the compassion to others which God created us to be able to express.

Myrto's exploration of the meaning of humanity, how we become dehumanized and the consequences of this for the king of Tyre, and indeed the 'everyman' within his story, framed so helpfully my understanding of our need for a gospel-centred approach to caring for people in poverty and those in need. Her comment that 'attempting to supersede one's humanity economically is precisely how one loses one's humanity and ends up as good as dead' reminds me of the words Jesus spoke, 'Those who find their life will lose it, and those who lose their life for my sake will find it' (Mt. 10.39 NRSV).

It is in walking the way of Jesus, in loving the poor and the needy at the expense of ourselves where we find our deepest humanity, where we are most like Christ and therefore the most human we could ever be.

21

Response to Ellie Hughes

Myrto Theocharous

Ellie Hughes's essay is extremely significant because it highlights the importance of self-perception among the women that she serves. I have seen this same element in my ministry when I have interacted with trafficked women. Of course, operations of rescue and opportunities for employment are invaluable, but they are often ineffective due to the low or completely distorted self-perception of these people. The personal affection, care and meaningful inclusion in the close circle of family, friends and church community is fundamental to the restoration of these souls. If they do not perceive themselves as genuinely loved and, most importantly, as sacred creation, they remain prone to abuse, manipulation and even self-destruction.

In my essay, I see the reverse problem of a distorted self-perception. The king of Tyre thought of himself in narcissistic terms, that is, as higher than others while on the contrary, the people we serve are made to think of themselves as lower than they are. Ezekiel shows that dehumanization occurs when people can no longer see their fellow humans as equals; thus, for Ezekiel, it is *not* the poor that are dehumanized. The one who views people as less than humans and himself as higher is the one who becomes 'dehumanized', that is, he loses something of his humanity. In this sense, I have used the word 'dehumanization' in a slightly different way than Ellie has.

Ellie mentions Gen. 1.26, 'Let us make humankind in our image', in order to show the communal being of God. This communion, also reflected in Gen. 2.18, 'It is not good for the man to be alone', argues against a human identity that is autonomous, self-sufficient and self-referential. This was the beginning of the king of Tyre's demise: he built his identity outside the sanctity of human and divine relationship and allowed his own intelligence and wealth production to be the determinative factor of his value and importance. His identity was exclusively self-referential and, in a paradoxical way, ended up 'removing' himself from the human race. For Ezekiel, a true Adam/human is one aware of his boundaries before God and of his responsibility towards others.

Ellie admits very honestly the existence of bleak moments. These are instances when we think change will never happen and it is the common experience of every social worker, activist and anyone who has dedicated their lives to the ministry of restoration. She uses Rom. 4.17 as her encouragement, reminding us that God 'gives life to the dead and calls into being things that were not'.

All of Christian history proceeds on this transcendent vision of restoration/resurrection. This vision is present in Ezekiel's vision of the valley of dry bones, as well as in most of the Old Testament prophets. There is something crucial about holding onto this 'irrational' inherited horizon of the dead living again and not succumbing to the acceptance of a world consisting of humans and dehumanized. I believe that it is extremely difficult, if not impossible, for us to work in the present for restoration and justice in the absence of a teleological, end-focused vision of the *fulfilment* of such restoration and justice.

22

The 'Undeserving Poor' in the Early Church

Fiona J. R. Gregson

The undeserving poor: A current debate

Following the 2008 economic crash and the UK 2010 election and in the lead up to 2015 UK elections, there was a lot of political rhetoric about 'strivers' and 'skivers', about those who deserved to receive from the benefit system and those who did not. Both Conservative and Labour language about those on benefits or affected by benefit cuts included references to or implied the idea of 'deserving' and 'undeserving', as Hannah Swithinbank's essay notes.

In the New Economics Foundation Blog, Stephen Reid highlights the use of 'striver' and 'skiver' language and questions the basis for such a distinction.[1] Chris Bowlby explores how to bring change in the welfare system and whether it is possible to distinguish between 'those who deserve help and those who do not',[2] while Ros Wynne-Jones, writing for the Joseph Rowntree Foundation, raises some of the ethical dilemmas for journalists writing about poverty and particularly about those who might be seen as 'undeserving'.[3] In these discussions, faith has been used to argue both for hard work and for provision for the poor.[4]

In *The Myth of the Undeserving Poor*, Charlesworth and Williams chart the re-emergence of the concept of the undeserving poor and note that both the numbers in poverty and negative attitudes towards those who are poor have increased.[5] They also highlight the increase in the number of people in work in poverty[6] and challenge the concept of the undeserving poor from a Christian perspective.

---

[1] Stephen Reid, 'Mythbusters: Strivers versus Skivers' http://tinyurl.com/ydb854ht (accessed February 2018).
[2] 'The Deserving or Undeserving Poor?' http://www.bbc.co.uk/news/magazine-11778284 (posted 18 November 2010, accessed July 2015).
[3] Ros Wynne-Jones, 'Deserving vs Undeserving', Joseph Rowntree Foundation (http://tinyurl.com/ycwolah3, accessed February 2018).
[4] 'The Deserving or Undeserving Poor'; and David Cameron, 'David Cameron's Easter Message to Christians' (https://www.premierchristianity.com/Topics/Society/Politics/David-Cameron-s-Easter-Message-to-Christians, accessed July 2015).
[5] Martin Charlesworth and Natalie Williams, *The Myth of the Undeserving Poor: A Christian Response to Poverty in Britain Today* (Tolworth: Grosvenor House, 2014).
[6] Charlesworth and Williams, *Myth*, 20.

To what extent are these ideas of 'strivers' and 'skivers' part of the biblical framework? Prov. 14.23 says, 'All hard work brings a profit, but mere talk leads only to poverty', yet it is easy enough to find passages that speak of other causes of poverty (Prov. 23.4-5), and the same chapter notes, 'It is a sin to despise one's neighbour, but blessed are those who are kind to the needy' (14.21). Similarly, in the New Testament (NT), there is a focus on giving to those in need: 'Sell your possessions and give to the poor' (Lk. 12.33); 'Go, sell everything you have and give to the poor' (Mk 10.21); 'All they asked was that we should continue to remember the poor, the very thing I had been eager to do all along' (Gal. 2.10); and 'It is more blessed to give than to receive' (Acts 20.35). Yet there are also verses where Paul encourages the Thessalonian Christians to 'mind your own business and work with your hands . . . so that you will be not be dependent on anybody' (1 Thess. 4.11-12) and gives that rule, 'Anyone who is unwilling to work shall not eat' (2 Thess. 3.10).

This essay considers whether the concept of the 'undeserving poor' is one that is present in the NT. It provides a brief overview of giving and poverty in the NT before considering three case studies, two where money is given to those in need (Acts 11.19-30; 2 Cor. 8–9) and one where limits are placed on provision (1 and 2 Thessalonians).

What about the NT?

Concern for the poor and provision for those in need is a key strand in NT thought.[7]

Jesus's teaching

Jesus, in his teaching, addresses those in need and encourages giving to those in need. In Lk. 4.18, Jesus announces that he has come 'to proclaim good news to the poor' and in the Sermon on the Mount teaches about giving to the needy, focusing on the how to do it, not whether to do it (Mt. 6.1-4). Jesus does not just encourage some people to give but praises the poor widow for giving (Lk. 21.1-4) as well as challenging the rich young ruler (Mk 10.17-22).

The Actions of Jesus and the Early Church

Giving to those in need is also seen in the actions of Jesus and the early church. One of the ways that Jesus and his disciples use the common purse is to provide for the poor (Jn 13.29).[8] The early church in Jerusalem, as they shared together, gave to those in need (Acts 2.45; 4.34) and responded when the Hellenistic widows were left out in the daily provision (Acts 6.1-7). We also find support being sent to Jerusalem for

---

[7] For more in depth studies of poverty/giving/money in the NT see Craig L. Blomberg, *Neither Poverty nor Riches: A Biblical Theology of Material Possessions*, NSBT (Leicester: Apollos, 1999); Ben Witherington III, *Jesus and Money* (London: SPCK, 2010); Martin Hengel, *Property and Riches in the Early Church* (London: SCM, 1974).

[8] Fiona J. R. Gregson, *Everything in Common? The Theology and Practice of the Sharing of Possession in Community in the New Testament* (Eugene, OR: Wipf & Stock, 2017), 9–10, 12–13.

the church community when they were affected by famine and other challenges (Acts 11.27-30; 1 Cor. 16.1-4; 2 Cor. 8–9; Rom. 16.1-4).[9]

The Letters

Similarly, the teaching in the letters includes concern for those in need. In Romans, Paul instructs his readers to share with those in need (12.13) and to feed their enemies (12.20). In Galatians, Paul has been asked to remember the poor (2.10) and then encourages the Galatians to 'do good to all people' (6.10). The Corinthians are encouraged to give generously to those in need, knowing God's provision for their giving (2 Corinthians 8–9). Paul expects Christians to care for those in need within their families and their church communities, but also limits those who should be put on the list of widows to receive (1 Tim. 5.4-16). James is concerned that his readers' actions match their faith in providing for those in need (2.14-17) and speaks against favouritism based on wealth (2.1-11) and oppression of workers (5.1-6).

Underlying many of these exhortations is an understanding of God's actions: for example, God's choice of the poor to be rich in faith (Jas 2.5), God's generosity and undeserved grace (2 Cor. 9.6-15; Rom. 12.1), and Jesus's grace and giving (2 Cor. 8.9).

What's expected?

The concern for those in need and encouragement to give does not seem in most instances to be dependent on whether those in need are deserving or undeserving, but on the presence of the need. However, there are examples where some sense of expectation of action is present. We have already mentioned the example of the widows in 1 Timothy 5. There is the example of the ἀτάκτοι (idle/disruptive) in the Thessalonian letters which we will look at later. Paul himself says that he works so that he is not a burden (1 Thess. 2.9) and encourages those who were formerly thieves to work so that they are able to share with those in need (Eph. 4.28).

A wider welcome

Charlesworth and Williams, in *The Myth of the Undeserving Poor*, point to NT passages which may not be directly about poverty or giving to the poor but which suggest an openness to those who would be seen as undeserving by others. For example, Jesus associates with the poor and values even those that others shun (Lk. 4.18; 5.27-32);[10] Jesus heals all the lepers, not simply the one who is thankful (Lk. 17.11-19);[11] and the landowner in Mt. 20.1-20 does not reject those who turn up later at the market place.[12]

It also seems probable that the question of blame for circumstances was a live issue at the time. In the instance of the tower of Siloam (Lk. 13.4-5) and the man

---

[9] As we will consider later, this giving is not simply because it is the church in Jerusalem but is due to their needs. Paul anticipates that such giving will occur in other directions (2 Cor. 8.14).

[10] Charlesworth and Williams, *Myth*, 2.

[11] Ibid., 86.

[12] Ibid., 62.

born blind (Jn 9.1-3), Jesus rejects the idea that their circumstances are caused by the individuals' actions. While Jesus is not speaking about poverty in either example, he is addressing areas where individuals at that time could be seen as being deserving of their circumstances.

Overview

Concern for and exhortation to care for the poor can be found throughout the NT. In most cases, the provision for those in need seems to be due to their need rather than their worthiness, although there are examples where limits are placed on those who are to receive. The majority of NT examples are about care within the Christian community rather than for those in need in general. However, there are passages that point to wider care for those in need. In Gal. 6.10, Paul encourages the Galatians, 'Let us do good to all people, especially to those who belong to the family of believers', and in 1 Thess. 5.15, 'Strive to do what is good for each other and for everyone else'.

Jesus's teaching is less specific about whether it is those inside or outside the group of Jesus-followers who are to receive. Jesus's command to love enemies (Mt. 5.44) might point to provision beyond the Christian community. The example of the early church beyond NT times suggests that the church's interpretation of these passages included care for those outside the Christian community. Emperor Julian notes, 'The impious Galileans support not only their poor but ours as well' (362 CE),[13] while Dionysius notes the way that Christians cared for the sick in the second great epidemic (c. 260 CE).[14]

We turn now to consider in more detail three examples of giving within the NT and to examine to what extent these include the concept of the 'undeserving poor'. In doing so, we will also explore how these examples compare to patterns in the surrounding cultures.[15]

Responding to famine: Acts 11.27-30

Here, the church in Antioch responds to a prediction of worldwide famine by sending a gift to the believers in Jerusalem. Given that the prediction was of widespread famine, we may wonder why the Antiochenes chose to provide assistance to the believers in Jerusalem rather than anywhere else. There are three reasons that the Antiochenes may have focused on Judaea as the recipients of their help.

First, they already had an existing link to Judaea and Jerusalem in particular. It was believers from Jerusalem who had first evangelized in Antioch (11.21).

---

[13] Julian the Apostate, *Letters* 3.22 (1923, *Works* vol. 3, 2–235; trans. W. C. Wright) (http://www.tertullian.org/fathers/julian_apostate_letters_1_trans.htm, accessed June 2016).

[14] Eusebius, *Hist. eccl.* 22.7 (http://www.ccel.org/ccel/schaff/npnf201.iii.xii.xxiii.html, accessed June 2016).

[15] In this we focus on Graeco-Roman culture, while acknowledging the continuity with the care for the poor in the Jewish tradition.

Secondly, the Antiochene church had an ongoing relationship with the believers in Jerusalem. This relationship started with the men of Cyprus and Cyrene, who first shared the faith (11.20), and continued with Barnabas being sent (11.22) and then the prophets who came (11.27). So the Antiochene believers would have known some of the Judaean believers and would also have been aware of their specific circumstances. The arrival of the prophets would have provided an update.

Thirdly, the believers in Jerusalem faced specific challenges which would have made them more vulnerable to food shortages. Some of these challenges were issues that affected Jerusalem and Judaea as a whole: the number of people who returned from the Diaspora to Jerusalem in their old age, the confiscation of land by Herod the Great, the increase in the number of large land holdings, the greed of high priestly families and high taxes and tithes.[16] It is also likely that a sabbath year was approaching, which would have exacerbated any other difficulties, particularly the food shortages mentioned earlier.[17]

Other challenges in Jerusalem were specific to those who followed Jesus. We have already noted the persecution and scattering out from Jerusalem. Those who remained may have faced ongoing persecution or, at the least, may not have been able to access help if they were seen in a negative light. They may have included people who had come from Galilee with Jesus (and those who had come for Pentecost and come to faith in Jesus) and had stayed in Jerusalem and therefore were away from their main occupation and would have found it more difficult to earn. Various scholars suggest that that the community of goods in Acts 2 and 4 may have depleted resources and created need.[18] However, Cassidy notes that Luke does not indicate that the community of goods led to the later need, and Finger argues that the community of goods may have actually helped the Jerusalem community survive in the surrounding challenges.[19]

The needs of the Jerusalem believers seem to be mainly due to the circumstance in which they find themselves. However, those who had come from outside Jerusalem could have chosen to go home.

The Antiochene believers, with their ongoing relationship with the believers in Judaea/Jerusalem, are probably aware of the specific challenges that the Jerusalem believers face, and, therefore, when they hear the prediction of famine, they know that the Jerusalem church will face particular difficulties and choose to send help to them. There is no mention of whether the believers in Jerusalem are deserving or undeserving, but rather, it is a response to a known need.

---

[16] S. E. Johnson, 'The Dead Sea Manual of Discipline and the Jerusalem Church of Acts', in *The Scrolls and the New Testament*, ed. Krister Stendahl (London: SCM, 1958), 129–42, here 133; Gerd Theissen, *Social Reality and the Early Christians* (Edinburgh: T&T Clark, 1992), 89–90; S. Guijarro, 'The Family in First-Century Galilee', in *Constructing Early Christian Families*, ed. Halvor Moxnes (London: Routledge, 1997), 42–65, here 43–46; Hengel, *Property*, 23.

[17] Joachim Jeremias, 'Sabbathjahr und neutestamentliche Chronologie', *ZNW* 27 (1928): 98–103, here 99.

[18] Richard J. Cassidy, *Society and Politics in the Acts of the Apostles* (Maryknoll, NY: Orbis, 1987), 29; F. F. Bruce, *The Book of Acts*, NICNT, 3rd edn (Grand Rapids, MI: Eerdmans, 1988), 101; Jacques Dupont, *The Salvation of the Gentiles* (New York: Paulist, 1979), 94.

[19] Cassidy, *Society*, 29; Reta Halteman Finger, *Of Widows and Meals* (Grand Rapids, MI: Eerdmans, 2007), 140.

The Antiochene believers respond to the need they see and provide help. In Acts 11.29 each of them gives 'as they are able' (καθὼς εὐπορεῖτο *kathōs euporeito*), and there is an element of individual decision ('each of them', ἕκαστος αὐτῶν *hekastos autōn*). However, the verb 'decide' here is in the plural (ὥρισαν *hōrisan*), suggesting that while there are individual contributions to the collection, it is seen as a *corporate* venture. Further, when at this point Luke writes about the Antiochene believers sending the gift to Jerusalem, he calls them 'disciples' (μαθητῶν *mathētōn*), which might indicate that Luke saw such provision as being key to learning to follow/being discipled by Jesus.

The Antiochenes then entrust the gift to Barnabas and Saul – so it is clearly seen as an important task, as it would have taken two key teachers away from the community for some time. Barnabas and Saul then take the gift and hand it over to the elders in Jerusalem, who presumably then decide how it is used.

Having considered how the Antiochenes respond to the prediction of famine, we now turn to examine whether they respond to the prediction of famine just as any other Graeco-Roman community would have, or were there ways in which their response was distinctively Christian? To discern the answer to this question, we will compare the example of the Antiochene church to how the Graeco-Roman world responded to famine.

Food crises were an ongoing issue in the Roman Empire and, therefore, strategies were developed to respond in times of need. Outside Rome, usually an individual or a group of individuals would be appointed as the *curator annonae* to be responsible for subsidizing the grain market.[20] In return, they would receive honour: they might receive titles, or a monument might be erected in their honour.[21] Sometimes, money might be distributed. For example, in Oenoanda, an inscription notes that the town clerk 'gave a distribution in money to each of the citizens – ten denarii'.[22]

When we compare the Graeco-Roman response to famine to how the Antiochene believing community responded to famine, we see a number of differences. First, the focus in appointing a *curator annonae* is not necessarily those in need. The poorest may well have been unable to buy the subsidized grain. While in the Oenoanda example, money is provided to individuals, it is provided to citizens who may well have been better off to begin with. Also, the way that the appointment of a *curator annonae* worked would mean that the incentive of honour was one of the attractions of providing in this way. In contrast, while the Antiochene believers' actions are noted in Acts 11.29, there does not seem to be the same expectation or receipt of titles and honour for their actions, and the main focus seems to be the need of the believers in Jerusalem. Secondly, the Antiochene believers do not simply choose one or two richer believers to provide the gift; rather, each of them is involved as they are able. Thus, the focus of the giving is more specifically the needs of the community, and giving in response to need is seen as something for each person to participate in.

[20] Bruce W. Winter, 'Acts and Food Shortages', in *The Book of Acts in its Graeco-Roman Setting*, ed. David W. J. Gill and Conrad Gempf, BAFCS 2 (Grand Rapids, MI: Eerdmans, 1994), 59–78, here 72–74.
[21] A. R. Hands, *Charities and Social Aid in Greece and Rome* (London: Thames & Hudson, 1968), 42–43, 53.
[22] *IGRP* III 493.

Plenty supplying need: 2 Corinthians 8–9

In 2 Corinthians 8–9, Paul writes to persuade the Corinthians to contribute to the gift for the church in Jerusalem/Judaea. The fact that Paul organizes a collection for the church in Jerusalem suggests that the initial community of goods in Jerusalem and the gift from Antioch did not enable the Jerusalem believers to provide for themselves and they continued to be in need. While Rom. 15.27 indicates Jewish believers in Jerusalem were owed this help by Gentile believers elsewhere, the Corinthian church included Jewish believers (Acts 18.1-8), so it is not just a gift from Gentiles to Jewish Christians. In addition, Paul emphasizes that the gift is voluntary and to supply need (8.8, 13-14). He also anticipates that in the future, plenty in Jerusalem might provide for the Corinthians (8.14).

Paul spends chapters 8 and 9 encouraging the Corinthians to give and explaining why and how they should give. Paul has already written to the Corinthians about the collection (1 Cor. 16.1-4) and he now writes to encourage them to finish the work they started (2 Cor. 8.11).

The example of the Macedonians

He begins with the example of the Macedonians who give in the midst of trials and poverty (8.2) and also give beyond their ability (8.3). Paul sees the Macedonians as rich in generosity (8.2, 13) and encourages the Corinthians to be wealthy in the grace of generosity (8.7).[23] Paul crafts his words carefully not only to encourage the Corinthians to participate but also to prompt their contribution to be freely given. He reminds them of their own desire to participate and by using 'to complete' (ἐπιτελέω *epiteleō*) Paul 'evokes the image of a benefactor who fulfils an obligation'.[24]

The example of Jesus

The ultimate example that Paul gives the Corinthians is that of Jesus and his grace in becoming poor for their sakes. The Macedonians gave beyond their ability (8.3), Jesus gave – becoming poor (8.9); however, Paul limits himself to encouraging the Corinthians to give according to what they have but not necessarily beyond that (8.12). Paul reassures the Corinthians that his aim is not to impoverish them or for them to suffer hardship (8.13),[25] but rather for equality[26] and relief from need. The Corinthians' plenty will supply the need in Jerusalem, and in due course, the plenty of those in Jerusalem will supply the Corinthians' need (8.14). Paul's reference to gathering manna speaks of each person having sufficient even though they gathered different amounts

---

[23] John M. G. Barclay, 'Because He Was Rich He Became Poor' (unpublished paper), 14.

[24] Jerry W. McCant, *2 Corinthians*, Readings (Sheffield: Sheffield Academic, 1999), 82.

[25] Murray J. Harris, *The Second Epistle to the Cornthians*, NIGTC (Grand Rapids, MI: Eerdmans, 2005), 589.

[26] Ernest Best, *Second Corinthians*, Int (Louisville: John Knox, 1987), 79.

(8.15), but may also remind the Corinthians not to hoard their plenty in the same way that manna could not be hoarded.[27]

Generosity based on God's generosity

As well as focusing on the Corinthians providing for what the Jerusalemites need, Paul is clear that the gift should not be given grudgingly (9.7). Paul's focus is less on the worthiness of the Jerusalemites and more on their need and the Christian imperative to be generous. Paul reminds the Corinthians of God's generosity and of the way that God provides for them to be generous (9.6-12) and is the ultimate provider,[28] so thanks is given to *God* rather than the Corinthians for the gift (9.12).

Paul's exhortation indicates that Christian giving and sharing is rooted in grace (8.1, 4, 6; 9.8, 14), is core to being a Christian (9.13), is rooted in Jesus and his example (8.9), provides for those in need (8.13-14), is voluntary (8.7, 8; 9.5, 7), involves generosity based in God's grace and provision (8.1, 9; 9.8), is active and practical (8.11), involves everyone (8.12; 9.7; see also 1 Cor. 16.2), is in relation to what they have (8.12), is relational and has relational effects (9.14), has potential reciprocity (8.13-14) and has God at the centre as the ultimate benefactor (9.8-15).[29]

Paul, as he writes to the Corinthians, uses patronage and benefaction language in his description of the collection.[30] In addition, Paul's refusal of support from the Corinthians (2 Cor. 11.9) is probably because he does not want to be seen as a client of the Corinthians and constrained to limit his preaching to that which will please them.[31] It, therefore, seems likely that the Corinthians would have seen the collection in terms of patronage/benefaction.

While Paul uses benefaction language, and there are some similarities between the giving that Paul encourages and patronage/benefaction, there are significant differences. First, Paul subverts patronage/benefaction expectations by bringing God into the equation as the supreme benefactor[32] who is the person to be thanked rather than the Corinthians for the gift, making it a three-way relationship. This contrasts with the expectation in patronage relationships that thanks and honour should be returned to the giver (Seneca, *Ben.* 2.35.1).

Secondly, Paul focuses on the need of the recipients (8.14), while in *De Beneficiis*, Seneca emphasizes that it is important to choose the right recipients:[33] those who will

---

27 Best, *Second*, 80; Kar Yong Lim, 'Generosity from Pauline Perspective: Insights from Paul's Letter to the Corinthians', *ERT* 37 (2013): 20–33, here 28.
28 Harris, *Second*, 646.
29 Ibid., 638.
30 McCant, *Corinthians*, 99; F. Danker, *Benefactor: Epigraphic Study of a Graeco-Roman and New Testament Semantic Field* (St Louis: Clayton, 1982), 320–62; David E. Aune, 'In Search of a Profile of the "Benefactor" (review of Frederick W. Danker, Benefactor: Epigraphic Study of a Graeco-Roman and New Testament Semantic Field)', Int 38 (1984) 421–25, here 424.
31 Craig S. Keener, *1–2 Corinthians*, NCBC (Cambridge: Cambridge University Press, 2005), 202; Ben Witherington III, *Conflict and Community in Corinth* (Grand Rapids, MI: Eerdmans, 1995), 413.
32 McCant, *Corinthians*, 96–99; Gary W. Griffith, 'Abounding in Generosity. A Study of Charis in 2 Corinthians 8–9' (PhD thesis, Durham University, 2005), 72.
33 G. W. Peterman, *Paul's Gift from Philippi. Conventions of Gift Exchange and Christian Giving*, SNTSMS 92 (Cambridge: Cambridge University Press, 1997), 67.

show gratitude (*Ben.* 1.1.2; 1.10.4) and who are worthy (*Ben.* 4.35.2–36.2)[34] but not necessarily those in need.

Thirdly, Paul encourages them all to participate in the giving rather than simply those who are more well-off.

Boundaries and expectations: 1 and 2 Thessalonians

Our third example is that of the ἄτακτοι *ataktoi*/those living ἀτάκτως *ataktōs*, whom Paul addresses in 1 and 2 Thessalonians. The Greek words are usually translated as 'the idle'/'those living idly', but they have a wider meaning which includes the idea of being disruptive, disorderly or standing against good order or out of line in battle ranks.[35] Does Paul see them as 'undeserving poor'?

The main passages where Paul addresses the issue about the *ataktoi*/those living *ataktōs* are 1 Thess. 5.14-15 and 2 Thess. 3.6-13. We will also look at 1 Thess. 4.9-12 as Paul addresses work in that section. Let us see what we can find out about the situation.

In 1 Thess. 4.9-12, Paul praises the Thessalonians for their love before responding to the issue. He links their love for one another to leading a quiet life, minding their own business and working with their hands. 'To have an ambition' (φιλοτιμεῖσθαι *philotimeisthai*) was used of political ambition and seeking honour (Philo, *Rewards* 11),[36] so it is an unusual word to use with 'to live quietly' (ἡσυχάζειν *hēsuchazein*). Paul goes on to instruct them to 'be concerned with your own affairs' (πράσσειν τὰ ἴδια *prassein ta idia*). The phrase is used in contrast with being a busybody (Plato, *Resp.* 433AB) and was used in the sense of affairs appropriate to the person.

The background to Paul's instructions may well be patronage, and Paul appears to be instructing the Thessalonians to seek to mind their own affairs rather than those of a patron and to make it their ambition to work quietly with their own hands rather than to make it their ambition to gain through patronage relationships.

Paul encourages them to work with their hands (although the idiom can refer to work in general),[37] so that they may have right relationships with the community outside and 'you may have need of nothing/no-one' (μηδενὸς χρείαν ἔχητε). 'Need' (χρείαν *chreian*) usually takes a thing rather than a person as its object.[38] This, together with Paul's example of sharing himself (1 Thess. 2.7-8), indicates that Paul does not intend this to be independence from every person. The lack of nothing could be individual, but it could also be collective, particularly as the verb is plural.[39]

---

[34] Seneca does instruct his readers that what is given should fit what the receiver might need. However, it is not in terms of the person receiving being in particular need; rather, it is about not giving something that is unwanted.

[35] David J. Williams, *1 and 2 Thessalonians*, NIBC 12 (Peabody, MA: Hendrickson, 1992), 96.

[36] Abraham J. Malherbe, *The Letters to the Thessalonians*, AB 32B (New York: Doubleday, 2000), 246; B. Rigaux, *Saint Paul: Les Épitres aux Thessaloniciens* (Paris: Lecoffre, 1956), 520.

[37] Earl J. Richard, *First and Second Thessalonians*, SP 11 (Collegeville, MN: Liturgical, 2007), 220.

[38] Williams, *Thessalonians*, 78.

[39] Robert Jewett, 'Tenement Churches and Communal Meals in the Early Church: the Implications of a Form-Critical Analysis of 2 Thessalonians 3.10', *BR* 38 (1993), 23–43, here 42; Reidar Aasgaard, *'My Beloved Brothers and Sisters!' Christian Siblingship in Paul* (London: T&T Clark, 2004), 165.

Later in the letter, having encouraged the Thessalonians to treat their leaders well (1 Thess. 5.12-13), Paul instructs the Thessalonians to admonish the *ataktoi*. Paul goes on to encourage them to avoid repaying evil with evil and to pursue good to each other and to all (5.15). The word Paul uses for pursuing 'good' (ἀγαθός *agathos*) has benefaction connotations,[40] and such good is to be done to outsiders as well as others in the congregation.

In 2 Thessalonians, Paul spends more time addresses the issue around the *ataktoi* (idle/disruptive) (2 Thess. 3.6-13)[41] and is sharper in his tone, commanding the believers to keep away from them. Paul contrasts the actions of these people with his own actions while he was with the Thessalonians and the way he and his companions worked and toiled so they would not be a burden despite the fact they had the right to help (3.8-9). He also reminds the Thessalonians of the rule he gave them while he was with them: 'Anyone who is unwilling to work shall not eat' (3.10). The present tense of the verb 'to work' indicates a habitual refusal to work[42] and the imperative (shall not eat) indicates that the community had the capacity to withhold food.[43] This suggests that the community was regularly eating together.

Paul identifies the ἄτακτοι as 'busybodies' (περιεργαζομένοι *periergazomenoi*), a word used of people concerning themselves with affairs that are not their own (Polybius, *His.* 18.51.2) and of correcting others but not one's own behaviour (Plutarch, *Mor.* 516A).

Paul addresses these disruptive people directly, instructing them to work quietly and eat their own bread. Paul goes on to encourage the Thessalonians to 'never tire of doing what is good (καλοποιέω *kalopoieō*)', again using a word which was used in benefaction. Paul's instruction is not just a call to keep out of trouble, but rather an expectation of 'doing good which benefitted the lives of others'.[44]

What led the *ataktoi* to be disruptive and idle? One suggestion is that some Thessalonians expected Jesus to return imminently and therefore did not see any point in working, or thought that the most important activity in such a situation was evangelism. While Paul addresses both issues in the two letters, he does so separately and does not link the issues.[45] Rather, he links the idea of work to love within the community.[46] If Jesus's return (the parousia) was the issue at hand, we might expect Paul to have said, 'All must work right up to the parousia', or 'All must work because the parousia might not come as soon as you suppose.'[47] It is possible that some Thessalonians may have felt that manual work was inappropriate for them now that

---

[40] Bruce W. Winter, *Seek the Welfare of the City: Christians as Benefactors and Citizens* (Grand Rapids, MI: Eerdmans, 1994), 35, 42.

[41] We are working on the basis that 2 Thessalonians is Pauline and was written after 1 Thessalonians (Gregson, 'Everything', 217–19).

[42] Leon Morris, *The First and Second Epistles to the Thessalonians*, NICNT (Grand Rapids, MI: Eerdmans, 1984), 254.

[43] Morris, *Epistles*, 255.

[44] Winter, *Welfare*, 57.

[45] Gordon D. Fee, *The First and Second Letters to the Thessalonians*, NICNT (Grand Rapids, MI: Eerdmans, 2009) 324; Malherbe, *Letter* 254; Ben Witherington III, *1 and 2 Thessalonians A Socio-Rhetorical Commentary* (Grand Rapids, MI: Eerdmans, 2006), 245.

[46] Charles A. Wanamaker, *The Epistles to the Thessalonians*, NIGTC (Grand Rapids, MI: Eerdmans, 1990), 162.

[47] A. L. Moore, *1 and 2 Thessalonians*, NCB (London: Nelson, 1969), 118.

they had freedom in Christ,[48] as only intellectual work was seen as appropriate for free men.[49]

Patronage may have lain behind the issue. We have seen how a number of the words Paul uses point to a patronage background to the issues around the situation of the *ataktoi*.[50] Paul encourages the Thessalonians to acts of benefaction (1 Thess. 4.12; 5.15; 2 Thess. 3.13)[51] in contrast to concerning themselves with the affairs of a patron (1 Thess. 4.11). It seems likely that the *ataktoi* presumed they could be dependent on a patron in return for concerning themselves with the patron's affairs. The *ataktoi* may have been looking for patrons within the Christian community[52] to avoid compromising their faith by being required to fulfill the expectations of a non-Christian patron.[53] They may have found it more difficult to find or continue with their work once they became Christians because of how they were perceived and, therefore, looked for support.[54] Paul is concerned about the Thessalonian believers' witness through their actions and thus encourages them to do good, in effect encouraging them to be patrons rather than to depend on patrons.

It is clear from Paul's letters to the Thessalonians that the Thessalonians have close familial relationships where they love and share with one another, with Paul and with believers further afield (1 Thess. 4.10). However, there is the issue of those who seem to be choosing to be dependent on others and disruptive. Paul praises the Thessalonians' love and sharing and uses love as the basis for encouraging work and placing boundaries on the sharing that is taking place. It seems likely that Paul's call not to be a burden is both individual and communal and that the call to benefaction encompasses the whole community.

While Paul uses patronage and benefaction language, his expectations are different from normal patronage expectations. First, the focus on work and not being a burden is different from patronage, where there was an expectation of being able to receive food and/or money from a patron. Secondly, who the benefactors are is different. Paul encourages all the Thessalonians to acts of benefaction rather than just a few, both within the community and then to outsiders in blessing.

Conclusion

We have seen in both the general overview of the NT and in the specific examples the way that concern for the poor is a key strand in NT thought. It is there in Jesus's

[48] Beverly R. Gaventa, *First and Second Thessalonians*, Int (Louisville: John Knox, 1998), 59.
[49] Ernest Best, *The First and Second Letter to the Thessalonians*, BNTC (London: A&C Black, 1972), 338.
[50] While Paul does not use the word 'client', this may be because it could be seen as being demeaning (Richard P. Saller, *Personal Patronage under the Early Empire* (Cambridge: Cambridge University Press, 1982), 9).
[51] David A. deSilva, *Honor, Patronage, Kinship and Purity. Unlocking New Testament Culture* (Downers Grove, IL: IVP, 2000), 147; Bruce W. Winter, 'If a Man Does Not Wish to Work . . .' *TynBul* 40 (1989): 303–15, here 314–15.
[52] Ronald Russell, 'The Idle in 2 Thess. 3.6–12: Eschatological or a Social Problem?', *NTS* 34 (1988): 105–19, here 112–13.
[53] Witherington, *Thessalonians*, 249.
[54] Peter Oakes, *Philippians From People to Letter*, SNTSMS 110 (Cambridge: Cambridge University Press, 2001), 90–92; Blomberg, *Poverty*, 180.

teaching; in the actions of Jesus, his disciples and the early church; and in the letters. The concern for the poor and provision for them is not generally based on whether those receiving deserve it, but on the existence of need, on the relationships between those involved and on God's action, grace and generosity.

While most NT examples are of care within the Christian community, there are pointers to care and provision for those outside the Christian community and this is borne out by the example of the actions of the church after the first century.

Giving in response to need has a greater emphasis in the NT tradition in comparison with Graeco-Roman culture. While Seneca is concerned with finding worthy recipients of gifts and a *curator annonae* would be concerned about honour and would not necessarily focus on those most in need, the NT witness repeatedly focuses on need as a reason for giving.

Giving takes place in situations of ongoing need and there is not necessarily an expectation that recipients will find their feet. With the church in Jerusalem, we see an ongoing situation of need – where the local church responds, then the church in Antioch and then a wider collection.

However, there are examples of *boundaries in giving* and providing for those in need. We have mentioned the widows in 1 Timothy, where there is an expectation that only those in particular need and without any other recourse would receive, and therefore an expectation that families would provide where they were able to do so. The position of 'widow' on the list also appears to be a specific ministry position rather than simply a way to help widows. There is also an underlying concern for the way widows in this ministry position reflected on the church.[55] In 2 Thessalonians, there is an expectation that individuals who are able to work will work (and presumably contribute and participate). It seems likely that those Paul labels *ataktoi* were not simply lazy, but that there were a mix of cultural and theological reasons why they were not working – it is quite possible that the ἄτακτοι thought they were doing the right thing. Paul writes to correct their misunderstanding and to encourage the community as a whole to work to support themselves and to continue to do good to those within the community and beyond.

There is, therefore, for those within the Christian community an expectation of participation in and contribution to the community where possible. More widely, giving and sharing are seen as key parts of being Christian disciples. In our overview of the NT and our case studies, we saw that there is a call on all Christians to be involved in giving, doing good and providing (patronage/benefaction) for those in need, even if they are not rich. This contrasts with patron-client expectations within the Graeco-Roman world where patronage expectations were usually of those who were more affluent, and also with the practice of the *curator annonae*. This call to all Christians to behave as patrons subverts the usual expectations of hierarchy. Together with Paul's emphasis on equality (2 Cor. 8.14), it suggests an equalising of relationships.

Underlying this subversion of the patronage system is the vision of God as the ultimate benefactor, and it is God's generosity that enables and provides for his people

---

[55] Thomas C. Oden, *First and Second Timothy and Titus*, Int (Louisville: John Knox, 1989), 153–8.

to be generous. Paul reminds the Corinthians of the way that God provides so that they are able to be generous (2 Cor. 9.6-15).

In conclusion, the NT does not, in general, support the concept of the 'undeserving poor'. In fact, the NT focuses on provision in response to need more strongly than the Graeco-Roman culture of the time. There are examples of boundaries on giving and on who is to receive and there may a possible link with the idea of the 'undeserving poor' is in the situation of the ἀτάκτοι in 1 and 2 Thessalonians with the expectation that they will not behave as clients. However, this is also about wanting the Thessalonians not to be concerned with the affairs of a patron rather than God. Within the NT there is also a wider call to participate in giving and sharing based on God's example and generosity rather than the status of the person to whom one is giving.

23

The 'Undeserving Poor' Today: The Rhetoric and Theological Development of a Problematic Category

Hannah Swithinbank

Introduction

What is poverty? Why do people find themselves living in poverty? What does it mean to be living in poverty and to be deserving or undeserving of support from your neighbours and fellow citizens – or to be thought to be so? Do we think of and talk about people as being the 'undeserving poor' today, and what does this kind of labelling do to our understanding of poverty and of people living in poverty – and what does it do to our society? These are all big questions, probably too big for one essay.

In this essay, I shall explore the way that we currently talk about poverty and the people who live in it, looking at one recent political debate to provide focus. I shall suggest that we do indeed have a concept of deserving and undeserving poor, one in which the ability to work is fundamental within an understanding of society that sees it as unfair for those who contribute to have to support those who do not. I shall then explore some of the consequences of this rhetoric in a world where poverty is complex and briefly suggest that the story of the Bible presents the church with an alternative perspective to which it could give a constructive public voice in our contemporary conversations about helping people out of poverty.

Definitions

To begin, it is worth briefly offering some definitions. First, *poverty*. We must begin by saying that it is probably impossible to define poverty simply, for the moment that any simple definition comes into contact with the experiences of those living in poverty, its inadequacy becomes clear and we start to feel the need to adjust it to encompass what we see and what people tell us about their lives. We may perhaps best describe poverty as *lack*. But lack of *what*? Here is a non-comprehensive list: money, food and water, housing, education, health, freedom, independence, dignity, community, power, hope.[1] A lack of any of the above – either absolute or relative to those among whom you live – may contribute to impoverishment. Tearfund, for whom I work, describe poverty in the following terms:

> Poverty is holistic: it is not just economic or physical but is also social, environmental and spiritual. It is complex and multi-faceted. The root cause of poverty is broken relationships which entered the world as a result of humanity's rebellion against God. At this time, we moved from a life of wholeness, living in perfect relationship with God, creation, ourselves and each other, into a life of broken relationships, broken off from God, family and community, broken off from others further removed from us (different communities, cultures or countries) – and even from ourselves, as a result of false images of identity and self-worth.[2]

In this, too, poverty is a *lack*, with the spiritual aspect of this lack clearly and specifically identified as the fundamental loss of relationship with a loving Creator God.

What might it mean to deserve to be poor?

To start with the above theological understanding of poverty, it might mean thinking that we all *deserve* some kind of poverty. If all have sinned and fall short of the glory of God, then perhaps we all deserve to live with the lack of that relationship and with the poverty that follows, in any or all of its aspects as they afflict us. Biblically, I suggest this is not quite the whole picture: the narrative in the Bible presents poverty as the consequence of the broken relations arising from human sin and the fall, and that this affects the whole of creation, separating us from God and damaging the way that we live together. We see this begin in Gen. 3.16-19, where God's pronouncement over Adam and Eve as he sends them out of the garden describes a brokenness in their relationships with God, each other and with the earth that will make it impossible to flourish as God intended. The world becomes a place where brother kills brother (Genesis 4) and where, as God says, 'The poor will be with you always' (Deut. 15.11).

Yet the narrative arc of the Bible presents God as a God on a mission to redeem his creation, reaching out to humanity and the wider creation which he loves in order to overcome the fall. We see this in the calling of Abraham (Genesis 12) and the establishment of the Israelites as God's people, and in the promise, the coming and the life, death and resurrection of Christ, which makes restoration to God possible.[3] That

---

[1] Helpful reflections on the nature of poverty include Steve Corbett and Brian Fikkert, *When Helping Hurts: How to Alleviate Poverty without Hurting the Poor . . . and Yourself* (Chicago: Moody, 2014), 51–68; Bryant Myers, 'Progressive Pentecostalism, Development, and Christian Development NGOs: a Challenge and an Opportunity', *International Bulletin of Mission Research* 39.3 (2015) 115–20.

[2] Tearfund, 'Overcoming Poverty Together' (internal document, 2012).

[3] See, e.g., Isa. 53, where verse 5 describes the Messiah as the restorer of *shalom*; Jn 1.1-14 and 14.6, which describe Jesus as coming to show humanity the way to the Father; and Eph. 2.1-10, in which Paul describes our salvation in Christ. For fuller discussion, see Christopher J. H. Wright, *The Mission of God* (Downers Grove, IL: IVP, 2006), 53–5, 62–6; N. T. Wright, *The New Testament*

God desires his people to flourish, free from oppression and injustice, can be seen in the exodus from Egypt and the final (long-delayed) establishment of the nation of Israel. What this should look like can be seen in the laws of Israel, particularly the Jubilee laws and the voices of the prophets, which call Israel to live in ways in which their love for the Lord their God goes hand in hand with their love for their neighbours.[4] In the synagogue in Nazareth, Jesus declares himself as the one who will bring this Jubilee and open the way to the Father through his death and resurrection.[5] He comes 'to reconcile to himself all things whether things on earth or things in heaven',[6] an act that will cumulate in the new heaven and new earth (Revelation 21).

Poverty may be a consequence of sin, but regardless of whether we really deserve to be poor or to be redeemed and lifted out of this situation or not, the Bible tells us that this is what God is doing.

In the day-to-day, however, defining poverty as *lack* means that to deserve poverty is to lack through some fault of one's own. This fault or failing, whatever it is, is then taken to mean that a person is undeserving of support because it would be a misuse of resources that would very likely go to waste. This assumes that people, fundamentally, do not change and have forfeited trust through their failure. The removal of support might be from government and taxpayers, from civil society bodies such as charities or churches, and even from immediate neighbours, friends and family.

However, *what* constitutes this kind of fault? What is considered a great enough personal failure to make a person undeserving? In their work *The Myth of the Undeserving Poor*, Martin Charlesworth and Natalie Williams discuss the evolution of the categorization of the poor in Victorian England through the administration of the Poor Laws: children, the aged and infirm, and the genuinely unemployed were to be given opportunities and relief, while the work-shy were to be given harsh corrective treatment in order to encourage them to change their wilful idleness.[7] Ideas have staying power – and the authors argue that this idea of an undeserving poor has never fully gone away. But what does this category look like now?

The rhetoric

In order to try and focus my discussion in what is a very large body of discourse about people living in poverty, both nationally and internationally, I have chosen to look

---

and the People of God (London: SPCK, 2013), 139–43; Craig Bartholomew and Michael Goheen, *The Drama of Scripture* (London: SPCK, 2014); and Kevin J. Vanhoozer, *The Drama of Doctrine* (Louisville, KY: Westminster John Knox, 2005), who uses the metaphor of a drama in a number of acts to illuminate this.

4 Leviticus 25 lays out the jubilee land laws. The fact that the jubilee is declared on the Day of Atonement connects Israel's restored relationship with God to the essential importance of restoring relationships with each other and with the land in which they live by allowing it to rest. See also Isa. 56.1 and 58 on the importance of pursuing justice; and Jeremiah 34, which explicitly references how, in a Jubilee year, the Hebrew aristocracy freed their slaves but then promptly re-enslaved them. The prophet directly connects the fall of Jerusalem and the exile in Babylon to Israel's failure to uphold the Jubilee and seek justice as the Lord had commanded.

5 Lk. 4.14-22; Jn 3.13-18; 5.24-27; 6.44-59.

6 Col. 1.20.

7 Martin Charlesworth and Natalie Williams, *The Myth of the Undeserving Poor: A Christian Response to Poverty in Britain Today* (London: Grosvenor House, 2014). section 2.1.

primarily at the discourse that surrounds the ongoing passage of the Welfare Reform and Work Bill through the UK Parliament in 2015. Of course, the joy of doing this is that the debate is ongoing and the proposals in question may change during it, and continue to do so after a paper is drafted or presented! However, as my focus is primarily on the rhetoric about the people and society affected by the proposals rather than on the proposals themselves, I hope that my analysis still holds.

The debate is still large – but I have tried to look at both the parliamentary debate (through *Hansard*) and the way both politicians and news media (especially print) have talked about the bill to the general public and electorate, and to look at a cross section.

I hope to draw out some of the key ideas that underpin the discussion about people who live in poverty. What this will reveal, I think, is a common framing in which some deserve support and some do not, and in which the arbiter of this status is whether or not a person contributes to society and whether, if they do not, this is through a genuine inability to do so, or not. Whether this understanding emerged with politicians, media or the general public is something of a chicken-and-egg question (and perhaps worthy of a hefty historical discourse analysis), but it currently seems to be seen by the majority of politicians and media as either undesirable or unproductive to challenge.

The debate has focused on the importance of ending in-work poverty and of work as the best way out of poverty. The key ambition (and catchphrase) for the current government is that Britain should become a 'high-wage, lower-tax, lower-welfare country'. This is a phrase used by Iain Duncan Smith in the parliamentary debates,[8] by the then-Prime Minister David Cameron in a speech in July, and it is the strong implication of George Osborne's comment piece in *The Guardian* on 19 July.[9] This is Duncan Smith's argument:

> In conclusion, ours is an approach that continues to provide a generous safety net and support for those who need it and expects people to face the same choices as those in work and not on benefits. At its heart, it is about moving from a low-wage, high-tax, high-welfare country, to a high-wage, lower-tax, lower-welfare country.[10]

There are certain ideological assumptions in this statement, specifically: earning more is good, paying more tax is bad, having a high welfare bill is bad. I do not want to get into an assessment of the ideology here – but I want to note its existence, as I think it has an effect on the way we talk about poverty and who deserves and does not deserve our support. There is, for example, a distinction made, as George Osborne did in a

---

[8] 'Welfare Reform and Work Bill: First Reading', 9 July 2015 (http://www.publications.parliament.uk/pa/cm201516/cmhansrd/cm150709/debtext/150709-0002.htm#15070957000011, accessed February 2018); 'Welfare Reform and Work Bill: Second Reading', 20 July 2015 http://www.publications.parliament.uk/pa/cm201516/cmhansrd/cm150720/debtext/150720-0002.htm#column_1256, accessed February 2018).

[9] Dan Bloom, 'Fears over Cameron's Tax Credits Raid That Would "Consign Workers to Poverty"', *Daily Mirror*, 22 June 2015; George Osborne, 'Calling All Progressives: Help Us Reform the Welfare State', *The Guardian*, 19 July 2015.

[10] 'Welfare Reform and Work Bill: First Reading', section 491.

piece for the *Guardian* in July, between *public services* (such as the NHS or schools) and *welfare* (i.e. benefits) which makes ideological claims about the role of the state, the support it should give and to whom. As he wrote, 'Furthermore, anyone who cares about well-funded public services such as the NHS and schools knows we have to control the costs of a welfare system that has become unsustainable and risks crowding out other areas of government spending.'[11]

Working or not?

In terms of who among people living in poverty is deserving and undeserving of government support, the primary divide is clearly between people working or actively seeking work and people not working. There is a general consensus that work is good and the best route out of poverty. This is Iain Duncan Smith in the child poverty debate: 'I believe work is the best route out of poverty. It provides purpose, responsibility and role models for our children.'[12] In the second reading of the Welfare Reform and Work Bill, the Labour MP Stephen Timms said, 'We stand for the right to work and the responsibility to work.'[13]

Connected with this is the idea that wages should be sufficient for those in work to live on – and acknowledgement of the fact that they are not is a factor in people remaining in unemployment (probably not an argument many would dispute). Thus, George Osborne: 'We are saying to working people: our new national living wage will ensure you get a decent day's pay, but there are going to be fewer taxpayer-funded benefits.'[14] Similarly, Iain Duncan Smith: 'Work is the best route out of poverty, and being in work should always pay more than being on benefits',[15] and Stephen Timms, in a continuation of the statement quoted above: 'We believe in making work pay so that people are always better off in work . . . work is the best route out of poverty.'[16]

Deserving or not?

Despite this divide, there are categories of people who are acknowledged as not working for valid reasons, and it is assumed and argued that these people deserve our support. As George Osborne wrote, 'We will protect the most vulnerable – disabled people, pensioners, who cannot change their circumstances, and those most in need.'[17] Similarly Iain Duncan Smith argues, 'Spending on the main disability benefits . . . will be higher in every single year to 2020 compared with 2010. Our commitment to protecting the most vulnerable is why we have protections in place on policies such

---

[11] Osborne, 'Calling All Progressives'.
[12] 'Child Poverty Debate', *Publications.Parliament.Uk*, 1 July 2015 (http://www.publications. parliament.uk/pa/cm201516/cmhansrd/cm150701/debtext/150701-0002.htm#column_1505, accessed February 2018). He continued to talk about the importance of education as preparation for work by providing skills for employment.
[13] 'Welfare Reform and Work Bill: Second Reading'.
[14] Osborne, 'Calling All Progressives'.
[15] 'Welfare Reform and Work Bill: Second Reading'.
[16] Ibid.
[17] Osborne, 'Calling All Progressives'.

as the benefit cap.'[18] Children are also on the list of those worthy of support, and ways of ending child poverty – including understanding what this looks like and how we measure it – have a debate of their own.

So, among the deserving are children, pensioners and those who are unable to work because of disability or chronic ill-health. One might categorize those who are 'deserving' as those experiencing personal misfortune, be it inevitable (age) or accidental (disability) – or more politely, those who do not have the capability to work. And the undeserving? Those who could work, but do not.

Fair or not?

Let us turn back to Osborne's argument for higher wages and fewer benefits: it includes an implicit argument that argument that it is 'ridiculous' for those not in work to receive more income in benefits than someone in work does from their wage – it is not fair.[19] He is not alone – and fairness is a major theme in the discussion about supporting people living in poverty. Thus, Stephen Timms: 'We believe in controlling the costs of social security so that it is fair on the working people who pay for it and so that it is there for people who need it because they cannot work or earn enough to live.'[20] Or this passage from a column in the *Daily Express* in June that focuses in particular on the question of immigration in relation to benefits:

> But in its quest to cut £12billion from the welfare budget the government should start with an even more absurd use of British taxpayers' money: paying child benefit and child tax credits to children who do not even live in Britain . . . *Fair* enough, if you are settled in Britain and have been *paying taxes* here for several years, the benefits system should not discriminate against you on the grounds that you are Polish.[21]

Here is Iain Duncan Smith during the first reading of the Welfare Reform Bill:

> For some time I have believed that the way tax credits operated distorted the system, so that there were far too many families not in work, living in bigger and bigger houses and getting larger while being subsidized by the state, while many others – the vast majority of families in Britain – made decisions about how many children they could have and the houses they could live in. Getting that balance back is about getting *fairness* back into the system. It is not fair to have somebody living in a house that they cannot afford to pay for if they go back to work, as it means that they do not enter the work zone and their children grow up with no sense of work as a way out of poverty.[22]

---

[18] 'Welfare Reform and Work Bill: First Reading'.
[19] Osborne, 'Calling All Progressives'. Osborne does not explicitly argue that to achieve balance we must take measures to make sure that those not in work are *worse off*, for example, by reducing their benefits, but this is a logical extension of his point.
[20] 'Welfare Reform and Work Bill: Second Reading'.
[21] Ross Clark, 'Why Must We Pay for Children Who Do Not Live in Britain?', *The Express*, 23 June 2015.
[22] 'Welfare Reform and Work Bill: First Reading'.

Implicitly, it is also unfair to those who work and make decisions about houses and families without relying on state subsidies.

Here we see an argument that effectively says that people who do not work do not deserve to have the same standard of life as those who do – and this implication is at an extreme end of the trope. Nevertheless, most people have an innate sense of what seems fair or not. Julia Hartley Brewer, writing in the *Daily Mirror*, expresses concern that the 'wrong people' are being hit by the bill – these being those with ill-health or a disability those who have been sanctioned because they missed a job centre appointment, and pensioners. However, she acknowledges,

> I'm one of the people who supports the principle behind the . . . welfare reforms. I think it's right that people who go out to work every day shouldn't be worse off than people who don't work, that people claiming Job Seeker's Allowance long-term should have to do more than fill out a form every fortnight to get their benefits. And I don't see why people living in social housing should be entitled to have a spare room when many hard-working people struggle to keep a roof over their family's heads.[23]

In other words, because it's not fair. Fairness is certainly not an argument to dismiss as we approach the details of social policy – but I think it is worth acknowledging that our instinct towards fairness means that we are all susceptible to the suggestion that some of those living in poverty are more deserving of support than others.

Contributing or not?

Key to the argument about fairness is the idea of making a contribution: if you do not contribute to society then, the rhetoric goes, you do not deserve support – because it's not fair. Those who do work should not be expected to subside those who do not, not without good reason.

Thus, Iain Duncan Smith: 'Spending on welfare should be sustainable and fair to the taxpayer while protecting the most vulnerable',[24] or George Osborne, 'For our social contract to work, we need to retain the consent of the taxpayer, not just the welfare recipient',[25] or Alan Mak, the Conservative MP for Havant: 'Will he [Chris Leslie MP] confirm that if a Labour government were ever to return to power, they would increase tax credits, and if so, which taxes on working people would they raise to pay for that increase?'[26] Here we see an argument that those who do not pay tax, who do not contribute, do not necessarily deserve to be supported.

At the same time, those who do earn deserve to keep more of the money they earn. For example, Frank Field MP argued, 'In the long build-up to the election, as well as during and after it, we heard that the one groups of people about which the

---

[23] Julia Hartley-Brewer, 'Iain Duncan Smith Is a Convenient Welfare Reform Bogeyman', *Daily Mirror*, 16 Aug 2014.

[24] 'Welfare Reform and Work Bill: Second Reading'.

[25] Osborne, 'Calling All Progressives'.

[26] 'Welfare Reform and Work Bill: First Reading'.

Conservatives, as a party and as a government, cared for most were the strivers, yet it is the strivers who will feel the worst effects of the Bill. People who have responded to the government's plea to become strivers, who are in work . . . will find themselves much worse off as a result of the Budget.'[27] Seeing the likely consequences of the bill differently, but sharing the same understanding of the importance of rewarding those who work and contribute, the *Daily Express* commented, 'The current government has emerged as the true supporter of working people . . . While the government seeks to end the dependency culture Osborne has also ensured that working people will be allowed to keep more of the cash they earn.'[28]

Making the right choices

The last idea I want to examine is the idea of choice, as people 'making the right choices' about their lives is an important element of deserving support. For example, one of Iain Duncan Smith's principles for the bill is that, 'People on benefit should face the same choices as those in work and those not on benefits.'[29] Here, he is arguing that people being supported by the state should make choices about homes and families – especially children – and about spending as those earning their own income.

Here we have a debate about children, lifestyle – and choice. So, Dr Eilidh Whiteford, a Scottish Nationalist MP, said, 'We need to recognize that bringing up children is expensive . . . but children are not some sort of luxury lifestyle accessory. Having children and encouraging family life is an essential, necessary and natural part of the human life cycle', followed by Pauline Latham, a Conservative MP:

> I am also disappointed. . . . I found it astonishing that she should be advocating that people on benefits should be allowed to have – encouraged to have – more than two children. Completely responsible people who recognize that children are expensive to bring up and cannot afford to because they are not on benefits subsidize those who the Hon. Lady would like to have three, four or five children. That is completely mad.[30]

In his *Guardian* piece, Osborne also questions government support of those who have more than two children (if they cannot afford them by working to earn income) and of single parents who do not go to work when their child turns three and is eligible for free childcare. Going (back) to work is also a choice here – one that the government needs to make it easier for people to make, by ensuring that systems for childcare are in place and that wages are enough for people to live on.

The argument is that those who make the 'wrong' choices ought to live with the consequences: they should not expect and do not deserve to be supported if their choices take them beyond their financial means. These people, by implication,

---

[27] 'Welfare Reform and Work Bill: Second Reading'.
[28] Leo McKinstry, 'Osborne Shows the Way to National Prosperity', *Daily Express*, 9 July 2015.
[29] 'Welfare Reform and Work Bill: Second Reading'.
[30] 'Welfare Reform and Work Bill: First Reading'.

are 'undeserving' of support: they have made their choices and must live with the consequences. More brutally, Richard Littlejohn in the *Daily Mail* writes about those, 'Who would rather spend their benefits on booze, drugs and big-screen televisions'[31] – those whose choices render them undeserving of our support.

A general consensus?

There is not a lot of debate about the question of whether or not we should be seeking to reduce our welfare bill: all the British political parties would like to spend less in this area. The British people would too, it seems. The 2014 British Attitudes Survey noted that the economic downturn had not reduced the general public view that benefits are too high:

> British Social Attitudes has previously reported that public support for welfare spending has been in long-term decline (Clery, 2012). In 1989, 61% agreed that 'government should spend more money on welfare benefits'. By 2009, this figure was just 27%. But since then not only have benefits been cut, but for at least three years the country continued to experience the depressing effects of the financial crisis on economic growth – both considerations that might have been expected to instigate an increase in support for welfare. Yet in 2014 support for more spending on welfare remained just 30%.[32]

The major argument against the Welfare Bill is not that we should not be seeking to reduce our welfare budget, but that this should not be done by cuts that will put people in greater poverty.

There is a sense that those in poverty deserve support – and at the same time, this is discussed in language that explains why they deserve support – continuing to buy in to the idea that there are some who do not. Much criticism of the bill focuses on arguments which claim that the 'wrong people' will be penalized by the cuts it makes. We have already seen Frank Field commenting that the 'strivers' will be worse off. Jeremy Corbyn, MP, opposed the Welfare Reform and Work Bill, saying, 'I am voting against the government on the Welfare Bill tonight because I believe it will increase child poverty.'[33] Children do not deserve to be poor. And Tim Farron, then leader of the Liberal Democrats, while taking issue with the practical implications of the legislation, said, 'The Liberal Democrats will stand up for families, whether they are hard-working or just desperate to be hard-working,'[34] leaving us with the suspicion, at least, that there are some families who are neither, who may not be deserving of our support.

---

[31] Richard Littlejohn, 'Ocado-Style Food Bank? I'll Have the Lobster', *Daily Mail*, 11 September 2015.

[32] NatCen Social Research, *British Social Attitudes 32*, *Bsa.Natcen.ac.uk*, 2015; Charlesworth and Williams, *The Myth of the Undeserving Poor*, section 2.2.

[33] Jon Stone, 'Welfare Cuts Vote: Labour Leadership Contender Andy Burnham Says He Won't Vote against Government', *The Independent*, 10 July 2015.

[34] 'Welfare Reform and Work Bill: Second Reading'.

Consequences

But what does this idea do within our society? The idea that for some poverty is a result of choice in this narrative has created an understanding of living on benefits as a lifestyle or a culture. As Michael Tomlinson, Conservative MP for Mid-Dorset and North Poole, commented, 'Does my Hon. Friend agree that, while the most vulnerable must be protected, welfare must be a safety net rather than a lifestyle choice?'[35] Or the *Daily Mail*: 'Britain's welfare bill alone is £220 billion. Work and Pensions Secretary Iain Duncan Smith's assault on the benefit culture has paid huge dividends in getting the idle into work but there is much more to do.'[36] Welfare is for those who deserve it, because they need it, because they do not currently have the capability to earn. It is not for those who do not choose to work.

The *Daily Telegraph* has referred critically to a '"Something-for-nothing" culture that has underpinned the benefits system'.[37] Writing in the *Guardian*, Zoe Williams more bitterly claimed, 'Citizenship, in modern British rhetoric, is conditional upon the money you bring in. The moment you are not economically productive, you are not just a non-citizen but a drain on other citizens.'[38]

There is a playground rhyme, 'Sticks and stones will break my bones, but words will never hurt me.' Even as children, we would like to believe this was true, but we really know better. The words and arguments we use to describe each other and the assumptions we make about people do have an impact on the way they view themselves and subsequently on the choices they make and the way they live. Many thinkers have discussed the way that rhetoric and discourse have a major role in the reproduction and reinforcement of societal values and systems.[39] Further, as Katie Harrison points out her essay in this book, fatalism and people's disbelief in their own agency is one reason why they struggle to get out of poverty.[40] Rhetoric about an 'undeserving poor' does not lessen this problem. Those who are told they do not deserve support from their society are unlikely to develop high self-esteem or to trust the world to give them an opportunity if they do go looking for it. People do not easily leave a culture that they feely understand them for one that they feel condemns them.

---

[35] 'Welfare Reform and Work Bill: Second Reading'.

[36] Daily Mail Comment, 'Osborne's Chance to Transform Britain', *Daily Mail*, 4 July 2015.

[37] Telegraph View, 'Welfare Reforms are Sensible and Right', *Daily Telegraph*, 24 August 2015.

[38] Zoe Williams, 'Immigration: The Big Issue that the Left Just Can't Get Right', *The Guardian*, 31 March 2015.

[39] E. Laclau and C. Mouffe, *Hegemony and Social Strategy: Towards a Radical Democratic Politics* (London: Verso, 1985); A. Giddens, *Profiles and Critiques in Social Theory* (London: Macmillan, 1982); J. G. A. Pocock, *Politics, Language, and Time: Essays on Political Thought and History* (Chicago: University of Chicago Press, 1989); Slavoj Žižek, *The Sublime Object of Ideology* (London: Verso, 1989); Michel Foucault, 'The Order of Discourse. Inaugural Lecture at the College De France, Given 2nd December 1970', in *Untying the Text: a Post-Structuralist Reader*, ed. R. Young (London: Young, 1981), 48–78; Michel Foucault, *Archaeology of Knowledge* (Oxford: Routledge, 2013).

[40] That the World Bank's Development Report of 2015 was entitled *Mind, Society and Behaviour* recognizes that some of the most crucial keys to unlocking people's potential are in the mind.

This is a cultural matter, but culture and associated lifestyles are not choices we easily enter and exit at will. Extricating ourselves from our cultural norms is difficult, even where we do not like the culture we are in. It cannot be done with one simple choice and action.

The assumption that people are deserving or undeserving of living in poverty or of being given support also assumes that personal responsibility is a key element in both falling into and getting out of poverty. As we have seen, 'bad choices' leave you in poverty, and 'good choices' – to work, to live with your means, will lift you out. Age or misfortune, such as ill-health or disability, might prevent this – but if it does, you will be deserving of support.

In this way, rhetoric about the 'undeserving poor' can lead people to ignore systemic factors that make poverty more or less likely for certain groups of people and that make it harder for them to work their way out of poverty. However, we know that there are systemic reasons why people struggle to live without welfare. Some of them have been mentioned already in the course of this book. On the other hand, it is important to recognize that there is a danger that emphasizing systemic factors while trying to avoid judging people living in poverty as deserving or undeserving of support, can lead people to overlook the importance of personal agency in well-being and its potential to play a role in getting out of poverty. It may lead us to talk about and treat people as powerless cogs in the machine.

A dominating rhetoric in which one's choices regarding welfare and work make one deserving or undeserving of support (assuming capability) in case of poverty within a situation where systemic and cultural issues are also at play leads to frustration, as we struggle back and forth between 'Why aren't you/they doing anything?' and 'What do you expect me/them to do?' This ultimately leads to alienation between the two, over time.[41] As Charlesworth and Williams point out, rhetoric that paints some people as deserving and some as underserving creates a conflictual frame of reference between those in work and those out of work,[42] between those who pay taxes and therefore deserve certain things in return and those who do not.

Not only that, our problems increase as rhetoric about dealing with poverty is entwined with ideological questions about the size of the state, the role of the government and our responsibilities as individuals and to each other as citizens of a society. The rhetoric about the 'undeserving poor' makes assumptions about the answers all of these questions, while we often do not raise them at all. I suspect that it will be hard to break free of this rhetoric and the stigma that it carries with it, without questioning those assumptions.

---

[41] It is equally possible, I should note, to see the opposite situation being created, in which a rhetorical focus on the systemic problems and a determination *not* to blame people for living in poverty or to describe them as undeserving of support, fails to acknowledge the potential that individuals do have to change their circumstances and can lead to people feeling disempowered or remaining static because they are not given the encouragement – the carrot rather than the stick – to embrace this potential.

[42] Charlesworth and Williams, *The Myth of the Undeserving Poor*, §2.2.

Conclusions

I have touched on the way that making choice and capability to work markers of the deserving or undeserving poor creates tensions as, despite best intentions, we struggle to think, talk about and enable responsibility and agency alongside engaging systemic issues in responding to those living in poverty. I suggest, as a point for further discussion, that the Bible offers the church a framework for understanding and navigating this tension, as it provides a picture of a world in which there are systemic problems and yet within which personal agency and responsibility matter. The Bible situates this current world in between a good creation and a promised good new creation, and offers individuals and the world the possibility of a change of status – through forgiveness and redemption – that our rhetoric about the undeserving poor (who, once fallen, do not deserve social support) lacks. That is, it offers salvation by grace and not by works.

We see, in the fall, the breaking of the harmony of God's good creation as sin enters the story, leading to pain and injustice, the division of humans from creation, each other and God. Poverty is one of the consequences of this state of the world. Nevertheless, we see throughout the Bible, individuals and communities being called upon by God to make a difference to this situation, given models (through the laws of Israel and the life of Jesus) for how to live and live together, allowing for personal agency and responsibility and for justice within a broken world. It is a picture of the world in which all have the capacity to act – and to change, in which all who are blessed are called to share that blessing with their communities and in which all have value and deserve their society's care – and all are offered love and freedom by Christ. I suggest that this understanding of the world could – and should – have an impact on the way that the church thinks about, talks about and engages with poverty and the people living in both, as well as with our society as a whole.

Response to Fiona Gregson

Hannah Swithinbank

The first thing I noticed about Fiona Gregson's essay was that we were both starting in the same place – a recognition that there is something happening in our contemporary discussion of poverty in the UK, in which personal responsibility and behaviour are being made key factors in answering the question, 'Who deserves to be helped, and how?' I think what works well about these two essays in partnership is that the discussion of what the Bible has to say about our responsibilities towards people living in poverty can prepare Christians to respond to the rhetoric – and the assumptions to which this rhetoric is tied – which I discuss in my essay.

There are two other issues which Fiona's essay and the two essays together raise. The first is the idea of people having *reciprocal responsibilities* in their relationships with others. It struck me, in Fiona's essay, that one of the ways that the biblical texts might take out the 'sting' of the question of being deserving or underserving is by making it clear that the primary expected response to generosity is not gratitude. As the essay points out, Jesus does not just heal or respond to those who say thank you, and yet Paul calls on the church to give because they have experienced God's generosity. At the same time, that does not seem to mean that there is no reciprocal relationship: it strikes me that there is an expectation that, while generosity should be expected from others, it should not be taken for granted.

The second thing is the question of whom we have these responsibilities to – as Christians and as citizens. By and large, the vast majority of people *do* operate on the assumption that we do have some kind of responsibility to support some of the many people living in poverty in some way, but to *whom?* Are our responsibilities to our families, our local neighbourhoods, our fellow citizens, the members of the global church or our other tribes, or those beyond our national borders? I think the discussion of the particular passages in Fiona's essay – and looking back to the Bible – can help Christians, at least, begin to work out our answers to that question.

Response to Hannah Swithinbank

Fiona J. R. Gregson

Hannah Swithinbank's paper reminds us of the impact of the fall and grace on Christian approaches to giving. In one sense, the fact that all have sinned means that everyone is 'in it together'. Christians know that they all, in some way, fall short and do not deserve the grace they have received, and this should, in many ways, make it more difficult to point at someone else as 'undeserving'. The centrality of grace in the New Testament (NT), particularly as we saw in 2 Corinthians 8–9, encourages Christians, who have seen and received grace in God's actions and attitudes to them, to then show that same grace to others. Therefore, the question addressed in the NT is more about why Christians should give, rather than who should or should not receive.

I think the NT emphasis on receiving that we may give provides a contrast in emphasis from the current questions that Hannah highlights about deserving or not deserving, fair or not fair, contributing or not. With the question of contributing or not contributing, I find the NT encouragement for all to be involved in beneficial acts, when that would not necessarily be the cultural norm, interesting – while there is a focus on giving to those in need, everyone is also encouraged to be giving, and praised for doing so, even when they are poor (2 Cor. 8.2-3; Lk. 21.1-4). My experience as a parish minister is that it is often those who are in difficult and precarious financial situations who are very generous, perhaps as they empathize more acutely with the situations of those they are giving to and are more aware of their dependency at times on receiving and the everyday vulnerability that can lead to poverty.

Hannah noted the different forms of poverty that exist, and our discussion of the papers and the example of people who are idle (ἀτάκτοι *ataktoi*) in the Letters to the Thessalonians raise the question about what someone's key need is: it may be financial, or it may be some other form of practical, relationship or spiritual help. The most pressing need may not be money.

Hannah explores the tension between individual and societal responsibility for poverty. The NT points to societal/external causes of poverty and encourages both individual and collective actions of generosity to those in need. For example, the Macedonians are not blamed for their poverty, and their poverty may be related to their affliction (2 Cor. 8.2-3). The Antiochene believers decide (corporately) each according to ability (individually) to provide help to the believers in Judaea (Acts 11.29).

The other thing that occurred to me as we discussed the two papers is that some questions – around how those in need are helped and how both societal and individual action and responsibility are encouraged – are easier to address in a more local relational setting or community, where individuals are known, where particular needs can be responded to and where personal agency can be encouraged. However, action would still be required for structural societal change.

26

The Early Church, the Roman State and Ancient Civil Society: Whose Responsibility Are the Poor?

Christopher M. Hays

Introduction

John the Baptist was, in some senses, Jesus's 'opening act'. He roamed the desert in his camel-skin toga, munching on locusts, in order to preach repentance in preparation for the Messiah. He told people to express their repentance by offering their second tunic to the bare-chested, and by sharing their food with the hungry (Lk. 3.11). Small surprise, then, that the Jesus movement that grew out of John's ministry also was concerned for the economically vulnerable.

Jesus endorsed almsgiving,[1] and counselled divestiture to that end;[2] people opened their homes and tables to the poor,[3] and to empty-pocketed itinerant preachers;[4] well-to-do women disciples took care of Jesus and the Twelve,[5] since they had abandoned stable jobs.[6] The Jerusalem Church set up a programme to feed local widows.[7] Paul sometimes got bankrolled by a church he planted,[8] but most of the time he worked a 'nine to five' job to take care of himself, his travelling companions and the indigent around him.[9] Paul even helped organize a couple of big international aid packages, for example, from the church in Antioch,[10] or the churches around the Aegean Sea.[11]

---

[1] Mt. 6.19-21//Lk. 12.33-34; cf. Acts 20.35; 1 Thess. 4.9-11; 5.14; Eph. 4.28.
[2] Mk 10.21//Mt. 19.21//Lk. 18.22; Lk. 12.33; 14.33.
[3] Lk. 14.15-24.
[4] Mt. 10.9-11; Mk 6.8-11; Lk. 9.3-5; 10.4-7.
[5] Lk. 8.1-3.
[6] Mt. 4.22; 9.9//Mk 1.20; 2.14//Lk. 5.11, 27-28.
[7] Acts 6.1-7.
[8] 2 Cor. 11.8-9; Phil. 1.5-7; 4.14-19. Julien M. Ogereau, 'Paul's κοινωνία with the Philippians: *Societas* as a Missionary Funding Strategy', *NTS* 60 (2014): 360–78 shows that the κοιν- language was typical of financial partnerships, and argues that Paul and the Philippians were partners in a *societas unius rei*, 'a partnership towards a particular, profitable or non-profitable, objective' (376–78). The church provided the money and Paul provided the skills and effort.
[9] Acts 20.34-35; 1 Cor. 4.12; 9.4-12; 2 Cor. 11.8-9; 1 Thess. 2.9; cf. Eph. 4.28.
[10] Acts 11.27-30.
[11] Rom. 15.25-26; 1 Cor. 16.1-3; 2 Cor. 8-9. This practice continued in subsequent centuries. For example, in the third century the church in Rome was known for its 'custom' (ἔθος *ethos*; Eusebius,

This much, we know. But when we talk about early Christian 'charity', we might tend to think of it as something that the church did in isolation from the power structures of its day. This chapter will examine to what degree that is actually the case. It will first ask how the ancient 'powers', that is, civil society and the Roman government, engaged with poverty, and then in that light, it will assess how the Early Church interacted with the methods of the powers. It will become readily clear that the church did not fob responsibility for the poor off on civil society or the state. Rather, the church variously resisted, redirected, cooperated with and led the powers because the church of the poor knew that all its members are agents of God's kingdom.

The church, the poor and the powers 1: Civil society

We begin our discussion of poverty and the powers by looking at 'civil society'. Civil society is often conceived in terms of organizations: Scouts, Tearfund, labour unions, universities, lawn-bowling clubs. So I will begin by introducing the closest ancient equivalent to a civic organization, before touching on early Christianity's engagements with three key expressions of civic munificence: banqueting, benefaction and patronage.

Voluntary associations

The best ancient Roman equivalent for the modern civic organization is the *collegium*, the 'voluntary association'. The reason for the vague English translation of *collegium* is that voluntary associations are notoriously slippery to define. Ancient *collegia* are sometimes categorized as occupational, cultic, or domestic, which is to say some were dedicated to a given profession (weavers, woodcutters, fullers, fishermen), or to a particular deity (Zeus, Dionysus, Aphrodite), and some were composed of members of an aristocratic household.[12] Still, this neat division is a bit misleading, because almost all *collegia*, even if not dedicated to a specific deity, all had a religious component.[13]

Collegia were basically ancient clubs, predominantly populated by the non-elite (freedmen, slaves, the poor and foreigners[14]), although they did include some wealthier members (and thus *collegia* helped mediate between the masses and the elite).[15] The association's community life centred around a communal meal (i.e. they would dine together regularly),[16] even if their stated *raison d'être* was religious or professional.

Hist. eccl. 4.23.9) of sending financial support to cities around the Mediterranean, even as far away as Syria and Arabia (*Hist. eccl.* 4.23.9; 7.5.2).

[12] Markus Öhler, 'Cultic Meals in Associations and the Early Christian Eucharist', *EC* 5 (2014): 475–502, here 477.

[13] John S. Kloppenborg, '*Collegia* and *Thiasoi*: Issues in Function, Taxonomy and Membership', in *Voluntary Associations in the Graeco-Roman World*, ed. John S. Kloppenborg and Stephen G. Wilson (London: Routledge, 1996), 16–30, here 18–19.

[14] Kloppenborg, '*Collegia*', 16–17, 23.

[15] Ibid., 27.

[16] Öhler, 'Cultic Meals', 476, 480–1.

And, while they certainly were not charitable organizations, the *collegia* would look out their members. For example, *collegia* would frequently provide for members' burial expenses;[17] some required members to post bail for one another.[18] They were funded by annual dues from their members,[19] on top of which the more-affluent members regularly infuse *collegia* with cash to help out members who could not pay their dues and sometimes provide the groups with facilities for their meetings.[20]

So why are *collegia* relevant to our discussion of the Early Church? After all, the church was not a big voluntary association. Organizationally speaking, churches had analogies to a few different institutions, such as the philosophical school or the household, and there is no doubt that in the earliest years and in churches with larger Jewish populations, the *synagogue*, not the *collegium*, was the church's closest organizational analogy. *However*, the more Christianity moved west, and the more predominantly gentile it became in composition, the more local churches would have appeared to be *collegia*.[21] As we will see the ensuing pages, lots of church activities would have looked like *collegial* activities as well. Christians had regular banquets; so did *collegia*. Christians acted as patrons and benefactors to their church communities; so did members of *collegia*. So, when members of local Christian communities engaged in practices like banqueting, benefaction and patronage, they would have looked a lot like collegial expressions of civic munificence. What is interesting, then, is the fact that Christians departed from collegial custom by applying these practices of civic munificence *to the poor*. Allow me to unpack this idea with a few case-studies.

Banqueting

One standard feature of early Christian worship, of the meetings of voluntary associations and of Jewish and Hellenistic social life, more broadly, was the community meal, the banquet. The banquet was an important venue for social manoeuvring (and, indeed, drama) in the Mediterranean world, and it was not initially conceived of as a mechanism by which to care for the needy. Christians, however, *transformed* ancient banquets into mechanisms by which to care for the vulnerable, and did so well aware of the sociocultural ramifications of that decision.

---

[17] Earlier scholarship tended to see these clubs as existing primarily to take care of funeral expenses, but Kloppenborg suggests that in the first century, even though many *collegia* took care of burial expenses, they were not defined as existing for that purpose. Rather, he argues that the existence the category of the funerary association, *collegium tenuiorum*, emerges during the reign of Hadrian. Kloppenborg, 'Collegia', 20–23.

[18] John S. Kloppenborg, 'Membership Practices in Pauline Christ Groups', *EC* 4 (2013): 183–215, here 200.

[19] For details, see F. Sokolowski, 'Fees and Taxes in the Greek Cults', *HTR* 47 (1954): 153–64.

[20] For epigraphic evidence, see Richard Ascough, 'Benefactions Gone Wrong: The "Sin" of Ananias and Sapphira in Context', in *Text and Artifact in the Religions of Mediterranean Antiquity: Essays in Honour of Peter Richardson*, ed. Stephen G. Wilson (Waterloo: Wilfrid Laurier University Press, 2000), 91–110, here notes 15–17; Markus Öhler, 'Die Jerusalemer Urgemeinde im Spiegel des antiken Vereinswesens', *NTS* 51 (2005): 393–415, here 405–6.

[21] Wayne O. McCready, '*Ekklēsia* and Voluntary Associations', in *Voluntary Associations in the Graeco-Roman World*, ed. John S. Kloppenborg and Stephen G. Wilson (London: Routledge, 1996), 59–73, here 62 (cf. 69–70).

Consider Luke 14. As Jesus sits in a conventional banquet setting, he criticizes the guests jockeying for seats of honour (vv. 7–11).[22] He has no time for the way banquets served as a venue for status-mongering (vv. 12–14) and tells his host that, on the occasion of planning his next banquet, instead of inviting the sort of people who could scratch the host's back in the future, he should 'invite the poor, the crippled, the lame, and the blind' (v. 13). The poor and handicapped were not typical guests at a banquet, and association with them certainly would not help the host's social standing. But they were the sorts of people to whom Jesus dedicated his attention (Lk. 4.18; 7.22; 14.21)[23] and, frankly, they were the sorts of people who really needed a good meal.

The banquet was not, historically, about feeding the hungry. That was a Christian innovation. Jesus took an institution that was about status maintenance and he turned it into practice that was about care for the poor (in line with what John the Baptist taught; Lk. 3.11). Thus, in Luke's laudatory depiction of the Jerusalem church in Acts 2, he underscores the fact that 'Day by day . . . they broke bread at home and ate their food[24] with glad and generous hearts' (Acts 2.46). While commensality certainly demonstrated and contributed to social unity within the church,[25] it was also very much about providing for those who did not have enough to eat. By eating together daily or weekly, the disciples would significantly ameliorate the financial burdens of the impoverished in the community, since food is the primary expense of a poor person.

It was not easy for the church to turn the banquet into the sort of communal meal that would care for the poor and honour Christ. First Corinthians 11 reveals that the socio-economic differences between believers could mar the celebration of the Lord's Supper. (The Lord's Supper remained a full communal meal for some decades, before being pared down to our modern wafers and thimbles of grape juice.) In Corinth, the meal's bread and wine were probably provided by richer Christians.[26] That was a good thing, as far as it went, but Paul still criticized them 'because when you come together it is not for the better, but for the worse' (1 Cor. 11.17).

> For when the time comes to eat, each of you [devours/goes ahead with] your own supper, and one goes hungry and another becomes drunk. What! Do you not have homes to eat and drink in? Or do you show contempt for the church of God and humiliate those who have nothing? . . . So then, my brothers and sisters, when you come together to eat, [receive/wait for] one another. If you are hungry, eat at

---

[22] Jesus criticizes the Pharisees for the same behaviour in Lk. 11.43 and in 20.46, but we know that this was not just a Jewish phenomenon; it also happened in voluntary associations that big donors got the best seats and special privileges during meals; Öhler, 'Cultic Meals', 480.

[23] For more detail, see Christopher M. Hays, *Luke's Wealth Ethics: A Study in Their Coherence and Character*, WUNT 2/275 (Tübingen: Mohr Siebeck, 2010), 130.

[24] The expression 'sharing food' (μεταλαμβάνον τροφῆς *metalambanon trophēs*) denotes the consumption of a real meal, not merely a symbolic rite; Andreas Lindemann, 'The Beginnings of Christian Life in Jerusalem according to the Summaries in the Acts of the Apostles (Acts 2:42–47; 4:32–37; 5:12–16)', in *Common Life in the Early Church: Essays Honoring Graydon F. Snyder*, ed. Julian V. Hills (Harrisburg, PA: Trinity Press International, 1998), 202–17, here 208.

[25] Santos Yao, 'Dismantling Social Barriers through Table Fellowship: Acts 2:42–47', in *Mission in Acts*, ed. William J. Larkin, Jr, and Joel F. Williams (Maryknoll, NY: Orbis, 2004), 29–36, here 29–32.

[26] This makes sense of why, per v. 14, the Corinthians expected that Paul would praise them.

home, so that when you come together, it will not be for your condemnation. (1 Cor. 11.21-22, 33-34 NRSV, adapted)[27]

It remains a bit unclear what precisely the Corinthians did to earn Paul's ire, but two explanations seem especially plausible.[28] The first possibility is that the rich may simply have begun their meals before the poor arrived and therefore eaten more than their fair share.[29] The second possibility is that the rich actually supplied themselves with superior fare, while extending only bread and wine to the poorer members of the community.[30] By either reconstruction, the outcome of this supposedly communal meal was that 'one goes hungry and another becomes drunk' (11.21).

From a sociocultural perspective, it is important to appreciate that common pagan practice legitimated the provision of the rich with both larger portions (per the first possibility) and better fare (per the second). In *collegia*, for example, all members paid regular dues to cover the costs of meals, but club officers had to make larger contributions[31] and therefore received larger portions. For example, the rules of a rather run-of-the-mill *collegium* in Lanuvium state (32 km south of Rome) that 'any member who has administered the office of the *quinquennalis*[32] honestly shall receive a share and a half of everything as a mark of honour'.[33] Thus, if the rich in Corinth provided the food for the Lord's Supper and tired of waiting around for poorer members to show up, they may have thought it justifiable to get a head start on dinner, even if they ended up with more booze and bread than the latecomers, who had not contributed anything to the meal anyway.

Similarly, classical literature reveals that hosts at banquets frequently provided better fare for their VIP guests and shabbier repast for the less-distinguished attendees. Consider the complaint from the incomparable Roman satirist, Martial, after his host, one Pontius, snubbed him at a banquet:

Since I am asked to dinner, . . . why is not the same dinner served to me as to you? You take oysters fattened in the Lucrine lake, I suck a mussel through a hole in a

---

27 The reconstruction of the conflict relates to the translation of two key verbs: προλαμβάνει *prolambanei* (v. 21) and ἐκδέχεσθε *ekdechesthe* (v. 33). If the conflict stems from the rich starting to eat before all the poor have arrived, then προλαμβάνει *prolambanei* (v. 21) is translated 'to take before, go ahead with' and ἐκδέχεσθε *ekdechesthe* is translated 'wait for', in the sense that the rich should wait for the poor to arrive before tucking in (so Barry D. Smith, 'The Problem with the Observance of the Lord's Supper in the Corinthian Church', *BBR* 20 (2010): 517–44, esp. 536–39). If the conflict results from differing fare for rich and poor, then προλαμβάνει *prolambanei* (v. 21) is translated 'to devour', and ἐκδέχεσθε *ekdechesthe* should be translated as 'receive', so that v. 33 exhorts the rich believers to include the poorer believers in all the dishes of the meal (so Gordon D. Fee, *The First Epistle to the Corinthians*, NICNT (Grand Rapids, MI: Eerdmans, 1987), 567–68; Bruce W. Winter, 'The Lord's Supper at Corinth: An Alternative Reconstruction', *RTR* 37 (1978): 73–82, here 76–80).
28 For a more detailed adjudication of the five major positions, see Smith, 'Problem', 517–44.
29 Smith, 'Problem', 521, 542–3.
30 See, e.g., Jerome Murphy-O'Connor, *St. Paul's Corinth: Texts and Archaeology*, GNS (Collegeville, MN: Liturgical, 1983), 167–69; Öhler, 'Cultic Meals', 498; Gerd Theissen, *The Social Setting of Pauline Christianity: Essays on Corinth*, trans. John H. Schütz (Philadelphia: Fortress, 1982), 155–9; Winter, 'Lord's Supper', 73–82.
31 Markus Öhler, 'Die Jerusalemer Urgemeinde im Spiegel des antiken Vereinswesens', *NTS* 51 (2005): 393–415, here 408.
32 This seems to have been a leadership role with a five-year tenure.
33 *CIL* XIV 2112; translation from Theissen, *Social Setting*, 154.

shell; you get mushrooms, I take hog funguses . . . Golden with fat, a turtledove gorges you with its bloated rump; there is set before me a magpie that has died in its cage. (Martial, *Epig.* 3.60; see also Pliny, *Ep.* 2.6)

Whichever reconstruction is more probable in the case of Corinth – that the rich gobbled up a disproportionate share of the food because they started before the poor arrived, or that the rich provided themselves with superior dishes – this differential treatment was perfectly in keeping with societal norms. The rich Corinthians even felt good about themselves for what they were doing (1 Cor. 11.17), because they *were* following Jesus's teachings about including the riff-raff in their banquets.[34] But Paul resists social convention, and tells the Corinthians to ensure that the poor and the rich are equal participants in the supper (11.33).[35]

Banqueting, thus, provides a clear example of how early Christians took a staple convention of civil society, which was not originally about charity, and transformed it into a mechanism of caring for the poor, even though doing so required the subversion of significant cultural suppositions.

This may seem a bit historically quaint at first blush. Most middle-class people worry about eating too much, rather than too little, such that the idea of meal-sharing might seem irrelevant as a means of caring for the poor. But regular hunger remains part of the lives of millions in the North Atlantic region[36] and, indeed, of hundreds of millions in the Majority World. In response to this reality, the Biblical Seminary of Colombia (the seminary at which I teach) has a program called the *Plan Tío* (the Uncle Plan), in which professors adopt a couple of students who are not getting three square meals a day; professors invite their 'nieces/nephews' to weekly meals in their homes and then subsidize the students' major daily meal on all the other days. Students were going hungry, and so the seminary, an organization of civil society, implemented a systematic but voluntary form of commensality.

Benefaction

Let us explore the way the New Testament (NT) appropriates another mainstay of ancient civic activism: benefaction (sometimes called 'euergetism').[37] On the positive side, some texts encourage Christians to be proactive in benefaction. First Peter, for example, is written to Christians in the context of local hostility and ostracism, and it advises readers to make the government an ally by engaging in community benefaction:[38]

---

[34] Theissen, *Social Setting*, 162.

[35] The practice of wealthier members providing food for the community meals continued in the second and third centuries, as we see in the writing of Justin Martyr (*1 Apol.* 67.1: οἱ ἔχοντες τοῖς λειπομένοις πᾶσιν ἐπικουροῦμεν 'Those of us who have [the means] supply those who lack' [my translation]).

[36] World Hunger Education Services, 'Hunger in America: 2015 United States Hunger and Poverty Facts' (http://www.worldhunger.org/articles/Learn/us_hunger_facts.htm, accessed May 2016).

[37] See further the discussion in Hays, *Luke's Wealth Ethics*, 58–63.

[38] Peter H. Davids, *The First Epistle of Peter*, NICNT (Grand Rapids, MI: Eerdmans, 1990), 101; W. C. van Unnik, 'The Teaching of Good Works in 1 Peter', *NTS* 1 (1954): 92–110, here 99; Bruce Winter,

For the Lord's sake submit to every human institution, whether of the emperor as supreme, or of governors, as sent by him to punish those who do evil and to praise those who do good (ἀγαθοποιῶν *agathopoiōn*). For it is God's will that by doing good (ἀγαθοποιοῦντας *agathapooiountas*) you should silence the ignorance of the foolish. (1 Pet. 2.13-14 NRSV, adapted)

Rom. 13.3, likewise, encourages believers, 'Do what is good (τὸ ἀγαθὸν ποίει),[39] and you will receive [the government's] approval.' The terminology (ἀγαθοποιέω, *agathapoieō*, etc.) utilized in both these texts frequently denotes, not just general do-goodery, but euergetism. So early Christians recognized the benefits that could accrue from benefaction.[40]

But ancient benefaction was not an unproblematic phenomenon, from a Christian perspective; it could be (and often was) a tool of self-aggrandisement. Therefore, Luke subverts the culturally dominant conception of benefaction. It is not that Luke avoids the terminology of euergetism. Quite the contrary – Luke describes God as a benefactor (ἀγαθουργῶν *agathourgōn;* Acts 14.17) who works through his brokers,[41] Jesus (who is called εὐεργετῶν *euergetōn*, a benefactor, Acts 10.38) and the apostles (who perform εὐεργεσία *euergesia*, a benefaction, Acts 4.9).[42]

Nonetheless, the deeds Luke describes with the benefaction language (e.g. healing and good harvests) are not actually *financial* benefactions; what Peter calls a benefaction in Acts 4.9, healing the blind man, is actually done *instead* of giving him money (Acts 3.6). On the flip side, when Barnabas gives the proceeds of the sale of his field to the apostles (4.36-37), he has effectively engaged in a benefaction to his *collegium*. But Luke does *not* use benefaction terminology to describe that donation; instead, he employs language that highlights the unity of the Jerusalem believers, in spite of their differing economic statuses.[43]

In other words, Luke calls miracles 'benefactions', even though his culture would not normally understand miracles in those terms, and he describes benefactions as evidence of Christian unity, even though pagans saw benefactions as ways to highlight one's superior status! In fact, the only time Luke speaks of benefaction in a normal, pecuniary fashion is when he *decries* it. 'The kings of the Gentiles lord it over them; and those in authority over them are called benefactors (εὐεργέται *euergetai*). *But not so with you*; rather the greatest among you must become like the youngest, and the leader

Seek the Welfare of the City: Christians as Benefactors and Citizens (Grand Rapids, MI: Eerdmans, 1994), 34–5, 38–9.
[39] Epigraphic evidence indicates that this is benefaction language: Winter, *Seek*, 34–5.
[40] Indeed, we see that, even when the government turned on Christians in later years, the Christian reputation for benefaction could work in their favour. The *Acts of Phileas* tell of a rich bishop (Phileas) who was so well known for his generosity that even when his episcopal status made him a target for state-persecution, the judge urged him to recant so that he could continue to be a benefactor to Alexandria (*Acts Phil.* 11.9–12.1).
[41] K. C. Hanson, *Palestine in the Time of Jesus: Social Structures and Social Conflicts* (Minneapolis: Fortress, 1998), 71.
[42] Halvor Moxnes, 'Patron-Client Relations and the New Community in Luke-Acts', in *The Social World of Luke-Acts: Models for Interpretation*, ed. Jerome Neyrey (Peabody, MA: Hendrickson, 1991), 241–68, here 257–61.
[43] For details, see Hays, *Luke's Wealth Ethics*, 200–209.

like one who serves' (Lk. 22.25-26). Why did Luke do this? Because, however important Luke knew benefaction to be, he did not want the care of the poor to undermine the unity and equality of the church.

In sum, early Christians did benefit from what Graeco-Roman society called benefaction. But Luke recognized the shadow side of benefaction, the way in which it cultivated grandiose delusions amongst benefactors. Benefaction was a useful convention of ancient civil society, but not one Christians took on uncritically.

Patronage

Moving on to a third convention, patronage, we can see the NT authors' views were similarly variegated. On the positive side, patronage supported the spread of Christianity. For example, Paul explicitly says that Phoebe, a 'deacon of the church in Cenchreae', 'was a patron of many, even of me myself (προστάτις πολλῶν ἐγενήθη καὶ ἐμοῦ αὐτοῦ)' (Rom. 16.1-2, my translation). This indicates she was likely a woman of means who offered aid and hospitality to Christians travelling through the port city in which she lived.[44] Lydia – who was a merchant in purple cloth, head of her own household and Paul's convert in Philippi – seems, likewise, to have become a patron of Paul, hosting him while he was in Philippi (Acts 16.14-16) and perhaps being one of his key financial supporters as he ministered in Corinth and Thessalonica (2 Cor. 11.8-9; Phil 1.5-7; 4.14-19).[45] So also the hosts of the early house churches, like Nympha (Col. 4.15) or Philemon (1–2),[46] should probably be thought of as patrons of their local ecclesial *collegia* as well.

On the more critical side, the Church sometimes reconstrued the concept of patronage. Consider the Parable of the Unjust Steward (Lk. 16.1-13). The parable describes how a steward, in the eleventh hour of his employment in one great house, writes off 500 denarii of the debts some affluent merchants owe to his current boss, in hopes of securing himself another white-collar job upon dismissal from his current post. In other words, the steward gets himself a new patron.[47]

Luke tells his readers to imitate the steward's example by using their mundane wealth wisely in order to receive true wealth in the future (16.11). This is conceptually the same as telling disciples to give alms and thereby secure treasure in heaven (Lk. 12.32-34). Thus, when Jesus applies the parable by saying, 'Make friends for yourselves by means of dishonest wealth so that when it is gone, they may welcome you into the eternal homes' (16.9), he is teaching that one makes 'friends' (φίλους *philous*) with the poor by giving one's earthly wealth, so that, after one dies, the poor welcome one into heaven.

---

[44] James D. G. Dunn, *Romans 9–16*, WBC 38B (Dallas: Word, 1998), 888–9; Douglas J. Moo, *The Epistle to the Romans*, NICNT (Grand Rapids, MI: Eerdmans, 1996), 916; *TDNT* 6:703.

[45] The same can probably also be said of Gaius (Rom. 16.23).

[46] Edward Adams has corrected the thesis that the vast majority of Christian churches met in believers' homes, though he affirms that something along the lines of traditional reconstructions is likely in the cases cited here. Edward Adams, *The Earliest Christian Meeting Places: Almost Exclusively Houses?*, LNTS 450 (London: T&T Clark, 2016), 18–21, 44.

[47] For detail, see Hays, *Luke's Wealth Ethics*, 140–2.

What does this have to do with patronage? The logic of the parable becomes clear when one realizes that the title 'friend' (*amicus*, φίλος *philos*) was a common euphemism[48] used between patrons and clients, since being called a *cliens* ('client') could be distasteful to a client of status or ambition.[49] This small historical insight illuminates Lk. 16.9. Normally in Graeco-Roman society, patrons cultivate clients through favours, such as financial gifts; by this logic, Jesus's instructions to give money to the poor would cast the giver as the patron and the poor recipient as the client, even though they refer to each other with the euphemism 'friend'. But, in 16.9, Luke makes it clear that it is the recipient friend who welcomes the giver into 'eternal homes', extending celestial hospitality. As the 'heavenly host', the friend who received the gift of earthly wealth becomes the eschatological *patron* of the formerly affluent donor friend.

This all makes good sense from Luke's perspective, since he considers the poor to be the blessed heirs of the kingdom (Lk. 6.20; 16.19-25; 18.18-27), in contrast to the rich, whose entrance into eternal beatitude is only the slimmest of possibilities (Lk. 6.24; 12.13-21; 16.19-31), largely contingent upon their care of the poor (Lk. 12.33-34; 14.12-14; 18.22; 19.8-10). Thus, according to the Parable of the Unjust Steward, the rich who are patrons to the poor today will be clients of the poor in the life to come.[50]

We have seen that early Christianity benefitted significantly from patronage as a mechanism of supporting its expansion. But the ideology of patronage, considering the poor inferior to the rich, ran contrary to the fundamental convictions of their faith. So Christians developed an eschatological vision in which the poor became the patrons of the rich, reflecting their abundance of true wealth.

Summary

To sum up the argument thus far, early Christian communities had many features in common with the practices and features of voluntary associations; like ancient *collegia*, churches were spaces for regular commensality, relationship across social classes, religious observance and mutual support. Christians recognized how patronage and benefaction could help support and expand their movement (thus the endorsement of benefaction in Romans 13 and 1 Peter 2, or the roles of Phoebe and Lydia in the ministry of Paul). They even saw how banqueting could be transformed into a space for commensality, feeding the hungry (Luke 14; Acts 2).

---

[48] The euphemism originally derives from the conventions of ritual/ideal friendship but came to be applied in the context of patron-client relations. While ritual friendship is an important idea for Luke, as seen in Acts 2.42-47; 4.32-35 (Hays, *Luke's Wealth Ethics*, 50–53, 200–209), ritual friendship is probably not in view in the Parable of the Unjust Steward. Although it is possible to read the term 'friends' in the more egalitarian sense, the literary context suggests the patron-client nuance, since (1) the steward would not become an equal to the debtors he released, but an employed inferior and (2) this seems to extend the central Lukan motif of the eschatological inversion of fortunes, according to which the poor and marginalized are elevated while the rich and powerful are brought low (Lk. 1.51-55; 6.20-26; 14.7-24; 16.19-31; 18.14).

[49] For detail, see Hays, *Luke's Wealth Ethics*, 53–4.

[50] The same idea gets developed in the Apostolic Fathers. In the Parable of the Vine and the Elm, the rich care for the poor so that the poor, who have 'pull' with God, will intercede on behalf of the rich (Herm. *Simil.* 2.5). Basically, the rich secure the poor as their patrons/brokers because, in the heavenly economy, the poor are the superiors of the rich, who can network on their behalf.

But the church also realized that civil structures and conventions came with baggage. They oftentimes fomented inequality, marginalized the poor and elevated the rich. So the church learned to be savvy in appropriating civil conventions, sometimes rejecting specific ideas (as Paul does in response to the unfair portions served at the Lord's Supper in 1 Corinthians 11) or transforming key terms (as in Acts 2 and 4), sometimes even inverting standard practices (as in Lk. 14.7-24 and 16.1-13). In brief, early Christians engaged robustly with civil society, they evaluated prudently and they revised unabashedly.

The Church, the poor and the powers 2: The state

Let us proceed to the subject of government. What can ancient history tell us about how the church and the *state* might interact on the subject of poverty? At first blush, the answer might appear to be 'not much', since in the first century, care for the needy was not, by and large, the responsibility of the government.

The paucity of centralized and systematic care for the poor by the state

First, it bears saying that the sort of distinction between religion and government one sees (theoretically!) endorsed in the United States did not exist in the first century. So, at least in regards to Judaism, one might surmise that the government did have an interest in caring for the needy; after all, the Old Testament has loads of legislation about providing for the impoverished (gleaning and reaping laws, Lev. 19.9-10; 23.22; second tithes for the poor, Deut. 14.28-29; debt remission in the sabbath years, Deut. 15.1-2; land restoration in the Jubilee years, Lev. 25.13, etc.). That surmise, however, would be erroneous.

First-century Judaea was part of the Roman Empire, but Rome devolved a fair amount of responsibility for regional governance to the seventy elders of the Sanhedrin. The Sanhedrin was, in the first place, a judicial and cultic body, and, at least in the post-Herodian decades, they also enjoyed some legislative powers (Josephus, *Ant.* 20.10.5 [20.251]).[51] But their interactions with matters of economics and finances were basically confined to maintaining the operations of the Jerusalem cult. Since religious laws were part of their remit, we could imagine that a violation of, for example, the second tithe could be brought before them, but unfortunately there is no record of them ruling on matters of this sort (at least as far as the present author is aware). So, if

---

[51] For a fulsome account of the Sanhedrin's functions see Sidney B. Hoenig, *The Great Sanhedrin: A Study of the Origin, Development, Composition and Functions of the Bet Din ha-Gadol during the Second Jewish Commonwealth* (Philadelphia: Dropsie College, 1953), 85–104; cf. Emil Schürer, Geza Vermes, Fergus Millar and Martin Goodman, *The History of the Jewish People in the Age of Jesus Christ (175 BC-AD 135)*, 4 vols, revised edn (Edinburgh: T&T Clark, 1973–86), vol. 2/1, 184–95; Graham H. Twelftree, 'Sanhedrin', in *Dictionary of Jesus and the Gospels*, ed. Joel B. Green, Jeannine K. Brown and Nicholas Perrin, 2nd edn (Downers Grove, IL: IVP Academic, 2013), 836–40, here 839.

there was a social welfare system in Judaea in the first century, the Sanhedrin did not run it.[52]

The Roman *frumentatio publica*, the imperial 'dole', is perhaps one of the better first-century analogies to state-sponsored welfare. Any adult male citizen residing in the city of Rome could take part in the lottery to receive this regular imperial benefaction, which was available to about 20 per cent of the city's population.[53] The dole was not, however, primarily about care for the poor.[54] Generally women and children are not on the lists; neither are non-citizens, foreigners, nor slaves,[55] and the very rich were just as eligible as the poorest male citizen. In other words, some needy, male, citizen plebs would have received the dole (as a matter of chance), but the most-marginalized people in Rome were excluded.[56]

Outside the city of Rome, there is not much more that looks like systematic state-sponsored care for the needy.[57] The first-century geographer Strabo did comment that, on the island of Rhodes, there were liturgies to care for the needy:

> [T]hey wish to take care of their multitude of poor people. Accordingly, the people are supplied with provision and the needy are supported by the well-to-do; and there are certain liturgies [λειτουργία *leitourgia*] that supply provisions so that at the same time the poor man receives his sustenance and the city does not run short of useful men, and in particular for the manning of the fleets. (Strabo, *Geogr.* 14.2.5)

Liturgies were benefactions designed for the service of the community, which the city in varying degrees foisted upon its richer members. The Rhodian liturgies had at least the partial purpose of ensuring that the island did not run out of sailors and oarsmen

---

[52] Rabbinic literature reveals that the Jewish communities maintained a community chest (קוּפָּה) and a 'soup kitchen' (תַּמְחוּי) which helped provide for the needs of the poor (*m. Pe'ah* 8.7; *t. Pe'ah* 4.2–9; *b. B. Bat.* 8a-9a), but these institutions do not seem to have been in effect prior to the destruction of the Jerusalem temple in 70 CE; Brian J. Capper, 'The Palestinian Cultural Context of the Earliest Christian Community of Goods', in *The Book of Acts in its Palestinian Setting*, ed. Richard Bauckham, BAFCS 4 (Grand Rapids, MI: Eerdmans, 1995), 323–56 (350–51); Hays, *Luke's Wealth Ethics*, 226; David Peter Seccombe, 'Was There Organized Charity in Jerusalem before the Christians?', *JTS* n.s. 29 (1978): 140–3, esp. 140–2. For an extended discussion of Jewish wealth ethics in the Old Testament and Second Temple periods, see Hays, *Luke's Wealth Ethics*, 25–49.

[53] Dio Chrysostom, 55.10.1; *Res Gestae* 3.15; Suetonius, *Aug.* 40.2; cf. 42.3.

[54] For further details, see Hays, *Luke's Wealth Ethics*, 60; Bruce W. Longenecker, *Remember the Poor: Paul, Poverty, and the Greco-Roman World* (Grand Rapids, MI: Eerdmans, 2010), 88–89.

[55] Peter Garnsey, *Famine and Food Supply in the Graeco-Roman World: Responses to Risk and Crisis* (Cambridge: Cambridge University Press, 1988), 238.

[56] The Roman Empire did also establish some alimentary schemes to support children in Italy, and while I am inclined to think that sentimental or humane considerations helped stimulate the establishment of these schemed, the public explanation for the schemes tended to focus on supporting a dwindling rural population of Italy or fortifying the ranks of the Roman military. For the history of the debate over the purposes of *alimentae*, see Jesper Carlsen, 'Gli *alimenta* imperiali e privati in Italia: Ideologia ed economia', in *Demografia, sistemi agrari, regimi alimentari nel mondo antico*, ed. Domenico Vera, Pragmateia (Bari: Edipuglia, 1999), 273–88 (274–8).

[57] The only Roman province with a dole was Egypt, during of the second and third centuries, but that dole too included only a sector of the local Hellenized elite. Garnsey, *Famine*, 263–6; Greg Woolf, 'Food, Poverty, and Patronage: The Significance of the Epigraphy of the Roman Alimentary Schemes in Early Imperial Italy', *Papers of the British School at Rome* 58 (1990): 197–228, here 213.

with which to populate their fleet (no small matter for a tiny island). We should not assume that the Rhodian practice was entirely unparalleled in the ancient world,[58] but it is telling that even the world-traveller Strabo considered the Rhodian liturgies to be a novelty. They are the exception that proves the rule.

Centralized and systematic care for the poor by the church and its impact on the state

So one finds minimal evidence of anything equivalent to state-sponsored welfare systems in the early Roman Empire. Christians, however, began to develop welfare structures quite early on, even without a government model to imitate. Acts 6 indicates that the apostles organized a regular distribution for widows in Jerusalem (vv. 1–7), and that practice spread and developed. In second-century Rome, Justin Martyr describes how

> they who are well-to-do and willing give what each thinks fit; and what is collected is deposited with the president, who succours the orphans and widows and those who, through sickness or any other cause, are in want, and those who are in bonds, and the strangers sojourning among us, and in a word takes care of all who are in need (*1 Apol.* 67.6; translation *ANF*)

By the mid-third century, the Roman community chest sustained 46 presbyters, 42 acolytes, over 1,500 widows and needy people, and 52 exorcists, readers and doorkeepers (Eusebius, *Hist. eccl.* 6.43.11). The church also employed 14 deacons and subdeacons to administer this formidable welfare operation at the behest of the bishop (*Apos. Trad.* 8.3; 13).

In some degree, it seems that the church set out mechanisms and models for governments to fund and follow. For example, Constantine the Great became a major patron of the church's charitable efforts, radically increasing the Christians' resources for helping the poor.[59] In reaction, Constantine's son-in-law, Emperor Julian (generously nicknamed 'the Apostate'), established major subsidies of the pagan cult so that they would care for the poor, precisely in reaction to the Christian and Jewish examples. Julian instructed the high priest of Galatia,

> 30,000 modii of corn shall be assigned every year for the whole of Galatia, and 60,000 pints of wine. I order that one-fifth of this be used for the poor who serve the priests, and the remainder be distributed by us to strangers and beggars. For it is disgraceful that, when no Jew ever has to beg, and the *impious Galilaeans [i.e. the Christians] support not only their own poor but ours as well*, all men see that our people lack aid from us. (Julian, *Epistle* 22 [Wright, LCL] my italics)

---

[58] Longenecker, *Remember the Poor*, 85.

[59] Robin Lane Fox, *Pagans and Christians in the Mediterranean World from the Second Century* AD *to the Conversion of Constantine* (London: Penguin, 1986), 667–68; Justo González, *Faith and Wealth: A History of Early Christian Ideas on the Origin, Significance, and Use of Money* (Eugene, OR: Wipf & Stock, 2002), 150–1.

In brief, Christians independently developed a rudimentary welfare system for their own co-religionists and thereby helped the Roman Empire to be more organized in care for the needy. Christians were not originally looking for the government to care for the poor.

Towards a more nuanced church-state engagement on economic justice: The analogy of criminal justice

This is not, however, a primer for some sort of Christian libertarianism. I do not want to argue from the NT's silence that secular governments should stay out of the welfare business. There are all sorts of marvellously God-honouring institutions that the NT never mentions simply because the relevant ideas (or types of political systems!) would not emerge for centuries (one thinks of national parks, state-funded universities, public radio, free motorways). In order to move beyond the NT's silence on government welfare, we can examine the church's view of the state's role in *criminal* justice and then extrapolate to the analogous issue of *economic* justice.

In the first place, there is a long Jewish and Christian tradition that affirms that God uses governments (even pagan ones) to fulfil his redemptive purposes.[60] NT authors are clear that getting justice for the innocent and punishing the guilty is something the government *should* do (Rom. 13.1-7), and they sometimes seem sanguine that the Roman government will do as it ought. The book of Acts, for example, often depicts the Roman authorities as defending the innocence of apostles.[61] Rom. 13.1-7 affirms that the Roman government has been instituted by God for the purpose of rewarding good conduct and punishing evildoers, and for that reason encourages Christians to be diligent in paying their taxes (cf. 1 Tim. 2.1-2; 1 Pet. 2.13-14; Tit. 3.1).[62]

This is not to be naïve about the reality that governments often dramatically abuse their power. Paul writes the Epistle to the Romans in the period before Nero started torching Christians to light his gardens.[63] Likewise, composing Acts in the 80s or early 90s CE, Luke is quite aware that the Romans decapitated Paul; his positive depiction of Roman governance is probably calculated to avoid the real possibility that Rome might become even more hostile to Christians. Still, caveats notwithstanding, the presence of these positive comments about pagan justice reveal the early Christian sentiment that it was *in principle* good and right for governments to be agents of criminal justice.

---

[60] E.g. Isa. 45.1-4, 13; 1 Kgs 3.9-13; James R. Harrison, *Paul and the Imperial Authorities at Thessalonica and Rome: A Study in the Conflict of Ideology*, WUNT 273 (Tübingen: Mohr Siebeck, 2011), 301.

[61] Acts 18.12-17; 19.35-41; 23.16-35; 24.1-26; 25.14-22; 26.30-32; though see, e.g., 16.20-22. This is surely part of an apologetic agenda, to the effect that Christians should not be viewed as a threat by the Roman government, but the apparent plausibility of the strategy indicates that it was within the realm of reasonable possibility.

[62] This is very much in keeping with Jewish tradition; see Prov. 8.15-16; Wis. 6.3; Dunn, *Romans 9–16*, 761.

[63] Furthermore, James Harrison has shown that even Paul's apparently account of Roman authority is both a subtle relativization of typical and far more lofty depictions of Roman power and, in its warning to 'fear' the government's 'wrath', probably functions as a 'hidden transcript' warning Christians against provoking Rome's ire; Harrison, *Paul*, 308–13.

Nonetheless, NT authors would shift their depictions of the government during seasons when the Rome perverted justice. Mark's Gospel, for example, was written during the Neronian persecution. So Mk 12.17 depicts Jesus being cagey about paying taxes – not opposing Roman rule (as one might have expected of a militant messianic claimant) but also not celebrating how those taxes would be put to good use in defending the Christians against pagan abuse, as Paul did in Rom. 13.6-7. On the contrary, Mark's Jesus warns that Christians will be tried before governors and kings and will indeed be executed (Mk 13.9-13). Similarly, during Domitian's persecution, the Apocalypse characterizes Rome as 'the mother of whores and of earth's abominations' (Rev. 17.5), who is 'drunk with the blood of the saints' (17.6).[64] Obviously, these are not periods in which Christians are sanguine about getting justice from the empire.

Sometimes, matters of economic and criminal justice intersected in the Early Church, as we can see in the story of the martyrdom of St Lawrence. In 258 CE, the prefect of Rome summoned the archdeacon Lawrence to surrender the church's treasures in order to supplement the government's dwindling coffers. Cheekily, Lawrence feigned agreement and asked leave to collect the church's wealth. Returning a couple days later, Lawrence paraded before the prefect a rag-tag assembly of beggars, widows and cripples, all of whom were supported by the Christian charitable bureaucracy (Prudentius, *Perist.* 2.173–72, 297–300); Lawrence then waxed eloquent about how the poor are jewels in the temple of God. The prefect was not amused and had Lawrence barbecued alive on a gridiron. This story is significant because we know that the Roman Church of this period possessed a formidable community chest and included many rich members (such as the senators who bore off Lawrence's body for burial; Prudentius, *Perist.* 2.489–492). But insofar as Lawrence was confident that the state was not acting as an agent of justice, he chose to die rather than to cooperate with the regime financially.

These brief investigations of economic and criminal justice clarify that the church has no grounds for fobbing the poor off on the state, even though Christians can cooperate with governments when their endeavours coincide with Christian commitments. Even Cyrus and Nero can be God's servants (Isa. 45.1-4, 13; Rom. 13.1-7). But, as the latter example suggests, God's imperial servant can quickly become a foe of justice, and so the church's efforts at cooperation should never be uncritical. Accordingly, when Rome becomes the Great Whore, then cooperation may need to turn to resistance on behalf of the poor, even carrying the gridiron of St Lawrence.

The church, the state and poverty in modern Colombia

The Church of Colombia has a complex history of trying to ameliorate poverty with and against the state. It was in 1968, in the city of Medellin, that the Latin American Episcopal Conference (CELAM) officially affirmed liberation theology's opposition

---

[64] Revelation 18 celebrates her foretold destruction, exulting in the way that would bring to the end her trade in fine goods (vv. 11–14) and the impact that would have on the merchants and seafarers (vv. 15–20). Apparently, the seer was not worried about the effect that the drop in GDP would have on the livelihood of the Christian populace!

to governmental and economic policies that reinforced poverty in Latin countries. In continuity with this ideological commitment, some church leaders – like Fr Camilo Torres Restrepo – ended up fomenting violent revolution.[65] Fr Torres was a priest, a sociologist (co-founder of Colombia's first faculty of sociology, at the Universidad Nacional de Colombia), and he became a guerrilla in the Ejercito de Liberación Nacional (ELN, National Liberation Army), which is the largest guerrilla group in Colombia. Killed in combat during his first engagement, Fr Torres has become a martyr of the ELN, which now is officially called the Unión Camilista-Ejército de Liberación Nacional; his name figures prominently in the hymn of the ELN:

> Avancemos al combate, compañeros, que están vivas la conciencia y la razón de Camilo el Comandante guerrillero, con su ejemplo en la consigna **NUPALOM** [**ni un paso atrás, liberación o muerte**].[66]
>
> Let us advance to combat, comrades, for alive are the consciousness and the reason of Camilo, the guerrilla commander, with his example of the motto NUPALOM [not a step backwards; liberation or death]. (Author's translation)

In the wake of Torres, the ELN has been led by several Catholic priests (such as Fr Manuel Pérez Martínez) who, in varying degrees, continued to elaborate the group's ideology as a combination of liberation theology and Marxism.

This matrix of church/state/poverty issues has become poignant for us at our seminary in Medellín, as we engage with the humanitarian crisis of forced displacement. Just since 1998, over seven million Colombians have been dispossessed and impoverished by violence at the hands of the guerrillas, the drug cartels and the paramilitary groups. Over the past decades, the government's hands have not always been clean in these conflicts; even in their well-intentioned moments, Colombia's leaders have often exacerbated the poverty and suffering of the Colombian people. So, as our seminary seeks to mobilize the church in responding to the displacement crisis, we struggle with the question of how to cooperate with the government, while recognizing that, for some internally displaced persons (IDPs), the government has historically been part of the problem.

The powers and the church of the powerful poor

Up to this point, I have emphasized how the Church engages constructively and critically with the powers in sharing responsibility for the poor. But now I want to flip my own premise, first, because the church and the poor are not strictly distinct entities and, secondly, because the poor are not powerless.

---

[65] For an incisive, and not wholly unsympathetic, commentary on the role of priests in the guerrilla conflict, see the recent article by the current Provincial Superior of the Jesuit Order, Francisco de Roux, 'Decisiones de guerra y paz', *El Tiempo*, 14 October 2015 (http://www.eltiempo.com/opinion/columnistas/decisiones-de-guerra-y-paz-francisco-de-roux-columna-el-tiempo/16403831, accessed May 2016).

[66] Ejército de Liberación Nacional, *Himno* (1964) (http://www.eltiempo.com/archivo/documento/CMS-16403831, accessed May 2016).

One of the basic affirmations of Jesus's ministry is that the poor and marginalized are particularly valued by God. Jesus frames his preaching as good news for the poor (Lk. 4.18) and he calls the poor 'blessed' (Lk. 6.20: 'Blessed are you who are poor, for yours is the kingdom of God'; cf. Jas 2.5; Rev. 2.9), affirming their value in a context which often thought that poverty belied one's dignity and integrity.[67] Jesus himself is construed as one who accepted penury voluntarily (Lk. 9.58: 'And Jesus said to him, "Foxes have holes, and birds of the air have nests; but the Son of Man has nowhere to lay his head."'). And even today, in many contexts the church remains the assembly of the impoverished: for example, Africa has a population of nearly half a billion Christians (494,668,000) and they have an *average* income of 1.85 US dollars per day.[68] So, for theological and demographic reasons, when we say that the church has responsibility for the poor, we are affirming that the poor have responsibility for the poor.

But the NT does not simply construe the poor as beneficiaries of the kingdom; it affirms the *potency* of the poor as agents of God's mercy. John the Baptist elaborates an ethic of solidarity among the poor; sharing one of your two tunics (Lk. 3.10-11) is not an ethic aimed at the rich. Further, when Jesus discusses the widow's offering (Mk 12.41-44// Lk. 21.1-4), he celebrates that the greatest generosity was shown by the poor woman who gave '*out of her lack*' (my italics). Similarly, 2 Corinthians 8 lauds the munificence of the impoverished church of Macedonia:

For during a severe ordeal of affliction, *their abundant joy and their extreme poverty have overflowed in a wealth of generosity on their part.* ... They voluntarily gave according to their means, and *even beyond their means*, begging us earnestly for the privilege of sharing in this ministry to the saints (2 Cor. 8.2-4, NRSV, my italics)

Paul goes on to praise Jesus for becoming poor so that, by his poverty, the saints might become rich: 'For you know the generous act of our Lord Jesus Christ, that though he was rich, yet for your sakes he became poor, so that by his poverty you might become rich' (2 Cor. 8.9).[69]

The poor are also agents of *justice*, opposing the rich and powerful who often foment injustice. Jesus decries the exploitation and neglect of the powerful when he purified the Temple (Mk 11.15-19)[70] and when he excoriates the scribes who devour widows' houses (Mk 12.40//Lk. 20.47//Mt. 23.14).[71] Additionally, on the heels of his

[67] See Hays, *Luke's Wealth Ethics*, 27.
[68] Jonathan J. Bonk, 'Christian Finance, 1910–2010', in *Atlas of Global Christianity*, ed. Todd M. Johnson and Kenneth R. Ross (Edinburgh: Edinburgh University Press, 2009), 294–97.
[69] Indeed, Paul's arguments about the poor Macedonians and the poor Messiah serve the purpose of mobilizing the more-affluent Corinthians (see 2 Cor. 8.13-15).
[70] Some temple leaders employed bribery to gain power and resorted to thuggery to deprive poorer priests of their tithes; see Josephus, *Ant.* 20.8.8; 20.9.2; Richard Bauckham, 'Jesus' Demonstration in the Temple', in *Law and Religion: Essays on the Place of the Law in Israel and Early Christianity: by Members of the Ehrhardt Seminar of Manchester University*, ed. Barnabas Lindars (Cambridge: James Clarke, 1988), 72–89.
[71] Scribes would oversee the inheritances of illiterate widows and would sometimes embezzle from those funds; J. Duncan M. Derrett, '"Eating Up the Houses of Widows": Jesus's Comment on Lawyers?', *NovT* 14 (1972): 1–9.

denunciation of the Temple leadership,[72] Jesus launches his disciples into positions of authority; menial fishermen like Peter are appointed to replace the den of thieves that is the temple elite (so Mk 11.23-25//Mt. 21.21-22). Thus, the NT reminds us that the powers are often the problem, not the solution. God's response to the powers who fleece the poor involves leadership by the marginal, who follow the peasant preacher that the powers crucified.

It is true that the church, civil society and the state have moral responsibilities towards the poor, but one of those responsibilities is to recognize that the poor are potent people who can collaborate with the powers in transforming their own situations of oppression. Indeed, the poor will be more effectively loved and served to the degree that we affirm that they are not only the beneficiaries of the kingdom of God but also its agents.

In practice, this is not intuitive to me; I still flatter myself by strapping on the White Man's Burden, and I need to be reminded that education and good intentions do not qualify me as a messiah, that I am not more valuable to the kingdom than those who have nowhere to lay their heads. That awareness needs to shape my social activism. Thus, as our seminary develops responses to the Colombian displacement crisis, we are partnering with IDPs as co-researchers and genuine collaborators. We want to affirm and encourage IDPs as agents of God's kingdom, fostering its presence (Lk. 17.21) even after they have been expelled from their homes by heinous violence.

Concluding synthesis

This essay examined how the ancient church engaged with the structures, practices and ideology of civil society and the state in seeking to care for the poor. We certainly witness positive ecclesial engagement, adopting structures and conventions from civil society and looking for the government to act as God's servant. Still, the church's engagement was reflective, critically analysing to how secular ideologies clash with Christian commitments, altering pagan practices for Christian ends. Moreover, the church nurtured the poor when the state did not care, and she resisted the powers when they became agents of corruption.

Still, describing how the church and the powers share responsibility for the poor is insufficient. To riff on Abraham Lincoln's Gettysburg Address, which spoke of 'government of the people, by the people, and for the people', the church should be of the poor, led by the poor and for the poor. The poor are not just victims to be rescued by ecclesial, societal and governmental powers. They are powerful, and part of the answer to the powers' problems, for they are the body of the impecunious king who became poor that we might become rich.

---

[72] The cursing and withering of the fig-tree in Mk 11.12-14, 20-25, which form an *inclusio* around Jesus's cleansing of the temple, symbolically depict the doom of the Jerusalem leaders for failing to 'bear fruit' (cf. Lk. 13.6-9); see R. T. France, *The Gospel of Mark*, NIGTC (Grand Rapids, MI: Eerdmans, 2002), 339–41.

Poverty and the Powers Today

Stephen Timms, MP

Then and now

Dr Christopher Hays's fascinating essay shows us how the practice of the Early Church with regard to poverty shamed and subverted the powers at the time. That state, while not a 'nation state' of the kind we know today, was an imperialist Roman occupation. Our modern UK nation state is a democracy. If people dislike what the state is doing, the government can fairly readily be replaced. The aims of the state are different as a result.

Dr Hays tells us that a rudimentary form of welfare was established by the Roman government, partly under pressure from the practice of Christians. In the New Testament, we read in Acts that the Early Church in Jerusalem was able to ensure that 'there were no needy persons among them' (4.34) through those with resources sharing them with those who lacked them. That was an impressive achievement, making a big impression on observers.

Two thousand years ago, the church was a unique organization in the way it sought to alleviate the suffering of people around it. Today, in another big contrast, we have large numbers of well-developed charities who share that aim: there are in total over 160,000 registered charities in the UK.[1] The generosity of individuals and trusts, along with support from local and national government, enables them to thrive.

What should we be expecting the state to do today? It could never meet every need. Its agencies and their processes are often inflexible and its resources are limited. For example, a husband who walks out on his wife and children on a Friday night, taking all financial provision with him, would leave his family without the means to pay for basic necessities over a weekend – the state would not be equipped to respond.

However, since the work of the Labour government which followed World War II, we have assumed that the state would provide general protection against destitution.

[1] 'Charity Commission Annual Report and Accounts 2016–17', 4 (https://www.gov.uk/government/uploads/system/uploads/attachment_data/file/628747/Charity_Commission_Annual_Report_and_Accounts_2016_17_web.pdf, accessed December 2017).

That assumption is starting to be questioned. It has been the policy of governments in recent years not just to acknowledge the inevitable limitations of its reach but also to withdraw from earlier areas of support. Problems which used to be regarded as unacceptable failures by the state are increasingly regarded as not necessarily the role of the state. The Trussell Trust reports that almost 30 per cent of food bank referrals result from administrative delays in payment of benefit.[2] The Secretary of State for Work and Pensions for the five years before the 2015 general election – far from being punished for such delays – was reappointed after it.

Food banks are necessary, not only because of benefit delays or unexpected events, but because in the UK we have an economic system in which people can be in full-time work and still live below the poverty line. A mother can be sanctioned by the Job Centre for staying with her baby overnight in an intensive care ward. The postcode a person grew up in still has a big impact on their life expectancy.

The Resolution Foundation's Low Pay Britain 2015 Report states that the private sector accounts for 85 per cent of all low-paid jobs.[3] Initiatives such as the Living Wage Campaign – the result of a largely faith-based coalition which started in East London[4] – gives us one example of a reshaping of the economic system in a way that benefits the poorest.

While we live in a country with these characteristics, it surely remains as important a duty for the church and its members to press political parties on their policies as it is to provide vital services to those in need.

Church impact today

There is a widespread impression that the church is gently fading away. Regular reports of declining church attendance convey an impression of faith-based organizations in terminal decline. In reality, it seems to me that the opposite is the case. Certainly in London, where there are also very large non-Christian religious congregations, church attendance has been rising for some years.[5] The Church of England is building its first new churches in London since the 1950s.[6] I suspect we will start to see the decline in attendance going into reverse on a larger scale in the future.

---

[2] The Trussell Trust, 'Foodbank Use Remains at Record High', 15 April 2016 (https://www.trusselltrust.org/2016/04/15/foodbank-use-remains-record-high/, accessed November 2015).

[3] Adam Corlett and Laura Gardiner, *Low Pay Britain 2015* (London: Resolution Foundation, 2015), 24, 42 (http://www.resolutionfoundation.org/app/uploads/2015/10/Low-Pay-Britain-2015.pdf, accessed June 2017).

[4] Living Wage Foundation, 'History' (http://www.livingwage.org.uk/history, accessed November 2015).

[5] Diocese of London, 'Rise in Young People Attending Church in London', 7 May 2013 (http://www.london.anglican.org/articles/rise-in-young-people-attending-church-in-london/, accessed November 2015).

[6] Bishop Richard Chartres, 'Bishop of London Delivers Lambeth Lecture on Church Growth in the Capital', Diocese of London, 1 October 2015 (http://www.archbishopofcanterbury.org/articles.php/5621/bishop-of-london-delivers-lambeth-lecture-on-church-growth-in-the-capital, accessed November 2015).

However – whatever the picture on church attendance – the impact of churches and of other faith-based organizations is today clearly on the rise. The best known example is the food bank movement. The Trussell Trust has developed an extraordinary network of 424 food banks around the country, every one of which is based on a church. Forty thousand people – by no means all church members – volunteered with them in 2016–17.[7] I see colleagues in Parliament – like the Roman authorities – being impressed by what the churches are doing in providing for others.

If we had had a discussion ten years ago about what would happen if hundreds of thousands of people could no longer afford sufficient food, many would not have predicted that the churches would be the ones to come forward with help. But that is what has happened. It has turned out, in Britain in 2015, that it has been uniquely the churches which have had both the motivation and, perhaps more surprisingly, the capacity to take on the challenge of food poverty. No other organization or network has been able to do so on anything like this scale. And, my goodness, they have made a difference.

The relationship between the Trussell Trust and the government is interesting. The Trussell Trust should qualify as the prime example of (then) Prime Minister David Cameron's Big Society in action. It is voluntary action on an extraordinary scale. However, ministers do not celebrate its achievements. The problem for the government is that the Trussell Trust does not just hand out food. It also insists – despite enormous pressure from ministers to stop – on publishing data about how many people use food banks and the reasons why. For months, ministers refused to meet the Trussell Trust, accusing them of having a political agenda against welfare reform. Finally – answering a question I put to him in the House of Commons – David Cameron agreed to meet them in 2015. But the government remains deeply uncomfortable. The Trussell Trust and its statistics present an unsettling challenge to ministers about what the real effects of their policies are. The church is shaming the authorities. Unlike Emperor Julian,[8] our state does not yet feel the need to change its ways in response.

My Christian understanding is that government has a responsibility to build an economic system that is just. A million visits to food banks in each of the years 2014–15, 2015–16 and 2016–17 – in many cases by people who are in work – suggest we have a long way to go.[9] Alleviating poverty requires being proactive in tackling the drivers of poverty as well as being reactive to the effects of poverty. The rise in the national minimum wage which the government has proposed will help, but other factors in the economy will need to change too.

A new role for the church

With the state now retreating, the church has the possibility of a new role. In Mark 12, Jesus provided two commandments for his followers:

[7]   The Trusell Trust, 'End of Year Stats' (https://www.trusselltrust.org/news-and-blog/latest-stats/end-year-stats/, accessed February 2018).
[8]   See Christopher Hays, 'The Early Church, The Roman State and Ancient Civil Society: Whose Responsibility Are the Poor?', 172 in this book.
[9]   Trussell Trust, 'End of Year Stats'.

'The most important one', answered Jesus, 'is this: "Hear, O Israel: The Lord our God, the Lord is one. Love the Lord your God with all your heart and with all your soul and with all your mind and with all your strength." The second is this: "Love your neighbour as yourself."' (Mk 12.29-31)

The command to love our neighbour as ourselves was not a throwaway line. It was a mandate for a mission which should be at the foundation of the Christian life. For as long as economic and social injustices exist, while some people are forgotten and have no voice, the church has a duty to seek to pick up those who have been left behind.

It is important in Christian belief that individual responsibility is maintained and not seen as being delegated to the church by the giving of money. In Matthew 25, Jesus tells the story of the sheep and the goats. Near the end he says,

They also will answer, 'Lord, when did we see you hungry or thirsty or a stranger or needing clothes or sick or in prison, and did not help you?' He will reply, 'Truly I tell you, whatever you did not do for one of the least of these, you did not do for me.' (Mt. 25.44-45)

No matter how much money the individual gives, he or she is still called on to interact directly with the poor.

Examples of how the churches changed things in our history – particularly from the eighteenth and nineteenth centuries – are well known: the abolition of slavery and the spread of education are examples. But it is happening today too, and not just through food banks.

The *Jubilee 2000* campaign – initiated in the churches and drawing most of its support from them, albeit attracting wider support too – campaigned in the years before the millennium for the cancellation of the debts owed to Britain by the poorest countries in the world. I was a minister in the Treasury at the time. The Treasury was inundated with *Jubilee 2000* postcards with £1 coins sellotaped to them, and a human chain formed around the building on one occasion. That was followed by the Make Poverty History campaign, which culminated in 2005.

Those campaigns – which were not exclusively church-based, but which drew the large majority of their support and their energy from the churches[10] – changed Britain's political culture. They delivered a cross-party consensus which survived the changes of government in 2010 and 2015, and which means that Britain is today for the first time[11] delivering the UN target that 0.7 per cent of our gross domestic product should be committed to overseas aid.[12] No one other than the churches could have delivered that. A more partisan campaign certainly could not have delivered it.

---

[10] 'Jubilee 2000' (http://tinyurl.com/y84suaqd, accessed February 2018).
[11] Department for International Development, 'Statistics on International Development 2015', 3 December 2015, 6 (https://www.gov.uk/government/uploads/system/uploads/attachment_data/file/482322/SID2015c.pdf, accessed June 2017).
[12] United Nations, 'Integrated Implementation Framework' (http://iif.un.org/content/official-development-assistance, accessed November 2015).

In 1996, John Kirkby founded Christians Against Poverty (CAP). Its local projects, all based in local churches, have enabled countless people to escape from debt and provided advice to many more. There are 290 CAP debt centres and 145 job clubs that have been established. By 2021, CAP aims for 1,000 local projects.[13]

These examples show the potential impact of faith-based initiatives today. Through hard work, a clear vision and an unmatched capacity to enlist volunteers, they can succeed in changing hearts and reaching out where others have drawn a blank.

A strategic choice for the churches

The church's increased role in programmes and services across the country poses a strategic – and moral – question about the level of its involvement. Is increased involvement a positive sign of effective civic engagement, or a negative impact of abdication by the state? Is the church compromised by both taking money from local or national government while seeking to offer critique of that government's policies and actions? Should the church welcome a bigger role, or deplore the necessity for it?

There certainly is not a problem with the quality of provision that churches can offer. Youth work, debt counselling and marriage preparation are areas where churches are providing invaluable help to people with and without faith. Sometimes the issue can be raised that opportunities for direct evangelism and witness are limited in such situations, where local government provides financial support – and there is a challenge here to churches to find creative ways of engaging in direct evangelism alongside their social engagement.

The church is present in every community. Its local branches interact regularly with vast numbers of people. That gives the capacity to identify fast changing needs and to adapt to meet them. I welcome the church playing an increased role in society. It should not be merely a reactionary role. The church and faith-based organizations have a unique opportunity to see the consequences of government policy. They are in a good position to feed back to the government observations about what works and what does not. As our society takes the fight to poverty, we need to look for new ways that the different powers of today can interact and work with one another better.

Christianity has spread across the world. It is forecast that by 2030, China will have more churchgoers than the United States.[14] In many cases, unlike China, Christianity is entwined in the constitution of nations, such as in the UK. Nevertheless, the church's mission and objectives, to champion the cause of the least and the lost, remain the same as 2,000 years ago.

In the UK, the churches have to tackle cynicism and scepticism. A fear by some 'secular' funders of aggressive proselytizing, or of bias in favour of faith group members,

---

[13] Christians Against Poverty, 'How it All Started' (https://capuk.org/about-us/the-cap-story, accessed November 2015).

[14] Tom Phillips, 'China on Course to Become "World's Most Christian Nation" within 15 Years', *The Telegraph*, 19 April 2014 (http://www.telegraph.co.uk/news/worldnews/asia/china/10776023/China-on-course-to-become-worlds-most-Christian-nation-within-15-years.html, accessed November 2015).

can prevent a faith organization from being given funding to deliver a service or recognition that it deserves. In 2013, the think tank Demos undertook a study on the role of faith in British society.[15] Among the case studies of faith-based providers that it examined, there was no evidence of aggressive proselytizing. The services provided were not biased in favour of believers but met the needs of people from a wide variety of backgrounds. The government – and, in particular, the local government – needs to be more confident in the potential contribution of faith-based providers.

It would be a mistake to try to drive the faith out of a faith-based organization. Quite the opposite. It is the faith of many of the volunteers and workers for these organizations which compels them to become more involved and to serve their community. The Demos report found that people who belonged to a religious organization were much more likely to volunteer than those who did not. Government should appreciate the dynamism that comes from people of faith, their enthusiasm for serving and interacting with people from different backgrounds. That contributes possibilities that the state on its own could not achieve.

I chair the All Party Parliamentary Group on Faith and Society. It exists to draw attention to the contribution which faith-based organizations make in their communities, to help celebrate them and – where appropriate – to help address the policy and regulatory constraints which sometimes hold them back. As a group, we have become aware of the serious tensions which seem to arise – in particular – between local authorities and faith-based organizations in their areas. We have drawn up what we call a Covenant for Engagement, the text of which is on our website,[16] which is intended to be signed up to by both local authorities and faith groups in their area wanting to be commissioned to provide services. The first local authority to sign up, in 2014, was Birmingham City Council, the largest local authority in Europe. I was in Halifax in 2015 for the adoption by Calderdale Borough Council of the Covenant there.

The church and faith-based providers can shape our culture through the services they provide and the voice they present. The nature of the services being offered and the manner they are delivered in areas left by the rest of society can prompt wider action. Britain's political culture can be changed as a result.

Church and state

In a society where the eradication of poverty was a central mission, the powers of today – including national and local governments, and faith-based groups – would work together and use their strengths and abilities in tandem with each other. There would be respect for differences in beliefs and an eagerness to work across theological, political and social divides. The state would aim for an economic system in which

---

[15] Jonathan Birdwell and Stephen Timms, MP, eds, *Exploring the Role of Faith in British Society and Politics* (London: Demos, 2013) (https://www.demos.co.uk/files/DEMOS_The_Faith_Collection_-_web_version.pdf, accessed June 2017).

[16] 'Covenant for Engagement', All-Party Parliamentary Group on Faith and Society (http://www.faithandsociety.org/covenant/, accessed November 2015).

everyone can work – in which individuals can apply for jobs and promotions without fear of discrimination – and in which those paid least in society can still afford to live decently.

The church and faith-based providers have always been creative in addressing formidable challenges. It is important to underline that that is not just a historical observation, as we are seeing from – alongside the examples I have already mentioned – organizations like CAFOD and Traidcraft, and initiatives like Street Pastors.

Churches and church-based organizations need to be both inward- and outward-looking. They must nurture and deliver programmes to the people they already serve, while also always imagining and dreaming about better ways of serving others in need. Churches and faith-based organizations see gaps, where the state lacks the resources or is too inflexible to respond and individuals are unable to cover these gaps themselves. They can fill caring gaps and help ensure vulnerable people are cared for.

Conclusion

Poverty in Britain was driven down over centuries through the combined work of the state, churches, charities and individuals. Today, progress seems to have stalled. Our society has become increasingly unequal. The powers in Britain do have the skill, expertise and enthusiasm to ensure that poverty can be eradicated. The question is whether they will work together to make it happen. The role of the churches will – in my view – be key in determining whether we resume progress or give up.

28

Response to Christopher Hays

Stephen Timms, MP

The notion that a core purpose of a national government is to focus on the condition of its poorest citizens has become a political norm. Christopher Hays's fascinating historical and biblical analysis shows how the idea of society caring for the poor had origins in the actions of the church and its members. The Early Church adapted and subverted ideas and institutions which were common at the time – voluntary associations, banqueting, benefaction, patronage – in order to pursue its calling.

From the very inception of the Christian Church, the Lord's Supper became a place where societal and class divisions were broken down, and that went a long way to break the notion that greater wealth conferred greater importance or value in society. At one stage, as Dr Hays explains, the Roman emperor felt obliged to provide welfare to the poor out of embarrassment that the Christians were supporting 'not only their own poor but ours as well'.[1]

Dr Hays shows that Graeco-Roman society had a different approach to benefaction: to benefit the givers' own social status, rather than primarily to benefit the poor. Today, voluntary giving to the poor is to be encouraged and lauded. But state programmes and initiatives show how helping others less fortunate than yourself as a primary motivation for giving has been embraced and promoted by the modern institutions of government. Dr Hays does not argue that the church set out to change the mission of the state, but that was the powerful consequence of the church's setting about its mission.

No matter how selfless philanthropists are, or how effective charity relief programmes are, underlying institutional structures which perpetuate unequal outcomes will undermine their good intentions. Some Christians are sceptical about the ability of government to bring about effective social change and improvements to the lives of its poorest citizens. Believing that God is in ultimate power, some are more comfortable with welfare coming from benevolent believers than from the state. But this overlooks the scale of the challenge, how wide the reach of government is and its demonstrable potential to do good.

[1] Christopher Hays, 'The Early Church, The Roman State and Ancient Civil Society: Whose Responsibility Are the Poor?', in this volume.

Communication and collaboration between the state – in particular, at times, the local state – and the church need improvement. Both must realize the strengths and weaknesses of each other. The flexibility and dynamism of church organization can be complemented by the size of the state and its greater resources and reach.

Dr Hays is right to highlight the power of the poor and to show how the New Testament does so. In our system, policies and procedures are often directed to recipients without any discussion. This leads to policy mistakes and alienates the poor from politics. People must be seen and spoken to as people, not merely as an economic unit or a national insurance number. Solutions to economic injustice cannot be found just by talking to people – however well meaning – who have never experienced it. Listening to people who are experiencing injustice and understanding and valuing their insights and contributions are vital steps in eliminating structural poverty.

29

Response to Stephen Timms, MP

Christopher M. Hays

Governments tend to get something of a drubbing in academic conferences. This may happen because academics have a keen awareness of the shortcomings of the state (and, perhaps, especially the political parties with which they do not identify), although at times one uncharitably suspects these critiques may have something to do with the scholarly self-importance! That notwithstanding, the tenor of the exchange following Stephen Timms's presentation was notably (and refreshingly) constructive, no doubt in good measure because of the tone Mr Timms himself set.

I am encouraged by Mr Timms's illustrations of how, in *word* and *deed*, the church can and has beneficially engaged with the government in order to ameliorate poverty. In *word*, the church communicates with the government (affirmatively and critically). Mr Timms explains how the intimate community knowledge of local congregations renders them uniquely capable of providing feedback to the government about which new policies and programmes are having a positive impact, and which measures require revision. He also affirms the critical role that churches and faith-based organizations can play in response to government failings; a case in point is the Trussell Trust's publication of the fact that the largest single reason people recur to their services is benefit delays.[1]

In *deed*, the Church acts where the government falls short, and even pioneers new paths. Mr Timms celebrates the fact that when hunger afflicts people in Britain, Christian organizations do more than just rail against the state; they also take matters into their own hands, creating food banks and providing financial counselling and career services (e.g. the Christians Against Poverty debt centres and job clubs). But the church is not just the maid which picks up after the government; she also innovates and pioneers. Thus, Mr Timms rightly highlights initiatives like the *Jubilee 2000* campaign, Traidcraft and Street Pastors. Perhaps Mr Timms is especially attuned to the diverse ways in which the church and state can cooperate to heal poverty because of his role as chair of the All Party Parliamentary Group on Faith and Society. But his testimony makes it clear that, in nations like the United Kingdom, the church most robustly

---

[1] The Trussell Trust, 'Primary Referral Causes in 2014–2015 to Trussell Trust Foodbanks' (https://www.trusselltrust.org/what-we-do/, accessed May 2016).

serves the poor when she cooperates with the state, in both critical and constructive capacities.

There is, naturally, more that could be said, beyond the themes Mr Timms had space to explore, although perhaps one theme is particularly noteworthy. During our days together in London, conference participants repeatedly affirmed the potency, personal resources and insights of the marginalized themselves, cautioning against the dangers of primarily viewing the poor as passive recipients of the church's and government's aid. The model of Asset-Based Community Development popped up time and again, since that approach recognizes the assets and skills possessed by members of low-income communities and fosters the mobilization of those community members in response to local challenges.[2] These same commitments are integral to the Umoja model practised around the world in Tearfund's 'Church and Community Mobilisation' programmes.[3] These are exciting strategies, and the adoption of such approaches could help the church to continue to recover her identity as a community of the marginalized, a community in which the blessed poor bless the world. As my closing query for Mr Timms, I would be curious to hear about whether the UK government has mechanisms in place not only to seek out the regular feedback of low-income and even homeless citizens but also to engage them as constructive agents who can contribute to solving some of the nation's social problems.

---

[2] For more information, see the seminal book by John P. Kretzmann and John L. McKnight, *Building Communities from the Inside Out: A Path toward Finding and Mobilizing a Community's Assets* (Evanston, IL: Institute for Policy Research, 1993).

[3] See, e.g., Francis Njoroge, Tulo Raistrick, Bill Crooks and Jackie Mouradian, *Umoja: Co-ordinator's Guide* (Teddington: Tearfund, 2009).

30

The Poor Will Always Be among You: Poverty, Education and the Catholic Ideal

Francis Campbell

Introduction

Poverty remains a major issue in today's world. As a Catholic university, St Mary's has a duty to stimulate and engage in discussion about how we can work to eliminate poverty, and my paper will be reflecting on St Mary's as a 'case study' of what it might look like for a Christian institution of higher education to contribute to that important goal. So I am delighted that we have been able to join with Tearfund and Caritas to stage a conference and to produce this book. I am also delighted that we practised what we preach by ensuring that part of the registration fee for the conference went to the Riverbank Trust, a local charity which works with vulnerable single mums and their families in Richmond.[1]

A preference for the poor

My starting point must be the first half of my title, which will be familiar to you as the words spoken by Jesus to some of his disciples when Mary Magdalene anointed him with oil, not long before his crucifixion. His disciples were indignant, because they felt she had disobeyed Jesus's instructions to sell luxury items in support of the poor. They regarded her use of expensive perfume as a waste and counter to his teaching. Yet Jesus admonished them by saying, 'You will always have the poor among you, but you will not always have me' (Jn 12.8). Jesus was not, of course, intending to be dismissive of the poor. He continually spoke out in support of the poor and famously said it was easier for a camel to squeeze through the eye of the needle than for a rich man to enter the kingdom of God (Lk. 18.25).

His teachings are responsible for the Church having an explicit preference for the poor. That is something that the current Pope is, of course, extremely concerned about. As he has said, the Catholic Church should be 'a poor Church for the poor'. He used

---

[1]   See Ellie Hughes, 'Poverty and Dehumanization', in this book.

that phrase to demonstrate his concerns about stories concerning the lavish lifestyles of some members of the Church hierarchy, which he believed were serving to alienate the faithful. As a consequence, Pope Francis has been determined to adopt a more visibly austere approach, eschewing big apartments and most recently using a Fiat to get around New York rather than the Popemobile. Some have attacked those actions as political stunts. They are certainly intended to send out a political message – but I would not dismiss them as stunts. Rather, those actions are important symbols which push us to examine how we behave and live, and that means each of us.

As I will come on to later, the Pope's warning about the alienation caused by extravagance should resonate with those of us involved in education, and higher education in particular.

Putting God first

So concern for the poor and the need to relate to the poor is absolutely embedded in the DNA of the Catholic Church. Jesus was not signalling indifference to the poor when he referred to them as always being with us. The point he was making was captured in what he said next: 'You will not always have me' (Jn 12.8). His message was that our first duty is to love and serve God. How is that relevant to our discussion about poverty, education and the Catholic ideal?

Poverty, education and the Catholic ideal

First, I would say it is highly relevant in the context of the UK and some other Western countries which have witnessed a trend of rising secularism in recent years. Many Catholic educational institutions founded in such pluralistic societies face the temptation or indeed the pressure to blend into secular societal norms rather than to promote their distinctiveness. That temptation, that pressure, is greater in societies that have become hostile or indifferent to Christianity and unsupportive of the benefit that faith-based institutions bring to the wider community.

Material and professional pressures

As the education system places increased emphasis on professional metrics and academic standards, as funding is increasingly tied to performance in league tables and as students are turned into consumers by a system of fees, the focus of schools and universities is inevitably drawn towards the daily grind and the demands from meeting statutory targets and material expectations. The space for attention relating to the core gospel-centred identity of these institutions becomes squeezed. As a result, a number of Catholic educational bodies have decided to weaken their religious affiliation. However, that seems to me a betrayal of their history and purpose. Catholic schools and universities should not just hang on to their core identity; it should be their central foundation. It is a strength upon which to build, not a burden to be cast aside.

The Catholic ideal

In November 2015, Catholic academic leaders gathered in Rome for the Congregation for Catholic Education's World Congress on Catholic Education to explore the role of Catholic identity in today's Catholic schools and universities. In a world where educators can be focused on university rankings, athletic team competitiveness and the future monetary gain of students, we discussed how Catholic institutions provide parents and students with a holistic education that is focused on developing character.

As I have seen at St Mary's University, focusing on Catholic identity can strengthen Catholic schools and universities, enabling them to better serve their pupils and students, better serve society and more actively engage in public debate. So what does a Catholic educational institution look like? And how does it engage with the issue of poverty?

Catholic education rooted in the poor

To answer those questions, let us begin by considering the origins of Catholic education in this country – a story in which St Mary's played, and continues to play, an important and influential role.

The Catholic Church was the first provider of schools and universities in England, but the Reformation saw significant upheaval in the centuries following. It was not until the nineteenth century that there was a significant formal expansion of Catholic education in England, largely in response to the wave of Catholic immigrants entering English towns and cities from Catholic Ireland. In 1847, a unique partnership was agreed with the State, and the Catholic Poor-School Committee was established by the Bishops of England and Wales to focus on the promotion of Catholic elementary education for this growing – largely poor Catholic – population.

Since the Church has always viewed education as vital to the formation and development of the whole person, the Catholic Bishops in England decided that educating the poor was to be the Catholic community's first priority. They even put the creation of schools for the Catholic community ahead of building churches, often using those schools in the early days as the place for worship for the parish.

The establishment of Catholic schools inevitably made teacher training a priority, and so a number of teacher training colleges were established. St Mary's, established in 1850, is one of the oldest. In keeping with the Catholic missionary tradition, which continues to play an absolutely vital role in educating the poor in all parts of the world, St Mary's was originally built on the labours of six French priests who arrived in England on a mission to teach the poor. Since then, St Mary's has sent generations of teachers out into the schools of England and more widely. It remains absolutely central to the mission of our university.

Open, accessible, diverse – and Catholic

So a concern to educate the poor has always lain at the heart of the Catholic ideal of education. For that reason, the issue of accessibility is a critical aspect of the identity of

Catholic schools and universities. They are not intended to be elitist or exclusive. They are intended to be comprehensive, open to all.

At St Mary's, we have a community of nearly 7,000: about 5,000 undergraduates, 1,000 postgraduates and just under 1,000 staff on a beautiful fifty-acre campus by the banks of the Thames at Twickenham in south-west London.[2] An important part of our story is that only a small minority of our students and staff are practising Catholics. Like other universities, we have on our books large numbers who are of other faiths or of no faith. We have the utmost respect for all faiths and a very strong belief that our community – in particular its intellectual rigour – is enhanced by the presence of people who come from different traditions.

Nonetheless, you may ask how an institution can claim to be Catholic if most of the people inside it do not belong to the Catholic faith. The answer is that the Catholic nature of our university is not located in any individual or groups of individuals but in the general ethos of the university – the 'spirit' of the place. Many people – staff, students and visitors – remark on the powerful community spirit that is present in St Mary's. No doubt that comes in part from our size, our beautiful location and the fact that we have all our facilities on one site, but I think there is more to it than that. Part of the strength of community life at St Mary's stems from the core Catholic foundation that recognizes the intrinsic dignity of every human person. That is what underpins our commitment to ensuring that everyone who enters our university feels included on an equal basis.

Another key aspect of our Catholic ethos is the emphasis on offering a service to the wider world and a determination to stand up for justice, fairness and ethical values. That ethos informs the direction and focus of our work. It runs through everything we do – from sport through to education.

Now, in saying that, I should stress that we are not a seminary. We are an autonomous institution. We value academic freedom, independent thought and a diverse but inclusive community, but we are motivated by a desire to develop rounded students through a philosophy that can be traced back to Cardinal Newman's vision of a university education which reunites intellect and virtue.[3] It is that emphasis on the whole person – the mind, body and spirit – which creates the community spirit of St Mary's and holds a powerful appeal to students past, present and future.

Furthermore, we are guided by our Catholic identity to raise the tone of intellectual debate and to pursue work that is ultimately designed to make the world a more just, peaceful and compassionate place. That is a very deliberate decision. If an institution truly wants to retain its Catholic identity, then it needs to decide that Catholic values will underpin its activity and work, and work out how they can be given practical expression.

It is a philosophy that runs through everything we do, not just on the academic side but also in the way we run the institution. For example, we are mindful that our students and ancillary staff find it hard to make ends meet, particularly in times of

---

[2]   Numbers are as of the 2017–18 academic year.
[3]   John Henry Newman, *The Idea of a University* (London: Longmans Green, 1852; now freely available on the internet).

recession and economic difficulty. That is why we were first out of the traps to pay the London Living Wage. That is why as a matter of policy we do not outsource services even though there is a financial cost. It is also why we have a concern to avoid the sort of extravagant salaries and expenses that have brought senior leaders in other higher educational institutions into disrepute. It is an example of St Mary's fulfilling its words about a commitment to dignity and social justice with actual deeds.

Conclusion

We do not just bear our Catholic identity as a label to be stuck on brochures or deployed in marketing materials. We live it, as an open and inclusive institution that is driven by a guiding concern to integrate faith and reason in pursuit of the common good. That seems to me to encapsulate the enduring Catholic ideal for education – an education that is available to everyone, rich or poor, and is aimed at providing academic excellence and moral virtue.

In conclusion, as a Catholic university, we must be a pole of opposition to the clear trend that has witnessed an increasing tendency to excessive individual acquisitiveness and growing inequalities in the distribution of economic wealth and political and social power. But more than that, we must be a beacon of positive light and hope in promoting the social values of a shared community – compassion, justice, awareness of the needs of others – and if we believe this and wish to act on it, then we are inevitably placed close to the poorest in our society. Now these are not exclusively Catholic values, but we as a Catholic-based institution are required by our faith to give a lead in promoting them, and we must be prepared to build alliances with like-minded people in society. At the end of the day, we are reminded that it is by our fruits that we shall be known.

Part Two

Responding and Reflecting

31

Review: Responding and Summarizing

Craig L. Blomberg

By way of introduction, this essay reviews some of the highlights of each of the essays in this volume and reflects on a few of the questions that arise from them. Although I have written two medium-size works on riches/poverty and stewardship[1] and experienced at least a little bit of life in thirty-two countries, including a few very poor ones, and a few very poor neighbourhoods in other, more affluent countries overall, I have neither the track record of scholarship on these issues nor the extensive periods of time overseas, especially in contexts of extreme poverty, that many of the contributors to this volume have. So I hope my summary comments can prove at least a little useful.

Justin Thacker opens the volume with a contrast between what he deems to be individualistic and relational approaches to poverty, its solutions and even the image of God in humanity. As a counterbalance to analyses that treat only individuals and their plight, it is an excellent reminder of what is more commonly called systemic injustice and which often requires systemic solutions. I wonder, however, if the either-or mentality of the chapter is the most helpful, especially since it takes individuals to create relationships. Thacker begins with the account of a Ugandan widow named Charity who has been prevented from earning an adequate wage for her children and her because she will not sleep with her boss. Somehow, we in the West are implicated in this, and there is the hint that if we were less capitalistic and individualistic, the problem would be mitigated. Yet, as Thacker implicitly acknowledges, one solution is to replace the corrupt boss with a fair one, a legal issue that seems unrelated to the particular system of economics of the society, even as it has everything to do with cultural systems of morality and justice. Jesus's world more closely resembled this African context than modern Western ones; is there a lesson to be learned from the parable of the persistent widow that Jesus told (Lk. 18.1-8), both at the literal and spiritual levels, that might prove more effective than implicating former British colonial models (as if African tribal ones were less hierarchical) or re-defining the image of God?

Lynn Cohick and Katie Harrison look at poverty and its causes, first in the ancient Mediterranean world of the New Testament (NT) and then today. Cohick identifies

---

[1] Craig L. Blomberg, *Neither Poverty nor Riches: A Biblical Theology of Material Possessions* (Leicester: Apollos, 1999); Craig L. Blomberg, *Christians in an Age of Wealth: A Biblical Theology of Stewardship* (Grand Rapids, MI: Zondervan, 2013).

four main causes in antiquity: disease and malnutrition, the inability to work to earn enough money, injustices that allowed only those in power to benefit from government policies or behaviour and the clash of Roman ideologies with those of Rome's subjugated peoples. She is most interested in the latter two causes of poverty and develops them at greater length. For me, most significant, however, is her contrast between the data of Classical Studies and archaeological investigations and the theories of the social scientific disciplines where they are applied to the first-century Roman Empire. Against the social scientific analysis that extrapolates from empires in the ancient world in general, Cohick observes that the actual data and primary sources available to us suggest a much more economically diversified population than we are otherwise led to believe. Especially in more urban contexts, while there were certainly plenty of 'dirt poor' people, there was also a definable middle class – at least to the extent that they had enough surplus to survive one year of drought or bad harvests. We must not envision Jesus and the Twelve, or his first followers around the empire, as coming from the most destitute of circumstances, as in some forms of liberation theology, but reflecting a broader cross section of socio-economic strata.

Harrison highlights how broken relationships invariably stand behind the plight of the homeless and the most destitute of our world today, leaving people without the support systems of family, neighbourhoods or, at times, even social services. Natural disasters and governmental corruption also produce a lot of problems. She rightly stresses that government and the private business sector have their responsibilities towards meeting the needs of the poor; the problem should not be left entirely to the church and para-church movements, who come nowhere close to having the resources to meet the world's huge needs. Indeed, what people in all three communities do is crucial; more study needs to determine which community accomplishes which tasks the best. Then we might come closer to meeting some of the UN goals for the elimination of poverty in our world.

In passing, both authors raise questions for me as they distinguish between absolute and relative poverty. Absolute poverty means the inability to access resources to maintain even the most minimum of decent standards of living with respect to having shelter, food, clothing, clean water, medicine and the like. Relative poverty occurs when the disparity becomes too great between what one individual or group of people have and the standard of living of the most well-off in a given society. Harrison, in particular, believes we have an obligation to meet the needs of those who live in relative poverty as well as absolute poverty, but this raises some troubling questions. As technology and access to it increases, even the relatively poor can live comparatively comfortable lives. Are we really expected to work so that all these people can then become what now is called the middle class?

Put sharply, we can make a huge dent in absolute poverty; one study suggests that we have moved from having 1.9 billion people beneath the UN poverty line to 900 million in the world in the last twenty-five years. However, if Christians think they have the responsibility to address relative poverty, then we could one day face a situation in which most of the people in our world live above the poverty line but are still considered relatively poor compared to the richest individuals. We could face the 'guilt trip' caused by the suggestions that the wealthy have to divest themselves of their resources *simply* because they have 'too much' rather than because others also have 'too little' (borrowing the terms from 2 Cor. 8.13-15). We need much more Christian reflection and instruction on the kinds of personal lifestyles, economic investments and governmental policies that help meet basic human needs without squelching the human desire to improve one's own situation and create new wealth, some of which can then be shared – and we must resist the temptation to continually redefine basic human needs.

Bruce Longenecker and John Coleby each address benefaction. Longenecker's central point contrasts the macro-scale benefaction seen in the Graeco-Roman world with what was at most a micro-scale equivalent within pre-Constantinian Christianity. Even if early Christians came from a diversity of socio-economic brackets, none that we know of represented the wealthiest of the well-to-do, the kind of people who had the resources to underwrite major building projects or meet the basic needs of the poor in an entire community. We can draw a direct line, however, Longenecker argues, between the micro-scale efforts of the first Christians and the larger undertakings of post-Constantinian Christianity. Indeed, the notion of helping large numbers of poor people, apart from the corn dole in Rome just for citizens, seems to have been a quite distinctive contribution of the Judaeo-Christian tradition. Even pagan writers in the second and third centuries commended the efforts of Christians to care for their own and for the needy who were not believers, when most pagans refused to do so.

Coleby follows this overview of the ancient Mediterranean world with an array of fascinating statistics about generosity in the UK today. Given the probably overstated rhetoric in many circles about the demise of the church in Britain, the relative health of the benefaction of its people was encouraging indeed. The statistics show generosity in both Christian and non-Christian sectors of society, including government giving in foreign aid, while recognizing that Christians are, understandably, responsible for giving to distinctively Christian causes.

Both papers reflect briefly on the question of motivation, which raises a host of interesting questions. Since ancient benefaction was geared to create a certain sense of indebtedness among the people helped, how should Christian benefaction operate? Is it appropriate to realize one's indebtedness only to God as benefactor but not to fellow human beings? Is motivation for earthly giving by the hope of heavenly treasure any more noble than if we think we will receive recompense in this life? A theme to add in both essays is discussion of Christian benefaction or stewardship motivated simply by one's gratitude for all that God in Christ has done for us that we could never have deserved. Giving out of gratitude is arguably the most central and/or distinctively Christian motive. Have our appeals for benefaction too quickly followed worldly models?

Closely related to benefaction is patronage. Steve Walton and Helen Hekel lead us through consideration of this topic in antiquity and today. Wealthy patrons in the ancient Graeco-Roman world gathered around themselves an entourage of 'clients', who greeted them every morning, waited on them in various ways, worked odd jobs for them and received enough sustenance to stay alive when full-time or self-sustaining work was not available. They accompanied them in public, singing their praises, and supported them in the ancient equivalent of political campaigns. Reciprocity was the key glue of patron-client relationships. One can understand, therefore, why Paul, even after vigorously arguing for the responsibility of Christians to help meet their leaders' material needs, refused to accept money for ministry whenever he sensed it might come with strings attached. He would place himself under no one who might attempt to limit what he could do, where he could go or what he would say in preaching the gospel and winning as many for Christ as possible. Walton walks us through Paul's tightrope act in Philippians, as Paul wanted to express his heartfelt appreciation for the financial gift they sent him without wording it in any way that would suggest he recognized that he owed them something in return.

Hekel's treatment of patronage today is more narrative and personal, and raises important questions about ways in which Christian attempts to help the poor today resemble ancient systems of patronage. We are becoming more aware than ever of what one writer has dubbed 'toxic charity'.[2] It is not enough to meet short-term needs, while setting up mechanisms of aid that merely 'enable' those we help (in the psychological sense of that term), and creating dependence on the helpers in the long term. Given humanity's inherent sense of entitlement, it becomes far too easy to rely on others, whether for foreign aid or welfare at home, rather than working to become self-sustaining. On the other hand, Paul's metaphor of the body of Christ and his understanding of the gifts of the Spirit[3] also means that we are created to rely on each other; those with the gift of 'giving' need people who are willing to receive their gifts.

All this raises the interesting question of whether there are acceptable and unacceptable forms of patronage today or whether Christians should eschew all forms of patronage. Jonathan Marshall's recent work, *Jesus, Patrons and Benefactors: Roman Palestine and the Gospel of Luke*, defends the thesis that early Christianity practised no form of patronage, only benefaction.[4] Benefactors, Marshall argues, were characterized by generosity, often giving lavish gifts, sometimes unexpectedly, perhaps to entire communities, in ways that no one could ever pay back. Patrons, on the other hand, entered into more formal relationships, providing the necessities of life to others, who were expected to reciprocate with definable forms of support for the patrons. Marshall limits his analysis to Luke, so it would be good to ask, even if he is correct, whether or not other NT writers take different tacks.

John Barclay broadens the conversation to gifts more generally. Central to his discussion is the observation that a gift was meant to establish a relationship, even at times a friendship. Unlike today, where we usually assume that calling someone a 'friend' means treating them like a peer, friends were not always equals in the ancient world. Certain kinds of gifts could establish friendship, with conventional forms of response understood. An anonymous gift would have been virtually oxymoronic: How could you establish a relationship if you did not know who provided the gift? Barclay applies these concepts to 2 Corinthians 8–9 and Paul's fundraising efforts among the wealthier Corinthians to aid the most impoverished in the church in Judaea.

[2] Robert D. Lupton, *Toxic Charity: How Churches and Charities Hurt Those They Help (and How to Reverse It)* (New York: HarperOne, 2011).
[3] See 1 Cor. 12.12-31 and Eph. 4.11-13 for both metaphors used together.
[4] Jonathan Marshall, *Jesus, Patrons, and Benefactors: Roman Palestine and the Gospel of Luke*, WUNT 2/259 (Tübingen: Mohr Siebeck, 2009).

A long-distance relationship was difficult, as was accountability for proper use of gifts. Corinthian interest in this project has clearly waned, so Paul focuses on its importance for the Corinthians rather than trying to highlight the Judeans' need. Second Corinthians 8.13-15 proves particularly important as Paul stresses that the Corinthians may find themselves in a position needing help, whether material or spiritual, from the 'mother church' in Jerusalem. The key term *isōtēs*, used twice in these verses, is usually translated 'equality', but is better understood as a fair balance. It is neither possible nor desirable that all enjoy the identical economic standing, but there is something called 'too much' as long as some have 'too little'. Paul does not call on the rich and poor to trade places but for people to give out of their surplus. We might add, however, that we need to be ruthlessly honest with ourselves about how much is surplus.

Virginia Luckett is the one practitioner who does not quite address the identical topic as the biblical scholar preceding her. Instead, her title was 'Engaging with Poverty in the Early Church and Today'. As a fundraiser for a charity, she clearly deals with gifts, at least from the perspective of one who makes regular appeals for money for Christian para-church ministry. She describes some of the best success stories around the world of those who have used micro-loans to become self-sustaining and help entire neighbourhoods or small communities. She strongly defends the need for the existence of the para-church organization as the bridge between the church and the world in areas where specialized expertise is required that many churches will not be able to develop on their own. Nevertheless, she also insists that para-church ministries do as much as possible with the aid and under the guidance of the local church in communities they try to help.

These descriptions of ancient and modern gift-giving raise, but leave largely unanswered, a variety of questions about specific methods. Is it appropriate to promise rewards for giving to motivate greater generosity? I think, especially in the American context, of the tradition of 'naming gifts' – large donations that ensure that one's name will be attached to a certain building or charitable endeavour – or the more modest practice of simply publishing the names of all those who give above various levels. There is no doubt that the methods work, but should Christians use them? One institution I was involved with thought that the way to avoid improper motivation was to put donors' names on buildings only after they gave large gifts and without telling them ahead of time they were going to do so. However, most people seeing donors' names on those buildings will assume the more standard practice was followed and then wonder about their motivation – a perception not lost on the donors who were actually rather upset that their names had been used in this fashion!

Myrto Theochauros offers the only exegesis of the Old Testament in this collection by showing in detail how Ezekiel defines the primal sin as economic injustice, the accumulation of wealth by unjust means, especially with its picture of the unholy king of Tyre and his aspirations. This imagery forms part of the background for Revelation 18, in which the merchants of the world lament their inability to pursue their trade any longer. If one combines the picture of Revelation 18 with the imagery of chapter 17, one discovers John's vision as depicting the evil empire of the last days as the most powerful political, (ir-)religious and economic force in its day. Reflecting on possible parallels in our day does not require one to leave the world of the powerful Western multinational corporations, even if partial parallels can be found in the increasing power of China, Russia or the oil-rich Islamic nations.

Ellie Hughes offers the most sophisticated and insightful of the practical theology papers with her discussion of poverty and dehumanization today. Precisely because government-originated social services must limit the time and expense spent on any individual person or family, they are not able to do what the church or para-church can – walking with people throughout life. Long-term relationships are the key to getting people back on their feet, or on their feet for the first time. No one is meant to have to go it alone through life, especially not those whose lives are broken through whatever combination of poor choices and adverse circumstances. When functioning properly, para-church organizations should hand people over to a healthy local church as soon as possible, since their resources are finite as well. However, at least para-church ministries have the potential for more holistic and integrated care than government-sponsored services can provide, above all, in intertwining the spiritual and the material.

The one unanswered question from Hughes's paper is the issue of priority. Mt. 25.31-46 is almost certainly not about helping all poor people indiscriminately, despite a recent history of misinterpretation in this direction. Both 'the least' and 'brothers' are terms used in Matthew without exception, when not referring to literal size or biological siblings, for spiritual kin. The parable of the sheep and the goats is about the world's response to *Christian* poor in a culture in which welcoming the messenger meant welcoming the message.[5] Gal. 6.10 captures the Christian's priority: we must do good to all people but especially to those of the household of faith. If we help unbelievers as much as believers, we lose the incentive for people to become Christians because of the unique community created by those filled with the Holy Spirit. If we help only Christians, we tempt people to become believers for all the wrong motives or, worse, to pretend to come to faith simply for the sake of the material help they can receive.

Fiona Gregson and Hannah Swithinbank address the debate about deserving and undeserving poor. The NT certainly gives examples of undeserving recipients of God's grace, most notably the hungry enemy that believers are to feed (Rom. 12.20). That said, it also asks believers to establish boundaries – the widows to be enrolled on the list of those receiving church support must not be those whose families are in position to care for them (1 Tim. 5.4-16), and the idle who are unwilling to work in Thessalonica should not be given help in getting something to eat (1 Thess. 5.10). In most of the calls to help the poor, no restrictions enable us to limit our giving to those who are more deserving. Like Barclay, Gregson uses 2 Corinthians 8–9 for her most extensive example. However, she does not discuss the most commonly mentioned reason for Paul's making the collection such a priority – his desire to unite Jewish and Gentile wings of the church, given the false rumours being spread about him and his antinomianism.

---

[5] See further Craig L. Blomberg, *Interpreting the Parables*, 2nd edn (Downers Grove, IL: IVP Academic, 2012), 396–403, and the literature there cited.

Swithinbank observes that charitable givers regularly operate with the concept of the 'undeserving poor'. She properly reminds us that, theologically speaking, we could probably all be said to deserve poverty or, better put, that none of us deserves the good life. Finite resources will always lead to differentiation of distribution along some lines. We all know at least a few who, in some fashion, take advantage of any system that is set up. We often do not realize that some are hurt by the system intended to help them. Legislation can create such disparities. The line at which taxes jump from one bracket to the next encourages those who might make just enough more to move up to the new bracket to stay below the dividing line so that their net income does not actually go down. The single mother with a chance to get off welfare often discovers that the job will not pay enough to make up for the childcare and transportation costs she now has to be able to afford. Overall, Swithinbank stresses that in her experience, there are almost always reasons like this, even if at times less obvious, for why people remain on the dole. So these kinds of inequities could be abolished if we had the will to do so. The 'bottom line' is that we are all *un*worthy of being offered love and freedom offered by Christ – but he offers them anyway, and, therefore, so should we.

Christopher Hays turns to the topic of how the church has engaged the society and the state both creatively and critically in helping the poor. The 'powers', a term in Scripture with a pejorative connotation and even a hint of the demonic, can be helpful. They still remain under God's sovereignty, and fallen humans in positions of power remain created in God's image. But they often get in the way and sometimes become exceedingly corrupt. The poor are, in fact, part of the answer to the powers' problems. If the powers will pay attention to them, they will recognize the need to engage them, to temper their heavy handedness and, on occasion, to become weaker and more vulnerable like them. Romans 13 is not the only chapter in Scripture relevant to how Christians should view the government; sometimes the picture of Revelation 13 is more relevant. Given both models, the church should avoid so withdrawing from society that it is no longer relevant and can no longer speak to the powers. On the other hand, it dare not become so enmeshed with them that it cannot address them prophetically when it is necessary.

Appropriately, Stephen Timms, a Christian Member of Parliament, follows Hays with reflections on the powers from within the system. He perceives a trend over his years in government that what once were considered unacceptable failures are now often considered acceptable. The church should, therefore, press the powers on key issues. Like Coleby, he writes optimistically about the church in the UK. In the Greater London area, the church is growing significantly. Despite some continual downward trends in other parts of the country, Timms rejects the notion that it is in terminal decline in Britain. The conference where these essays were first presented was indicative of communication and cooperation across Roman Catholic, Pentecostal and evangelical (including Anglican) lines, which is occurring with encouraging frequency today. The Food Bank movement is an excellent, encouraging example that, even as recently as ten years ago, one would not have predicted that the churches would have been primarily responsible for. The church is actually shaming the current Conservative government, which refuses to own up to the extent of the needs in the UK, especially among those who are employed but with very low wages. The Jubilee campaign from 2000 is a longer-term example, which received much of its support from the churches. No other institution could have achieved this in such a non-partisan fashion. Timms, likewise, raises the question of which sector is best equipped for which portion of ameliorating poverty. We kid ourselves if we think we do not need the church, the private business sector and the government all committed to the goals of helping the poor.

Francis Campbell concludes the collection by reflecting on the slogan of a 'preferential option' for the poor and Jesus's remark that 'the poor you will have with you always' (Mk 14.7 and parallels). He observes that the important part of Jesus's statement is that Mary anointed him for his burial as a one-off gift of lavish love. He could strengthen his point even more by observing that Jesus alludes to Deut. 15.11, which goes on to stress that we can and must help the poor any time we can. Campbell quotes Pope Francis's reminder that we are a poor church living for the poor, which he is trying to lead by example in some noticeably more modest ways than recent Popes have modelled. Christian institutions of higher education can create an ethos of Christian commitment and justice for the poor even without having a majority of its staff or students being Christians themselves, which is what he is seeking to fashion at St Mary's University, Twickenham. This can be successful as long as a current administration keeps this as a clear vision and keeps confirming that it is in fact being modelled and that people understand why it is being modelled. The danger, as with so many once Christian private colleges and universities, especially in the United States, is that successive administrations will not share the same vision and there will be insufficient mechanisms in place to preserve its outworking.

As one reflects on the breadth of topics covered in this volume, it is clear that others could have been broached. At the time of writing, the worldwide refugee crisis was clearly the biggest issue among those under the category of helping the poor, but perhaps an entirely separate volume is needed for addressing that huge issue. A second key issue involves the balance between evangelism and social action. A generation ago, evangelicals were barely beginning to rediscover social justice as part of the gospel, while Catholics at times barely had any awareness of the need to stress life-transforming personal faith in Jesus. Today, both groups have made noticeable progress toward a better balance. But among millennials, at least evangelical ones, it is arguable that concerns for justice have eclipsed the need for salvation. A message of trust in Christ without any concern for someone's physical circumstances rings hollow, but a commitment to eradicating poverty, however successful, that leaves people lost and alienated from Christ, still sends them to an eternity apart from God and all things good.

An encouraging development in this volume is the mix of presenters. Both Catholic and Protestant authors appear, and the Protestants represent Pentecostal, classic evangelical and more middle-of-the-road perspectives. There is also a good balance of men and women, and they are not divided along the lines of biblical versus practical theology, with two women writing as Old or New Testament scholars and two men writing as practitioners. Americans and Europeans are included, although they are all white. The next step would be to include people of colour from the Majority World in a comparable anthology. Were the organizers and editors to be particularly daring, they could include poor people themselves, or at least those who have spent a significant portion of their lives in poverty. There *are* representatives of these communities with the education or experience to contribute to this kind of anthology with equally important perspectives. Meanwhile, the editors of this volume are to be commended for having organized an outstanding and collegial conference that included considerable audience input, and the audience did include at least a few representatives of these various underrepresented people groups. If all these dimensions cannot be reproduced in this published form of the proceedings, the papers at least are improved because of the opportunities their authors have had to revise them in light of the conference.

32

Between Today and Yesterday: Evidence, Complexity, Poverty and the 'Body' of Christ

Francis Davis

Introduction

In this collection, we have explored the power of benefaction, ideas of the deserving and undeserving poor and notions of who might be responsible for the poor. As we have seen, these are contested terms, and in this essay, I want to suggest that they are today all the more contested and contestable. On the one hand, I will argue, this is because the social challenges and contexts which poor people face, and in which they find themselves, are now more complex than ever before, and what we know about the sources of those challenges is both more and less complete than ever before. On the other hand, I will propose, this is because that complexity provides immense challenges for the Christian paradigms by which we seek to discern modern needs and, indeed, may be confronting the Christian social tradition with challenges so demanding to some of its assumptions that it leaves it in a kind of analytical bind. And, of course, 'today' we know much more than we did 'yesterday' about how the Christian Church itself performs in these regards.

First, I will turn to aspects of how this may shape our interpretation and notions of 'evidence' and so authority. Second, I will tease out some of the problems we may face in the light of new patterns of complexity. Third, I will explore how these factors may impact our ideas of poverty by reference to a particular set of human issues and, finally, set out some research areas that seem to be a natural development of the book's conversation.

Motivation, behaviour and 'evidence'

When, in 2008, my *Moral But No Compass: Church, Government and the Future of Welfare* was published, it caused a storm.[1] The *Times* and *Sunday Times* led with coverage of its

---

[1] Francis Davis, Elizabeth Paulhus and Andrew Bradstock, *Moral But No Compass: Church, Government and the Future of Welfare* (Cambridge: Von Hugel Institute and Marple: Matthew James, 2008).

findings and the BBC TV News as well.[2] Over the next days, the publication was the subject of leaders in every major UK daily newspaper, scrutiny through op-eds and lectures and comment by the Archbishops of Canterbury and York, and parliamentary debate. It then began its gradual percolation into the cycles of academic citation and discussion. What was notable throughout this period was that while those in the policymaking community reacted pragmatically to the 'empirical evidence' we had gathered on Anglican volunteering, philanthropic cashflows, capacity, capabilities and institutional reach, a variety of strands within the churches reacted, instead, against what they perceived to be an implicit assumption the publication had made, namely, that 'data' trumped theology. We were also accused of falling foul of 'government's tendency to want to "make use" of the church whose role is actually not to "do" anything but to "be" prophetic'.[3] One current senior Anglican bishop explains this as a reaction to a mirror being held up to the church's decision-making itself, but, either way, what was also conceivably at stake was an older dispute between the relative veracity – and authority – of the 'sacred' and 'social' sciences as intense as the one that Christians may have explored in more depth elsewhere, namely, that between 'science' and 'faith'.[4]

It is a repeated claim in modern English Christian discourse – especially that of evangelicals and some Catholics – that faith *motivates* social action. This elucidation of a continuum between religious conviction, an idea of responsibility and consequent behaviours is a constant theme in many fora and one that arises in parts of the papers in this collection. To question this linkage can attract furious Christian protest and accusations of being unbiblical and even 'lacking poetry'.[5] Thus, while Joachim Jeremias, in his classic study, may have given us an ability to interpret Jerusalem at the time of Jesus through an economic and social lens,[6] the challenge we face now is our ability to make sense of our present Christian claims in the context of the exponentially increasing scope of the social and political sciences. Disciplines such as geography, sociology which is rediscovering religion 'after' the secularization thesis, epidemiology

---

[2] E.g. Ruth Gledhill, 'Church Attacks Labour for Betraying Christians', *The Times*, 7 June 2008 (https://www.thetimes.co.uk/article/church-attacks-labour-for-betraying-christians-vhnmkfhf859, accessed March 2018); and Ruth Gledhill, 'Ignored and Spurned, the Church has lost its Faith in Government', *The Times*, 7 June 2008 (https://www.thetimes.co.uk/article/ignored-and-spurned-the-church-has-lost-its-faith-in-government-3qmhjqql06x, accessed March 2018).

[3] This was a challenge offered constructively by John Atherton when I gave the first Ronald Preston Lecture, outlining what would be in the report's findings at the University of Manchester (May 2010); and also the feedback of the head of public affairs of the Church of England to me, who, at a later public debate organized by the Church Urban Fund, suggested the arguments I made had a weakness of having 'no theology of sin' (Church Urban Fund/Diocesan Social Responsibility Officers' Conference, June 2010).

[4] See, e.g., the work of the Faraday Institute (http://www.faraday.st-edmunds.cam.ac.uk/, accessed March 2018) and John Cornwell's activities (https://science-human.org/, accessed March 2018), both in the University of Cambridge; and also Nick Spencer, *Darwin and God* (London: SPCK, 2009).

[5] I am thinking especially of Timothy Radcliffe, 'Relativising the Relativisers: A Theologian's Assessment of the Role of Sociological Explanation of Religious Phenomena and Theology Today', in *Sociology and Theology: Alliance and Conflict*, ed. David Martin, John Orme Mills and W. S. F. Pickering (Leiden: Brill, 2004), 165–77; Robin Gill, ed., *Theology and Sociology: A Reader*, new edn (London: Cassell, 1996); and also an intense exchange on choosing Nehemiah versus any other biblical book as a guide to the public sphere between the Jubilee Centre's Michael Schluter and the scholar and hermit Fr Thomas Cullinan (Epiphany Group, Prinknash Abbey, Jan 1990).

[6] Joachim Jeremias, *Jerusalem in the Time of Jesus* (London: SCM, 1969).

and psychology offer insights today previously unavailable to the churches and their scriptural scholars. Collectively, they are as widely, if not more widely, read than academic theology, and together they form a body of knowledge more likely to shape the perceived decisions of firms, governments, anti-poverty agencies and even the accounting functions of the churches than 'theology' or 'faith' as such. This is not just a feature of secularity but a concrete question of confidence in interpretive power. It might just be, then, that the things we know now about societies leave biblical texts more at risk of being rooted to the spot of the spaces and places from which they arose and the Christian social tradition not much more distinctive than, in effect, risking aping whatever the social structures and government habits in which they find themselves happening to be – all while protesting forcibly its unique ability to 'motivate' in modern times.[7] By avoiding the issue that Christian behaviour is conceivably indistinguishable from other behaviours, the Christian narrative weakens itself.

By way of example, in this context, the energetic turn in government, business and the academy to behavioural science, in general, and behavioural economics, in particular, seems to me to present evidence which begins to undermine much of the way Christians talk about poverty and public life. Behavioural economists contend that in contrast to linear relationships between ideas and behaviour, and *contra* rational choice theory of private choice or class preference – or, for that matter, 'faith' provoking or motivating 'action' – human decision-making and behaviours are the product of the intense aggregation of information conditioned by default perspectives on sources of trust, time, institution and (s)pace. Thus, famously, at Schipol airport in Amsterdam, exhortation to the common good, inspiration to higher social norms and incentivization applied to the problem of the cleanliness around male urinals of Amsterdam's busy airport had no observable impact on outcomes or choices of the male users of the facilities. Ultimately, the painting of an ergonomically placed fly upon the ceramics seemed strikingly to provoke just such a fundamental change in behaviour as male users were 'nudged' to direct fluid flows to points in the urinal which would maximize liquid capture and minimize cleaning costs round and about.[8] In policy terms, this is the source of the current requirement, while applying for a UK driving licence, to declare an intention or otherwise to become an organ donor. In theological terms, the success of nudge in the face of the failure of so many other approaches is a kind of decimation of the claim that 'faith motivates' (and trumps other variables) alone while undermining a raft of enduring Christian strategies to inspire behaviour change.

---

[7] See the special edition of *Public Money and Management* 29 (2006), ed. Francis Davis; and Francis Davis. 'The English Bishops, Caritas and "Civic Prophecy" after the 2010 Papal Visit', in *Catholic Social Conscience: Reflection and Action on Catholic Social Teaching*, ed. Keith Chappell and Francis Davis, revised edn (Leominster: Gracewing, 2011), 129–45.

[8] Richard H. Thaler and Cass R. Sunstein, *Nudge: Improving Decisions about Health, Wealth and Happiness* (Harmondsworth: Penguin, 2009); Ben Chu, 'Father of "Nudge Theory" Richard Thaler wins 2017 Nobel Prize in Economics' *Independent*, 9 October 2017 (https://www.independent. co.uk/news/business/news/richard-thaler-nobel-prize-in-economics-winner-2017-behavioural-economics-nudge-theory-a7990291.html, accessed March 2018); the government Behavioural Insights Team website (http://www.behaviouralinsights.co.uk/, accessed March 2018); and the 2010 launch of a specialist and far-reaching programme at Warwick Business School (https://warwick. ac.uk/fac/soc/wbs/subjects/bsci/, accessed March 2018).

Indeed, modelling that which did not work at Schipol airport, modern churches trail-blaze exhortation as a biblical norm for idea change leading to behaviour change – they call it preaching. Meanwhile, much economic analysis emerging from church headquarters regarding the 'common good' has a tendency to draw on classical economic frameworks even while claiming theological authority for new insights into human behaviour and flourishing.[9] It happens with 'fresh expressions' , too, when language about the need for intense spiritual conversion as the best next step for human flourishing is as often unreflectively combined with success criteria for evangelism uncritically adopted from the performance standards of trading institutions. One friend remarked to me recently that listening to the leaders of the pentecostal network Pioneer and the conservative Catholic Bishop of Portsmouth speak of outreach was like 'sitting in a sales strategy meeting at work'.

What is at stake here is the very possibility and idea of 'believing' conversion leading to concrete action when aggregation, belonging and other factors may be greater shapers of what may be possible or proceed from 'believing'. Evidencing 'what really works' is important, then, if benefaction, service and responsibility are to be concretely sustained, for 'faith' alone may tell us little. There is a risk in not doing such ground work in seeking to learn from our old history of service to, with and alongside the poor. It is that, in order to seek to make our prior models of analysis fit, we uncritically assume the traction of ideas, the agency of persons, the shaping of geographies, the relationality of choices or the presence of a grounded spirituality, where all those relationships have actually been split asunder by the complexity of contemporary society, by unnamed commodification and by behavioural insights that shred our pathways to authoritative insight. More work needs to be done here at the interface of the social, economic and political sciences, theology and the Bible, for it is likely that something is being lost to us 'today' that was available to us 'yesterday' and that some things available 'today' mean that old history and language are under pressure.

This difficult tension of discernment through religious eyes between the 'is' of the contemporary arena and the 'ought' of Scripture and tradition and our own narratives is helpfully exemplified in the encounter with the institutions, social forces and extreme complexity of step-change global urbanization. It is to this that I shall now turn.

Cities, complexity and urban bias

One of the great changes between the collation of the New Testament and the death of St Francis of Assisi was the emergence of the effervescing urban arena and its growth to large scale. And in the era between St Francis and the present ministry of Pope Francis, humanity became a majority urban species, and the first cities of more than ten million inhabitants came in to view. Most of us now live in cities. An increasing number of us

---

[9] For extended discussion of this conundrum, see Davis 'English Bishops'; Davis, Paulhaus and Bradstock, *Moral but No Compass*.

on every continent live in megacities, and, not least on mainland China, the size and number of cities continues to grow exponentially.

Modern cities as social constructs, of course, are absent from the Bible. Nor are they as clearly spatially and architecturally stratified as the first European ones that St Francis may have walked. Nor any longer can their conflagration of so many varying forces and populations easily have them located as beacons of modernity and so described as 'secular'.[10] For modern cities can be suggested to live beyond the normal confines of time and space being simultaneously pre-modern, modern and post-modern: trading 24/7 they are the meeting points of diasporas, global supply chains, telecommunications and the arrival and dispersal of new DNA chains and diseases. They are the hiding points of the most traditional and radical interpretations of religious traditions. They are the outing points of the most liberal and unconstrained choices of lifestyle, sexual and gender preferences. They are the new agents of diplomacy whose hard and soft power outstrips some national governments subverting claims to sovereignty with which many of us have grown up, and upending hierarchies of decision-making with which, especially, episcopal denominations are comfortable.

If Jesus and Mary came looking for an inn in modern Karachi, its swirling scale might both offer sheep to slaughter from familiar pens cobbled together on the roadside in the traditional manner while requiring digital literacy and access to credit to lock down a room for the night.[11] Indeed, as refugees or travellers they might have had it harder still: while the international refugee support community is much designed around rural 'camps', the slums, streets and tiny apartments of urban centres are as likely to house those fleeing now as those settled. Politically, such economic reach and population concentration can trigger new political behaviours on the part of elites, behaviours which privilege the political accommodation of those 'virtually' present through financial and trading systems and bodily present, by proximity, at the expense of rural domains that cannot present such a threat (or source of revenue) to those elites. If, in response to tiny, or even unexpressed, personal preferences an incoming user of a website can encounter – without knowing – thousands of personalized points of change in their customer journey at a bank whose 'branch' is on the same road – whose data is in the cloud and whose technicians are abroad – without ever speaking with or meeting a person how do we see the embodiment of human community, family, home?

---

[10] The classical study here is Harvey Cox, *The Secular City: Secularization and Urbanization in Theological Perspective* (New York: Macmillan, 1966), which the author has revisited more recently: Harvey Cox, *The Secular City: Secularization and Urbanization in Theological Perspective*, new edn (Princeton, NJ: Princeton University Press, 2013). See also 'Disability Inclusion', *The Ruderman Foundation* (https://rudermanfoundation.org/programs/disability-inclusion/, accessed March 2010).

[11] For the digitization of erstwhile offline services in Karachi, see the striking work of Seed Ventures (http://seedventures.org/, accessed March 2018). On a recent visit to Karachi, I was struck by the juxtaposition of livestock and high-tech dwellings, refugees and local ventures and discussed this with the Governor of Sindh at meetings hosted by Seed (https://farazkhan.org/portfolio-items/meeting-with-governor-of-sindh-mohammad-zubair-today-with-our-keynote-speaker-of-the-future-summit-prof-francis-davis-uks-ministerial-adviser-on-inclusive-enterprise-professor-of-innovation-at-st/, accessed March 2018).

Many issues, from the use of advanced digital strategies to shape urban life – in shorthand, termed 'smart cities' technology[12] – to the presence (or lack) of planning policy, to the function of architecture to the simultaneous concentration and dispersal of resources, to 'who' the poor are, 'where' they are and 'how' they might be 'cared' for, take on new dimensions as these spaces that are not physical places as we have known them. Indeed, they now are places which blend across time and space, spreading and developing their claims to ground the terrain on which humanity plants (or unhinges) itself.

Combined with the insights, trading opportunities and the traction of big and open data, these factors play out to leave the church under pressure once again as much as any other institution or community. For 'yesterday' Christ could share a language, geography, conversation, even with his oppressors, while today the urban age forces only fluidity into movement. Even if the church had committed to run with 'evidence' like that described above, it might, like others, find it impossible to gather it meaningfully.

This is unsurprising: the first urbanization of the medieval age eventually required the innovation of mendicant preaching sustained through new religious orders such as the Franciscans and Dominicans, so forcing a reshaping of the monastic structuring of the church on the urban outskirts and enabling that which was new to be really heard. Modern urbanization will require step changes in the form of mission as great, if not greater. For all the many Christian claims to ideas and motivation by believing, the institutions they create to embed those new efforts will be crucial.

Ideas, institutions and 'relationality'

As lines are blurred and silos built up and complexity slides so many information and decision points away from personal view, a certain kind of 'rigorous understanding' recedes for 'contingency' is the new norm everywhere. As a result, a kind of uncertain panic emerges for some Christian leaders used to certainty, and, in response, I want to suggest that we repeatedly risk trying to bottle five-pint-size challenges in quart-size pots.

So, a pentecostal fellowship of 2,000 members may wish to 'shed light' on 'the dark places of the city', may seek to 'transform relationality in our nation' and 'liberate the poor from the burden of debt'. Nevertheless, in response to these conceivably structural challenges found at complex scale, their first steps are all organized at a level they can touch and in a geography to which they can drive – namely, their own 'congregation'. Even in the Catholic case, where the enormous Caritas federation of agencies sits alongside the official *ecclesia*, they do so organized at the 'congregation' level first – and one way of interpreting Pope Benedict's approach to these bodies was to understand his key teaching letter on Catholic charity as much as an attempt to

---

[12] The Royal Institute of Chartered Surveyors discuss tech and 'smart' dimension cities at http://www.rics.org/uk/knowledge/glossary/smart-cities/ (accessed March 2018); see also the IBM Smarter Cities Challenge (https://www.smartercitieschallenge.org/, accessed March 2018).

bring them under episcopal control at the micro level as to constrain actions at large scale.[13] Indeed, in our debates surrounding one of the papers in the present collection, it was suggested by one interlocutor that to move beyond the congregational was to create a 'para-church' realm of institutions that would under-mine relationality and personal conversion.

I wonder here if a few things are going on which, in order to make good our solidarity with the weakest today, we need to work harder at surfacing.

First, it is not clear to me that the Christian defaults to shorthand ideas such as 'relationality' or the rhetorical device of 'the common good' offers any assistance in discerning our current context or future actions. Rather, it can simply shrink unfathomable complexity to comprehensible scale – to seemingly put the 'genie' back in the bottle, to make our theology cope again, not least by linking it to a metaphor of congregation. Thus, 'spiritual redemption' and congregationalism at the expense of community renewal and engaging at institutional scale is easier to handle, while also not challenging any ecclesiologies or patterns of power within and around the churches that have been carried forward from the past. Moreover, it is ironic, for, while it is grasped, controlled and brought to a 'relational' scale of insight, actions that are associated with it are often allocated with ever more energetic ideas and descriptions of meaning, purpose and spiritual significance. Thus, a church might claim to be 'remaking' a whole city in the light of Christ, while its city civic leadership thinks it simply opened a Free School for twenty and a community project with a turnover of about 0.000001 per cent of the local hospital, let alone the urban care system.

We have touched not only on behavioural economics already but also on the choices emanating from its insights as they encounter institutions and organizations that mediate religion, that shape culture, that unlock and mitigate social and spiritual impacts. We know that the 'same' Christian message preached by a pentecostal pastor has varying meanings in contexts as diverse as, say, the slums of Lusaka, the rural areas of the Zambian North and railtrack-side rallies in Livingstone on the Zimbabwe border. Intense financial centralization within the Mormons sheds a new light on 'local missions', while the third-world-ization of many Catholic religious orders and the South Americanization and Africanization of the US-centric Assemblies of God essentially mean the increasing capture by the Global South of Christian assets and institutions closely held for centuries in the Global North. Indeed, the 'same' Christian idea reaching the bureaucracy of Sierra Leone or Khartoum is not only *not* the same in its implications, but the actions that flow from it ought not to be the same as each other or those, say, in London or Dallas. Institutions – management – matters.

Further, of course, it is not only doing something at scale that is the answer. 'Relationality' and 'the common good' may be quick fixes of language that help us avoid tough policy and leadership decisions, but so is the shorthand reach for fashionable new 'liberations' being offered to the societies in which the church finds itself. Those facing female genital mutilation (FGM), human slavery and severe disability, for

---

[13] This would be my response to Pope Benedict XVI, *On the Service of Charity* (http://w2.vatican.va/content/benedict-xvi/en/motu_proprio/documents/hf_ben-xvi_motu-proprio_20121111_caritas.html, accessed March 2018).

example, have had as hard a time gaining traction for their voice within the mainline churches as within mainstream society, even while the liberal West has been loosening the legal shackles on the freedoms to be enjoyed by women and gay people in general.

In short, the tendency towards the avoidance of hard-headed institutional assessments can leave the poor being presented as 'liberated' by 'relationality' or 'set free' by the common good but practically untouched, unaided or unmobilized as the shape, scale and form by which the church sets out to respond, and the locations in which it speaks, are inadvertently limited by that which went before or by that which is currently fashionable in wider culture.

This not only constrains the church's service and public engagement, but it also has devastating impacts on its own self-understanding. For what we know about the churches today is that they have struggled to bring the good news.

Mind, disability, poverty and the body of Christ

Nowhere is the mismatch between the capabilities of how we use Scripture, the context in which Jesus lived, the contingencies of today, the constraints in our assessment of need, the position of the poor and the risky tendency to weak institutional analysis better shown than when we turn to the huge swathe of humanity who live with disability and mental ill health: according to the World Health Organization, one in four of humanity will live with a mental illness in our lifetimes.[14] An increasing number of us will experience post-partum, dementia- or trauma-related psychosis, in addition to those with environmental and genetic triggers. In total, about a billion people have disabilities, about 15 per cent of the globe's population, and, despite the weakness of some data, we know that many disabilities and conditions have global prevalence.

Christianity, of course, is a religion whose God had been disabled by trauma by the time he was lifted on to the cross. Subsequently pierced in the side and above the wrists with his legs probably broken, no matter what one Gospel says, he would have been laid in the tomb. Three short days later, he would have needed a wheelchair and a trauma counsellor were it not for the miracle of the resurrection. Those who had watched his demise were still in shock. Our God, by this account, is a disabled God and only 'deserved' those disabilities if we strangely accrue to Christ a power of 'choice' born of New Right political economy rather than biblical norms.[15]

This presents the Christian Church with some challenges. The last and present popes have only used the term 'schizophrenia' in relation to the human tendency to spiritual inconsistency and never in relation to the lived experience of psychosis. Across the Global South, draconian mental health laws – often inherited from colonial 'lunacy' legislation – which permit the sterilization and imprisonment of disabled women have been met with silence by church leaders while the failure of church hospitals

---

[14] WHO, 'Mental Disorders Affect One in Four People' (http://www.who.int/whr/2001/media_centre/press_release/en/, accessed March 2018).

[15] This was the contention of Margaret Thatcher in her speech to the Church of Scotland General Assembly (21 May 1988) (https://www.margaretthatcher.org/document/107246, accessed March 2018).

to consistently train nurses with mental health specialisms, psychiatrists and those seeking to specialize in disability are as marked as in any other community or service-providing contexts.

This is not surprising, as my researchers and I have been unable to find a single bishop of any denomination in the English-speaking world who was openly disabled on the day of appointment. In the wider church there are exceptions, with Joni Erikson Tada in evangelical circles and an eminent American Benedictine Abbot, but the omission in leadership becomes embedded across the church the further we look. Recently, I observed to an eminent Catholic canon lawyer that it struck me as a shame that the code of canon law had for many centuries found it difficult within its heart to permit those with disabilities to even *apply* to train for the priesthood. 'Think', I said, 'of the squaddie whose hands have been bombed away in Afghanistan, who found God as part of his recovery and wants to serve as priest.' The response from this totally compassionate person was that 'it was obvious, because without hands there was no way you'd be making the consecration [of the bread and wine at Mass]'. The body of Christ, it seems, is and ought to be as beautiful as the magazine covers it often decries as representing a decadent culture. Worse still, it is statistically more likely than almost any other institution and indeed even more likely than the secular world to exclude disabled people and those with mental ill health from its pathways of decision-making and ministry. Legal challenges to Gurdwaras alleging discrimination, and the heavy lifting which Boston's Ruderman Foundation has had to do to reshape Jewish attitudes to disability,[16] suggest that might be a wider religious problem too. This is especially so when a growing number of those who are disabled have been saved from termination by mothers resisting cultural norms and by medical advances that permit birth at an earlier phase of gestation, but with likely complications in the long term. In this context, this gulf in awareness and discourse is all the more striking in those denominations who speak of disability rights in the womb as part of pro-life political strategies.

The conundrum here may be one that touches on a wider question that we might wish to explore as we build on the papers in the present collection, namely, the question of how much agency the excluded have, whether the Church is open to reshaping and repurposing itself in the light of their experience and what the consequences might be for practical and other responses with the shifted paradigm of knowledge and insights that co-creation might unlock. Pentecostal and charismatic Catholic and other mainstream Christian responses to disability are only rarely in the realm of rights but are most often associated with pity, healing and subject status. Catholic dioceses speak of the 'sick and the disabled', pastoral letters on disability focus on care, not empowerment, and the language, habits and symbols of pilgrimage – especially to seek 'cures' – have ambiguous and possibly pernicious impacts on the ability of those made in the image of the disabled God to seize the significance of the potential in their own resurrection. With disability and severe mental ill health, we seem to be encountering

---

[16] 'UK Gurdwara Sued over Discrimination against Disabled', *Daily News and Analysis* website (http://www.dnaindia.com/world/report-uk-gurdwara-sued-over-discrimination-against-disabled-2074664, accessed March 2018); more broadly, see The Ruderman Foundation (http://rudermanfoundation.org/, accessed March 2018).

a profound systemic failure of Christian insight, and what goes with it is a deep and implicit assumption of a lack of agency on the part of disabled people which might in turn name this as a fundamental failing in our whole approach to benefaction, responsibility and service today and yesterday.

Conclusion

In this short essay, I have sought to respond to the rest of the collection and our conversations in a manner which would provoke conversation and further enquiry. I wondered, first, if the renewal of the social sciences now gives us more insight into human behaviour and choices than ever before and so runs the risk of relativizing the veracity of some of the claims that churches are in the habit of making about themselves and the society around them. This line of enquiry seems particularly significant if one turns to the intense complexity and morphing of traditional conceptions of many theological and other categories of enquiry that emerge from examining the majority urban world in which we now all live. The gap I suggested might be to relink, or properly disaggregate, religious ideas, other ideas, institutions and social practice, for without close attention to such detail, Christians risk mixing their rhetorical metaphors with the actual scale and reach of the institutions that they put to work. Finally, I set out how the unspoken, un-mobilized and uncared for swathe of humanity living with disabilities and severe mental ill health may be an exemplar case of the kinds of 'poverty' that become excluded from the language and the body of Christ when social analysis, organizations and social change are not combined.

Between today and yesterday is like a million years. Indeed, but the collection here points not only to the fruitfulness of the conversations we have had but also to the urgency of the work that remains to be done.

Select Bibliography

Aasgaard, Reidar. *'My Beloved Brothers and Sisters!' Christian Siblingship in Paul*. SNTW. London: T&T Clark, 2004.

Acemoğlu, Daron, and James A. Robinson. *Why Nations Fail: The Origins of Power, Prosperity and Poverty*. New York: Simon & Schuster, 2012.

Adams, Edward. *The Earliest Christian Meeting Places: Almost Exclusively Houses?* LNTS 450. London: T&T Clark, 2016.

Adams, Samuel L. 'The Justice Imperative in Scripture'. *Interpretation* 69 (2015): 399–414.

Alcock, Susan E. 'The Eastern Mediterranean'. In *The Cambridge Economic History of the Greco-Roman World*, edited by Walter Scheidel, Ian Morris and Richard Saller, 671–98. Cambridge: Cambridge University Press, 2007.

Alkire, Sabine, Christoph Jindra, Gisela Robles Aguilar, Suman Seth and Ana Vaz. 'Global Multidimensional Poverty Index 2015'. *Oxford Poverty and Human Development Initiative* (2015). Online: http://www.ophi.org.uk/wp-content/uploads/Global-MPI-8-pager_10_15.pdf (accessed May 2016).

Anderson, Gary A. *Sin: A History*. New Haven: Yale University Press, 2009.

Ascough, Richard S. 'Benefactions Gone Wrong: The "Sin" of Ananias and Sapphira in Context'. In *Text and Artifact in the Religions of Mediterranean Antiquity: Essays in Honour of Peter Richardson*, edited by Stephen G. Wilson, 91–110. Waterloo: Wilfrid Laurier University Press, 2000.

Aune, David E. 'In Search of a Profile of the "Benefactor" (review of Frederick W. Danker, *Benefactor. Epigraphic Study of a Graeco-Roman and New Testament Semantic Field*)'. *Interpretation* 38 (1984): 421–5.

Ayerst, D., and A. S. T. Fischer. *Records of Christianity, Vol. I: The Church in the Roman Empire*. Oxford: Blackwell, 1971.

Bar-Ilan, M. 'Infant Mortality in the Land of Israel in Late Antiquity'. In *Essays in the Social Scientific Study of Judaism and Jewish Society*, edited by S. Fishbane and J. N. Lightstone, 3–25. Montreal: Concordia University, 1990.

Barclay, John M. G. '"Because He Was Rich He Became Poor": Translation, Exegesis and Hermeneutics in the Reading of 2 Cor 8.9'. In *Theologizing in the Corinthian Conflict: Studies in the Exegesis and Theology of 2 Corinthians*, edited by R. Bieringer, M. M. S. Ibita, D. A. Kurek-Chomycz and T. A. Vollmer, 331–44. Leuven: Peeters, 2013.

Barclay, John M. G. *Jews in the Mediterranean Diaspora from Alexander to Trajan (323 BCE–117 CE)*. Edinburgh: T&T Clark, 1996.

Barclay, John M. G. 'Manna and the Circulation of Grace: A Study of 2 Corinthians 8:1–15'. In *The Word Leaps the Gap: Essays on Scripture and Theology in Honor of Richard B. Hays*, edited by J. Ross Wagner, C. Kavin Rowe and A. Katherine Grieb, 409–26. Grand Rapids, MI: Eerdmans, 2008.

Barclay, John M. G. *Paul and the Gift*. Grand Rapids, MI: Eerdmans, 2015.

Barclay, John M. G. 'Poverty in Pauline Studies: A Response to Steven Friesen'. *Journal for the Study of the New Testament* 26 (2004): 363–6.

Barr, James. "'Thou Art the Cherub": Ezekiel 28.14 and the Post-Ezekiel Understanding of Genesis 2–3'. In *Priests, Prophets and Scribes: Essays on the Formation and Heritage of Second Temple Judaism in Honour of Joseph Blenkinsopp*, edited by E. Ulrich, J. W. Wright, R. P. Carroll and P. R. Davies, 213–3. JSOTSup 149. Sheffield: Sheffield Academic, 1992.

Bauckham, Richard. 'The Economic Critique of Rome in Revelation 18'. In *Images of Empire*, edited by Loveday Alexander, 47–90. JSOTSup 122. Sheffield: Sheffield Academic, 1991.

Bauckham, Richard. 'Jesus' Demonstration in the Temple'. In *Law and Religion: Essays on the Place of the Law in Israel and Early Christianity by Members of the Ehrhardt Seminar of Manchester University*, edited by Barnabas Lindars, 72–89. Cambridge: James Clarke, 1988.

Berlyn, Patricia J. 'The Biblical View of Tyre'. *Jewish Bible Quarterly* 34 (2006): 73–82.

Best, Ernest. *The First and Second Letter to the Thessalonians*. BNTC. London: A&C Black, 1972.

Best, Ernest. *Second Corinthians*. Interpretation. Louisville, KY: John Knox, 1987.

Betz, Hans Dieter. *2 Corinthians 8 and 9: A Commentary on Two Administrative Letters of the Apostle Paul*. Hermeneia. Philadelphia: Fortress, 1985.

Birdwell, Jonathan, and Stephen Timms, MP, eds, *Exploring the Role of Faith in British Society and Politics*. London: Demos, 2013. Online: https://www.demos.co.uk/files/DEMOS_The_Faith_Collection_-_web_version.pdf.

Bishop, Matthew, and Michael Green. *Philanthrocapitalism: How the Rich Can Save the World and Why We Should Let Them*. London: A&C Black, 2008.

Block, Daniel I. *The Book of Ezekiel: Chapters 25–48*. NICOT. Grand Rapids, MI: Eerdmans, 1998.

Blomberg, Craig L. *Christians in an Age of Wealth: A Biblical Theology of Stewardship*. Grand Rapids, MI: Zondervan, 2013.

Blomberg, Craig L. *Interpreting the Parables*. 2nd edn. Downers Grove, IL: IVP Academic, 2012.

Blomberg, Craig L. *Neither Poverty nor Riches: A Biblical Theology of Material Possessions*. NSBT. Leicester: Apollos, 1999.

Bloom, James J. *The Jewish Revolts against Rome, A.D. 66–135: A Military Analysis*. Jefferson, NC: McFarland, 2010.

Bonk, Jonathan J. 'Christian Finance, 1910–2010'. In *Atlas of Global Christianity*, edited by Todd M. Johnson and Kenneth R. Ross, 294–7. Edinburgh: Edinburgh University Press, 2009.

Breeze, Beth, 'How Donors Choose Charities: The Role of Personal Taste and Experiences in Giving Decisions'. *Voluntary Sector Review* 4.2 (2013): 165–83.

Bretherton, Luke. 'Poverty, Politics and Faithful Witness in the Age of Humanitarianism'. *Interpretation* 69.4 (2015): 447–59.

Brown, Peter. *Poverty and Leadership in the Later Roman Empire*. Waltham: Brandeis, 2001.

Bruce, F. F. *The Book of Acts*. NICNT. 3rd edn. Grand Rapids, MI: Eerdmans, 1988.

Cafod, Tearfund and Theos. 'Wholly Living: A New Perspective on International Development'. London: Theos, 2010. Online: http://whollyliving.tearfund.org.

Callender, Dexter E., Jr. *Adam in Myth and History: Ancient Israelite Perspectives on the Primal Human*. Harvard Semitic Studies 48. Winona Lake, IN: Eisenbrauns, 2000.

Campbell, Joan Cecelia. *Phoebe: Patron and Emissary*. Collegeville, MN: Liturgical, 2009.

Capper, Brian J. 'The Palestinian Cultural Context of the Earliest Christian Community of Goods'. In *The Book of Acts in Its Palestinian Setting*, edited by Richard Bauckham, 323–56. BAFCS 4. Grand Rapids, MI: Eerdmans, 1995.

Cassidy, Richard J. *Society and Politics in the Acts of the Apostles*. Maryknoll, NY: Orbis, 1987.

Charlesworth, Martin, and Natalie Williams. *The Myth of the Undeserving Poor: A Christian Response to Poverty in Britain Today*. Tolworth: Grosvenor House, 2014.

Cohick, Lynn H. *Women in the World of the Earliest Christians: Illuminating Ancient Ways of Life*. Grand Rapids, MI: Baker Academic, 2009.

Collier, Paul. *The Bottom Billion: Why the Poorest Countries are Failing and What Can be Done about It*. New York: Oxford University Press, 2007.

Coogan, Michael D. *A Brief Introduction to the Old Testament: The Hebrew Bible in Its Context*. 2nd edn. New York and Oxford: Oxford University Press, 2012.

Cooke, G. A. *The Book of Ezekiel*. ICC. Edinburgh: T&T Clark, 1936.

Corbett, Steve, and Brian Fikkert. *When Helping Hurts: How to Alleviate Poverty without Hurting the Poor . . . and Yourself*. Chicago: Moody, 2014.

Corlett, Adam, and Laura Gardiner. *Low Pay Britain 2015*. London: Resolution Foundation, 2015.

Corral, Martin Alonso. *Ezekiel's Oracles against Tyre: Historical Reality and Motivations*. Rome: Editrice Pontificio Instituto Biblico, 2002.

Cox, Harvey. *The Secular City: Secularization and Urbanization in Theological Perspective*. New York: Macmillan, 1966; new edn: Princeton, NJ: Princeton University Press, 2013.

Crouch, Carly L. 'Ezekiel's Oracles against the Nations in Light of a Royal Ideology of Warfare'. *Journal of Biblical Literature* 130 (2011): 473–92.

Cypher, James M., and James L. Dietz. *The Process of Economic Development*. 4th edn. London: Routledge, 2014.

Danker, Frederick. *Benefactor. Epigraphic Study of a Graeco-Roman and New Testament Semantic Field*. St Louis: Clayton, 1982.

Davids, Peter H. *The First Epistle of Peter*. NICNT. Grand Rapids, MI: Eerdmans, 1990.

Davis, Francis. 'The English Bishops, Caritas and "Civic Prophecy" after the 2010 Papal Visit'. In *Catholic Social Conscience: Reflection and Action on Catholic Social Teaching*, edited by Keith Chappell and Francis Davis, 129–45. Revised edn. Leominster: Gracewing, 2011.

Davis, Francis, Elizabeth Paulhus and Andrew Bradstock. *Moral But No Compass: Church, Government and the Future of Welfare*. Cambridge: Von Hugel Institute and Marple: Matthew James, 2008.

Deneulin, Séverine, and Sabina Alkire. 'The Human Development and Capability Approach'. In *An Introduction to the Human Development and Capability Approach: Freedom and Agency*, edited by Séverine Deneulin and Lila Shahani, 22–48. London: Earthscan, 2009.

Derrett, J. Duncan M. '"Eating Up the Houses of Widows": Jesus's Comment on Lawyers?' *Novum Testamentum* 14 (1972): 1–9.

deSilva, David A. *Honor, Patronage, Kinship, and Purity. Unlocking New Testament Culture*. Downers Grove, IL: IVP Academic, 2000.

Downs, David J. *The Offering of the Gentiles: Paul's Collection for Jerusalem in Its Chronological, Cultural and Cultic Contexts*. WUNT 2/248. Tübingen: Mohr Siebeck, 2008.

Dunn, James D. G. *Romans 9–16*. WBC 38B. Dallas: Word, 1998.

Dupont, Jacques, *The Salvation of the Gentiles*. New York: Paulist, 1979.

Dyson, Stephen L. *Christian Origins and the Ancient Economy*. Eugene, OR: Cascade, 2014.

Dyson, Stephen L. 'Native Revolts in the Roman Empire'. *Historia* 20 (1971): 239–74.

Evans, A., and R. Gower. *The Restorative Economy: Completing our Unfinished Millennium Jubilee*. Teddington: Tearfund, 2015.

Fee, Gordon D. *The First and Second Letters to the Thessalonians*. NICNT. Grand Rapids, MI: Eerdmans, 2009.

Fee, Gordon D. *The First Epistle to the Corinthians*. NICNT. Grand Rapids, MI: Eerdmans, 1987.

Fee, Gordon D. *Paul's Letter to the Philippians*. NICNT. Grand Rapids, MI: Eerdmans, 1995.

Finger, Reta Halteman. *Of Widows and Meals*. Grand Rapids, MI: Eerdmans, 2007.

Finley, Moses I. 'Injustice or God's Will? Early Christian Explanations of Poverty'. In *Wealth and Poverty in Early Church and Society*, edited by Susan R. Holman, 17–36. Grand Rapids, MI: Baker Academic, 2008.

Finley, Moses I. *The Ancient Economy*. Updated edn. Los Angeles: University of California Press, 1999.

Fitzmyer, Joseph A. *Romans: A New Translation with Introduction and Commentary*. AB 33. London: Geoffrey Chapman, 1993.

Fowl, Stephen E. 'Know Your Context: Giving and Receiving Money in Philippians'. *Interpretation* 56 (2002): 45–58.

Fowl, Stephen E. *Philippians*. THNTC. Grand Rapids, MI: Eerdmans, 2005.

Fox, Robin Lane. *Pagans and Christians in the Mediterranean World from the Second Century AD to the Conversion of Constantine*. London: Penguin, 1986.

France, R. T. *The Gospel of Mark*. NIGTC. Grand Rapids, MI: Eerdmans, 2002.

Friesen, Steven. 'Poverty in Pauline Studies'. *Journal for the Study of the New Testament* 26.3 (2004): 323–61.

Garnsey, Peter. *Cities, Peasants and Food in Classical Antiquity: Essays in Social and Economic History*, edited with addenda by Walter Scheiden. Cambridge: Cambridge University Press, 1998.

Garnsey, Peter. *Famine and Food Supply in the Graeco-Roman World: Responses to Risk and Crisis*. Cambridge: Cambridge University Press, 1988.

Gaventa, Beverly R. *First and Second Thessalonians*. Interpretation. Louisville, KY: John Knox, 1998.

Gibson, E. Leigh. 'Jews in the Inscriptions of Smyrna'. *Journal of Jewish Studies* 56 (2005): 66–79.

Gill, Robin, ed., *Theology and Sociology: A Reader*, new edn. London: Cassell, 1996.

González, Justo. *Faith and Wealth: A History of Early Christian Ideas on the Origin, Significance and Use of Money*. Eugene, OR: Wipf & Stock, 2002.

Goodman, Martin. *The Ruling Class of Judaea: The Origins of the Jewish Revolt against Rome A.D. 66–70*. Cambridge: Cambridge University Press, 1987.

Gottwald, Norman K. *All the Kingdoms of the Earth: Israelite Prophecy and International Relations in the Ancient Near East*. Philadelphia: Fortress, 2007.

Green, Joel B. 'Good News to Whom?' In *Jesus of Nazareth Lord and Christ*, edited by Joel B. Green and Max Turner, 59–74. Grand Rapids, MI: Eerdmans, 1994.

Green, Joel B. *The Theology of the Gospel of Luke*. Cambridge: Cambridge University Press, 1995.

Greenberg, Moshe. *Ezekiel 21–37*. AB 22A. New York: Doubleday, 1997.

Gregson, Fiona J. Robertson. *Everything in Common? The Theology and Practice of the Sharing of Possessions in Community in the New Testament*. Eugene, OR: Pickwick, 2017.

Griffith, Gary W. 'Abounding in Generosity. A Study of Charis in 2 Corinthians 8–9'. PhD thesis, Durham University, 2005.

Guijarro, S. 'The Family in First-Century Galilee'. In *Constructing Early Christian Families*, edited by Halvor Moxnes, 42–65. London: Routledge, 1997.

Guy, C., and A. Burghart. *Breakthrough Britain 2015: An Overview*. London: Centre for Social Justice, 2015.

Hands, A. R. *Charities and Social Aid in Greece and Rome*. London: Thames & Hudson, 1968.

Hanson, K. C. *Palestine in the Time of Jesus: Social Structures and Social Conflicts*. Minneapolis: Fortress, 1998.

Harland, Philip A. 'The Economy of First-Century Palestine: State of the Scholarly Discussion'. In *The Handbook of Early Christianity: Social Science Approaches*, edited by Anthony J. Blasi, Jean Duhaime and Paul-André Turcotte, 511–27. Walnut Creek, CA: AltaMira Press, 2002.

Harris, Murray J. *The Second Epistle to the Corinthians*. NIGTC. Grand Rapids, MI: Eerdmans, 2005.

Harris, W. V. *Rome's Imperial Economy*. Oxford: Oxford University Press, 2011.

Harrison, James R. *Paul and the Imperial Authorities at Thessalonica and Rome: A Study in the Conflict of Ideology*. WUNT 273. Tübingen: Mohr Siebeck, 2011.

Harrison, James R. *Paul's Language of Grace in its Graeco-Roman Context*. WUNT 2/172. Tübingen: Mohr Siebeck, 2003.

Hays, Christopher M. *Luke's Wealth Ethics: A Study in Their Coherence and Character*. WUNT 2/275. Tübingen: Mohr Siebeck, 2010.

Hays, Richard B. *The Moral Vision of the New Testament: A Contemporary Introduction to New Testament Ethics*. San Francisco: HarperOne, 1996.

Hengel, Martin. *Property and Riches in the Early Church*. London: SCM, 1974.

Hochschild, A. *Leopold's Ghost: A Story of Greed, Terror and Heroism in Colonial Africa*. Boston and New York: Houghton Mifflin Harcourt, 1999.

Hock, Ronald F. *The Social Context of Paul's Ministry: Tentmaking and Apostleship*. Philadelphia: Fortress, 1980.

Holman, Susan R., ed., *Wealth and Poverty in Early Church and Society*. Grand Rapids, MI: Baker Academic, 2008.

Holmes, Stephen. *The Holy Trinity*. Milton Keynes: Paternoster, 2012.

Hopkins, Keith. 'Taxes and Trade in the Roman Empire (200 B.C.–A.D. 400)'. *Journal of Roman Studies* 70 (1980): 101–25.

Horsley, Richard A. 'Jesus and Galilee: The Contingencies of a Renewal Movement'. In *Galilee through the Centuries: Confluence of Cultures*, edited by Eric M. Meyers, 57–74. Winona Lake, IN: Eisenbrauns, 1999.

Ilo, Stan Chu. *The Church and Development in Africa*. 2nd edn. Eugene, OR: Pickwick, 2014.

Jewett, Robert. *Romans*. Hermeneia. Minneapolis: Fortress, 2007.

Jewett, Robert. 'Tenement Churches and Communal Meals in the Early Church. The Implications of a Form-Critical Analysis of 2 Thessalonians 3.10'. *Biblical Research* 38 (1993): 23–43.

Johnson, P. *A History of Christianity*. New York: Touchstone, Simon & Schuster, 1976.

Johnson, S. E. 'The Dead Sea Manual of Discipline and the Jerusalem Church of Acts'. In *The Scrolls and the New Testament*, edited by Krister Stendahl, 129–42. London: SCM, 1958.

Jongman, Willem M. 'The Early Roman Empire: Consumption'. In *The Cambridge Economic History of the Greco-Roman World*, edited by Walter Scheidel, Ian Morris and Richard Saller, 592–618. Cambridge: Cambridge University Press, 2007.

Jongman, Willem M. '"Gibbon Was Right": The Decline and Fall of the Roman Economy'. In *Crises and the Roman Empire*, edited by Olivier Hekster, Gerda de Kleijn and Daniëlle Slootjes, 183–200. Impact of Empire 7. Leiden: Brill, 2007.

Joubert, Stephan. *Paul as Benefactor: Reciprocity, Strategy and Theological Reflection in Paul's Collection*. WUNT 2/124. Tübingen: Mohr Siebeck, 2000.

Joyce, Paul M. *Ezekiel: A Commentary*. LHBOTS. London: T&T Clark, 2008.

Judge, Edwin A. 'Cultural Conformity and Innovation in Paul: Some Clues from Contemporary Documents'. *Tyndale Bulletin* 35 (1984): 3–24.

Kang, Ezer. 'Human Immunodeficiency Virus (HIV) Stigma: Spoiled Social Identity and Jürgen Moltmann's Trinitarian Model of the *Imago Dei*'. *International Journal of Public Theology* 9 (2015): 289–312.

Katzenstein, H. Jacob. *The History of Tyre: From the Beginning of the Second Millenium B.C.E. until the Fall of the Neo-Babylonian Empire in 538 B.C.E.* Jerusalem: Schocken Institute for Jewish Research, 1973.

Kearsley, R. A. 'Women in Public Life in the Roman East: Iulia Theodora, Claudia Metrodora and Phoebe, Benefactress of Paul'. *Tyndale Bulletin* 50 (1999): 189–211.

Keener, Craig S. *1–2 Corinthians*. NCBC. Cambridge: Cambridge University Press, 2005.

Kehoe, Dennis P. 'The Early Roman Empire: Production'. In *The Cambridge Economic History of the Greco-Roman World*, edited by Walter Scheidel, Ian Morris and Richard Saller, 543–69. Cambridge: Cambridge University Press, 2007.

Kelly, Matthew. *The Four Signs of a Dynamic Catholic*. Hebron: Beacon, 2012.

King, David P. 'Faith and Giving'. In *Achieving Excellent in Fundraising*, edited by Eugene R. Tempel, Timothy L. Seiler and Dwight Burlingame, 145–52. 4th edn. San Francisco: Jossey-Bass, 2015.

Kisangani, Emizet Francois. *Civil Wars in the Democratic Republic of Congo 1960–2010*. Boulder, CO: Lynne Rienner, 2012.

Klaasen, John. 'The Interplay between Theology and Development: How Theology Can Be Related to Development in Post-modern Society'. *Missionalia* 41.2 (2013): 182–94.

Kloppenborg, John S. '*Collegia* and *Thiasoi*: Issues in Function, Taxonomy and Membership'. In *Voluntary Associations in the Graeco-Roman World*, edited by John S. Kloppenborg and Stephen G. Wilson, 16–30. London: Routledge, 1996.

Kloppenborg, John S. 'Membership Practices in Pauline Christ Groups'. *Early Christianity* 4 (2013): 183–215.

Kretzmann, John P., and John L. McKnight. *Building Communities from the Inside Out: A Path toward Finding and Mobilizing a Community's Assets*. Evanston, IL: Institute for Policy Research, 1993.

Kvanvig, Helge S. *Primeval History: Babylonian, Biblical and Enochic: An Intertextual Reading*. JSJSup 149. Leiden: Brill, 2011.

Lampe, Peter. 'Paul, Patrons and Clients'. In *Paul in the Greco-Roman World: A Handbook*, edited by J. Paul Sampley, 499–523. Harrisburg, PA: Trinity Press International, 2003.

Larsen, Mik. 'The Representation of Poverty in the Roman Empire'. PhD dissertation, University of California, Los Angeles, 2015.

Lim, Kar Yong. 'Generosity from Pauline Perspective. Insights from Paul's Letter to the
    Corinthians'. *Evangelical Review of Theology* 37 (2013): 20–33.
Lindemann, Andreas. 'The Beginnings of Christian Life in Jerusalem according to the
    Summaries in the Acts of the Apostles (Acts 2:42–47; 4:32–37; 5:12–16)'. In *Common
    Life in the Early Church: Essays Honoring Graydon F. Snyder*, edited by Julian V. Hills,
    202–17. Harrisburg, PA: Trinity Press International, 1998.
Longenecker, Bruce W. 'Peace, Security and Prosperity: Advertisement and Reality in the
    Early Roman Empire'. In *An Introduction to Empire in the New Testament*, edited by
    Adam Winn, 15–46. Atlanta: SBL, 2016.
Longenecker, Bruce W. *Remember the Poor: Paul, Poverty, and the Greco-Roman World*.
    Grand Rapids, MI: Eerdmans, 2010.
Longenecker, Richard N. *Acts*. The Expositor's Bible Commentary. Grand Rapids,
    MI: Zondervan, 1995.
Lupton, Robert D. *Toxic Charity: How Churches and Charities Hurt Those They Help (and
    How to Reverse It)*. New York: HarperOne, 2011.
MacDonald, Margaret Y. *Early Christian Women and Pagan Opinion: The Power of the
    Hysterical Woman*. Cambridge: Cambridge University Press, 1996.
MacMullen, Ramsay. 'Women in Public in the Roman Empire'. *Historia* 29 (1980):
    208–18.
Maggay, Melba. 'The Influence of Religion and Culture in Development in the Phillipines'.
    In *Carnival Kingdom: Biblical Justice for Global Communities*, edited by Marijke
    Hoek, Jonathan Ingleby, Carol Kingston-Smith and Andy Kingston-Smith, 177–205.
    Gloucester: Wide Margin, 2013.
Malherbe, Abraham J. *The Letters to the Thessalonians*. AB 32B. New York:
    Doubleday, 2000.
Malina, Bruce J. *The New Testament World: Insights from Cultural Anthropology*. 3rd edn.
    Louisville, KY: Westminster John Knox, 2001.
Marshall, Jonathan. *Jesus, Patrons and Benefactors: Roman Palestine and the Gospel of
    Luke*. WUNT 2/259. Tübingen: Mohr Siebeck, 2009.
Marshall, Peter. *Enmity in Corinth: Social Conventions in Paul's Relations with the
    Corinthians*. WUNT 2/23. Tübingen: Mohr Siebeck, 1987.
Mathew, Susan. *Women in the Greetings of Romans 16.1–16: A Study of Mutuality and
    Women's Ministry in the Letter to the Romans*. LNTS 471. London: Bloomsbury T&T
    Clark, 2013.
Mattila, Sharon Lea. 'Revisiting Jesus' Capernaum: A Village of Only Subsistence-Level
    Fishers and Farmers?' In *The Galilean Economy in the Time of Jesus*, edited by David A.
    Fiensy and Ralph K. Hawkins, 75–138. Atlanta: Scholars, 2013.
McCant, Jerry W. *2 Corinthians*. Readings. Sheffield: Sheffield Academic, 1999.
McCready, Wayne O. '*Ekklēsia* and Voluntary Associations'. In *Voluntary Associations
    in the Graeco-Roman World*, edited by John S. Kloppenborg and Stephen G. Wilson,
    59–73. London: Routledge, 1996.
McKnight, John, and Peter Block. *The Abundant Community: Awakening the Power of
    Families and Neighborhoods*. San Francisco: Berrett-Koehler, 2012.
Mein, Andrew. *Ezekiel and the Ethics of Exile*. Oxford: Oxford University Press, 2001.
Meredith, Martin. *The State of Africa: A History of the Continent since Independence*.
    London: Simon & Schuster, 2013.
Meyers, Eric M., James F. Strange and Carol L. Meyers. *Excavations at Ancient Meiron, Upper
    Galilee, Israel, 1971–72, 1974–75, 1977*. Meiron Excavation Project 3. Cambridge, MA:
    American Schools of Oriental Research, 1981.

Middleton, J. Richard. *The Liberating Image: The* Imago Dei *in Genesis 1.* Grand Rapids, MI: Brazos, 2015.

Moltmann, Jürgen. *God in Creation.* London: SCM, 1985.

Moo, Douglas J. *The Epistle to the Romans.* NICNT. Grand Rapids, MI: Eerdmans, 1996.

Moore, A. L. *1 and 2 Thessalonians.* NCB. London: Nelson, 1969.

Morley, Neville. 'Narrative Economy'. In *Ancient Economies Modern Methodologies: Archaeology, Comparative History, Models and Institutions,* edited by Peter F. Bang, Mamoru Ikeguchi and Harmut G. Ziche, 27–47. Bari: Edipuglia, 2006.

Morley, Neville. 'The Early Roman Empire: Distribution'. In *The Cambridge Economic History of the Greco-Roman World,* edited by Walter Scheidel, Ian Morris and Richard Saller, 570–91. Cambridge: Cambridge University Press, 2007.

Morris, Leon L. *The First and Second Epistles to the Thessalonians,* NICNT. Grand Rapids, MI: Eerdmans, 1984.

Mott, S. C. 'The Power of Giving and Receiving: Reciprocity in Hellenistic Benevolence'. In *Current Issues in Biblical and Patristic Interpretation: Studies in Honor of Merrill C. Tenney Presented by His Former Students,* edited by Gerald F. Hawthorne, 60–72. Grand Rapids, MI: Eerdmans, 1975.

Moxnes, Halvor. 'Patron-Client Relations and the New Community in Luke-Acts'. In *The Social World of Luke-Acts: Models for Interpretation,* edited by Jerome Neyrey, 241–68. Peabody, MA: Hendrickson, 1991.

Murphy-O'Connor, Jerome. *St. Paul's Corinth: Texts and Archaeology.* GNS. Collegeville, MN: Liturgical, 1983.

Namikas, Lise A. *Battleground Africa: Cold War in the Congo, 1960–1965.* Stanford, CA: Stanford University Press, 2013.

Narayan, D., Raj Patel, Kai Schafft, Anne Rademacher and Sarah Koch-Schulte. 'Voices of the Poor: Can Anyone Hear Us?' Washington, DC: World Bank, 2000.

Newbigin, Lesslie. *The Gospel in a Pluralist Society,* London: SPCK, 1994.

Newman, John Henry. *The Idea of a University.* London: Longmans Green, 1852.

Njoroge, Francis, Tulo Raistrick, Bill Crooks and Jackie Mouradian. *Umoja: Co-ordinator's Guide.* Teddington: Tearfund, 2009.

Nouwen, Henri. *The Spirituality of Fundraising.* Nashville, TN: Upper Room Ministries and the Estate of Henri Nouwen, 2004.

O'Brien, Peter T. *The Epistle to the Philippians: A Commentary on the Greek Text.* NIGTC. Grand Rapids, MI: Eerdmans, 1991.

O'Mahony, Kieran J. *Pauline Persuasion: A Sounding in 2 Corinthians 8–9.* JSNTSup 199. Sheffield: Sheffield Academic, 2000.

Oakes, Peter. 'Constructing Poverty Scales for Graeco-Roman Society: A Response to Steven Friesen's "Poverty in Pauline Studies"'. *Journal for the Study of the New Testament* 26.3 (2004): 367–71.

Oakes, Peter. 'Jason and Penelope Hear Philippians 1.1–11'. In *Understanding, Studying and Reading: New Testament Essays in Honour of John Ashton,* edited by Christopher Rowland and Crispin H. T. Fletcher-Louis, 155–64. JSNTSup 153. Sheffield: Sheffield Academic, 1998.

Oakes, Peter. *Philippians: From People to Letter.* SNTSMS 110. Cambridge: Cambridge University Press, 2001.

Oakes, Peter. 'Using Economic Evidence in Interpretation of Early Christian Texts'. In *Engaging Economics: New Testament Scenarios and Early Christian Reception,* edited by Bruce W. Longenecker and Kelly Liebengood, 9–34. Grand Rapids, MI: Eerdmans, 2009.

Oakman, Douglas E. 'Execrating? Or Execrable Peasants!' In *The Galilean Economy in the Time of Jesus*, edited by David A. Fiensy and Ralph K. Hawkins, 139–64. Atlanta: Scholars, 2013.

Oakman, Douglas E. *Jesus, Debt, and the Lord's Prayer: First-Century Debt and Jesus' Intentions*. Eugene, OR: Cascade, 2015.

Oden, Thomas C. *First and Second Timothy and Titus*. Interpretation. Louisville, KY: John Knox, 1989.

Ogereau, Julien M. 'Paul's κοινωνία with the Philippians: *Societas* as a Missionary Funding Strategy'. *New Testament Studies* 60 (2014): 360–78.

Öhler, Markus. 'Cultic Meals in Associations and the Early Christian Eucharist'. *Early Christianity* 5 (2014): 475–502.

Osiek, Carolyn. 'Archaeological and Architectural Issues and the Question of Demographic and Urban Forms'. In *Handbook of Early Christianity: Social Science Approaches*, edited by Anthony J. Blasi, Paul-André Turcotte and Jean Duhaime, 83–103. Walnut Creek, CA: AltaMira Press, 2002.

Pakenham, Thomas. *The Scramble for Africa*. London: Weidenfeld & Nicolson, 1991.

Parker, A. J. *Ancient Shipwrecks of the Mediterranean and the Roman Provinces*. British Archaeological Reports International series 580. Oxford: Hadrian, 1992.

Patmore, Hector Michael. *Adam, Satan and the King of Tyre: The Interpretation of Ezekiel 28:11–19 in Late Antiquity*. JCP 20. Leiden: Brill, 2012.

Patterson, Kate. *The Promise of Blessing*. Edinburgh: Muddy Pearl, 2015.

Peterman, Gerald W. *Paul's Gift from Philippi: Conventions of Gift-exchange and Christian Giving*. SNTSMS 92. Cambridge: Cambridge University Press, 1997.

Peterman, Gerald W. '"Thankless Thanks". The Social-Epistolary Convention in Philipppians 4.10–20'. *Tyndale Bulletin* 42 (1991): 261–70.

Piketty, Thomas. *Capital in the Twenty-First Century*. Cambridge, MA: Harvard University Press, 2014.

Pontifical Council for Justice and Peace. *Compendium of the Social Doctrine of the Church*. New edn. London: Continuum, 2005.

Radcliffe, Timothy. 'Relativising the Relativisers: A Theologian's Assessment of the Role of Sociological Explanation of Religious Phenomena and Theology Today'. In *Sociology and Theology: Alliance and Conflict*, edited by David Martin, John Orme Mills and W. S. F. Pickering, 165–77. Leiden: Brill, 2004.

Rajak, Tessa. 'Jews as Benefactors'. In *Studies on the Jewish Diaspora in the Hellenistic and Roman Periods*, edited by Benjamin Isaac and Aharon Oppenheimer, 17–38. Tel Aviv: Ramot, 1996.

Renz, Thomas. *The Rhetorical Function of the Book of Ezekiel*. VTSup 76. Leiden: Brill, 1999.

Reynolds, Joyce, and Robert Tannenbaum. *Jews and God-fearers at Aphrodisias: Greek Inscriptions with Commentary*. Proceedings of the Cambridge Philological Society 12. Cambridge: Cambridge Philological Society, 1987.

Rhee, Helen. *Loving the Poor, Saving the Rich: Wealth, Poverty and Early Christian Formation*. Grand Rapids, MI: Baker Academic, 2012.

Richard, Earl J. *First and Second Thessalonians*. SP 11. Collegeville, MN: Liturgical, 2007.

Rieff, David. *The Reproach of Hunger: Food, Justice and Money in the Twenty-First Century*. New York: Simon & Schuster, 2015.

Russell, Ronald. 'The Idle in 2 Thess 3.6–12. Eschatological or a Social Problem?' *New Testament Studies* 34 (1988): 105–19.

Saller, Richard P. *Personal Patronage under the Early Empire*. Cambridge: Cambridge University Press, 1982.

Sandford, Michael J. *Poverty, Wealth and Empire: Jesus and Postcolonial Criticism*. NTM 35. Sheffield: Sheffield Phoenix, 2014.

Scheidel, Walter, and Steven J. Friesen. 'The Size of the Economy and the Distribution of Income in the Roman Empire'. *Journal of Roman Studies* 99 (2009): 61–91.

Schürer, Emil, Geza Vermes, Fergus Millar and Martin Goodman, eds, *The History of the Jewish People in the Age of Jesus Christ (175 BC–AD 135)*. 4 vols. Revised edn. Edinburgh: T&T Clark, 1973–86.

Seccombe, David Peter. 'Was There Organized Charity in Jerusalem before the Christians?' *Journal of Theological Studies* n.s. 29 (1978): 140–3.

Sen, Akire. *Development as Freedom*. Oxford: Oxford University Press, 1999.

Sen, Akire. 'Poor, Relatively Speaking'. *Oxford Economic Papers* 35 (183): 153–69.

Smith, Barry D. 'The Problem with the Observance of the Lord's Supper in the Corinthian Church'. *Bulletin of Biblical Research* 20 (2010): 517–44.

Sokolowski, F. 'Fees and Taxes in the Greek Cults'. *Harvard Theological Review* 47 (1954): 153–64.

Stearns, Jason. *Dancing in the Glory of Monsters*. Philadelphia: Public Affairs, 2012.

Stiglitz, Joseph E. *The Price of Inequality*. New York: Norton, 2013.

Strom, Mark R. 'An Old Testament Background to Acts 12:20–23'. *New Testament Studies* 32 (1986): 289–92.

Swart, Ignatius. 'Meeting the Challenge of Poverty and Exclusion: The Emerging Field of Development Research in South African Practical Theology'. *International Journal of Practical Theology* 12.1 (2008): 104–49.

Tanner, Kathryn. *Economy of Grace*. Minneapolis: Fortress, 2005.

Tearfund. 'Church and Community Mobilisation in Africa'. Teddington: Tearfund, 2017.

Tearfund. 'Partnerships for Change: A Cost Benefit Analysis of Self-help Groups in Ethiopia'. Teddington: Tearfund, 2013.

Tearfund. 'Saving for a Very Dry Day'. Teddington: Tearfund, 2017.

Thaler, Richard H., and Cass R. Sunstein. *Nudge: Improving Decisions about Health, Wealth, and Happiness*. New Haven: Yale University Press, 2008/Harmondsworth: Penguin, 2009.

Theissen, Gerd. *Social Reality and the Early Christians*. Edinburgh. T&T Clark, 1992.

Theissen, Gerd.*The Social Setting of Pauline Christianity: Essays on Corinth*. SNTW. Translated by John H. Schütz. Philadelphia: Fortress; and Edinburgh: T&T Clark, 1982.

Townsend, Peter. *Poverty in the United Kingdom*. Harmondsworth: Penguin, 1979.

Turner, Thomas. *Congo*. Cambridge and Malden: Polity, 2013.

Twelftree, Graham H. 'Sanhedrin'. In *Dictionary of Jesus and the Gospels*, edited by Joel B. Green, Jeannine K. Brown and Nicholas Perrin, 836–40. 2nd edn. Downers Grove, IL: IVP Academic, 2013.

van Unnik, W. C. 'The Teaching of Good Works in 1 Peter'. *New Testament Studies* 1 (1954): 92–110.

Veyne, Paul. *Bread and Circuses: Historical Sociology and Political Pluralism*. Abridged and translated by Brian Pearce. London: Penguin, 1990.

Volf, Miroslav. *Free of Charge: Giving and Forgiving in a Culture Stripped of Grace*. Grand Rapids, MI: Zondervan, 2005.

Wallace-Hadrill, Andrew. *Herculaneum: Past and Future*. London: Frances Lincoln/Los Alto, CA: Packard Humanities Institute, 2011.

Wallace-Hadrill, Andrew, ed., *Patronage in Ancient Society*. Leicester-Nottingham Studies in Ancient Society 1. London: Routledge, 1989.

Walton, Steve. 'Paul, Patronage and Pay: What Do We Know about the Apostle's Financial Support?'. In *Paul as Missionary: Identity, Activity, Theology and Practice*, edited by Trevor J. Burke and Brian S. Rosner, 220–33. LNTS 420. London: T&T Clark, 2011.

Walton, Steve. 'Primitive Communism in Acts? Does Acts Present the Community of Goods (2:44–45; 4:32–35) as Mistaken?' *Evangelical Quarterly* 80 (2008): 99–111.

Wanamaker, Charles A. *The Epistles to the Thessalonians*. NIGTC. Grand Rapids, MI: Eerdmans, 1990.

Welby, Justin. *Dethroning Mammon*. London: Bloomsbury Continuum, 2016.

Westermann, Claus. *Genesis 1–11*. London: SPCK, 1984.

Whelan, Caroline F. ''Amica Pauli': The Role of Phoebe in the Early Church'. *Journal for the Study of the New Testament* 49 (1993): 67–85.

White, L. Michael. 'Paul and *Pater Familias*'. In *Paul in the Greco-Roman World: A Handbook*, edited by J. Paul Sampley, 457–87. Harrisburg, PA: Trinity Press International, 2003.

Will, Elizabeth Lyding. 'Women in Pompeii'. *Archaeology* 32.5 (1979): 34–43.

Williams, Anthony J. 'The Mythological Background of Ezekiel 28:12–19'. *Biblical Theology Bulletin* 6 (1976): 49–61.

Williams, David J. *1 and 2 Thessalonians*. NIBC 12. Peabody, MA: Hendrickson, 1992.

Williams, Rowan. 'A Theology of Development'. Online: http://clients.squareeye.net/uploads/anglican/documents/theologyofdevelopment.pdf (accessed July 2015).

Williams, Travis B. *Good Works in 1 Peter: Negotiating Social Conflict and Christian Identity in the Graeco-Roman World*. WUNT 2/337. Tübingen: Mohr Siebeck, 2014.

Williamson, H. G. M. *He Has Shown You What is Good: Old Testament Justice Here and Now*. The Trinity Lectures, Singapore, 2011. Eugene, OR: Wipf & Stock, 2012.

Willis, John T. 'National "Beauty" and Yahweh's "Glory" as a Dialectical Key to Ezekielian Theology'. *Horizons in Biblical Theology* 34 (2012): 1–18.

Wink, Walter. *Engaging the Powers: Discernment and Resistance in a World of Domination*. Minneapolis: Augsburg Fortress, 1992.

Winter, Bruce W. 'Acts and Food Shortages'. in *The Book of Acts in its Graeco-Roman Setting*, edited by David W. J. Gill and Conrad Gempf, 59–78. BAFCS 2. Grand Rapids, MI: Eerdmans, 1994.

Winter, Bruce W. 'If a Man Does not Wish to Work . . .'. *Tyndale Bulletin* 40 (1989): 303–15.

Winter, Bruce W. 'The Lord's Supper at Corinth: An Alternative Reconstruction'. *Reformed Theological Review* 37 (1978): 73–82.

Winter, Bruce W. *Seek the Welfare of the City. Christians as Benefactors and Citizens*. Grand Rapids, MI: Eerdmans, 1994.

Witherington, Ben, III. *1 and 2 Thessalonians A Socio-Rhetorical Commentary*. Grand Rapids, MI: Eerdmans, 2006.

Witherington, Ben, III. *Conflict and Community in Corinth*. Grand Rapids, MI: Eerdmans, 1995.

Witherington, Ben, III. *Jesus and Money*. London: SPCK, 2010.

Woolf, Greg. 'Food, Poverty and Patronage: The Significance of the Epigraphy of the Roman Alimentary Schemes in Early Imperial Italy'. *Papers of the British School at Rome* 58 (1990): 197–228.

World Bank. *World Development Report 2015: Mind, Society and Behavior*. Washington, DC: World Bank, 2015. Online: http://www.worldbank.org/content/dam/Worldbank/ Publications/WDR/WDR%202015/WDR-2015-Full-Report.pdf.

Yao, Santos. 'Dismantling Social Barriers Through Table Fellowship: Acts 2:42–47'. In *Mission in Acts*, edited by William J. Larkin, Jr, and Joel F. Williams, 29–36. Maryknoll, NY: Orbis, 2004.

Zimmerli, Walther. *Ezekiel 2*. Hermeneia. Translated by James D. Martin. Philadelphia: Fortress, 1983.

Zizioulas, John. *Being as Communion*. Crestwood: St Vladimir's Seminary, 1985.

Index